CHIEF OF STAFF

CHIEF OF STAFF

The Principal Officers
Behind History's Great Commanders

2
VOL

World War II
to Korea and Vietnam

Maj. Gen. David T. Zabecki, AUS (Ret.)

NAVAL INSTITUTE PRESS
Annapolis, Maryland

Naval Institute Press
291 Wood Road
Annapolis, MD 21402

This book has been brought to publication with the generous assistance of Marguerite and Gerry Lenfest and Edward S. and Joyce I. Miller.

Library of Congress Cataloging-in-Publication Data

Zabecki, David T.
  Chief of staff : the principal officers behind history's great commanders. Vol. 2, World War II to Korea and Vietnam / Maj. Gen. David T. Zabecki, AUS (Ret.).
      p. cm.
  Includes bibliographical references and index.
  ISBN 978-1-59114-991-0 (alk. paper)
  1. Command of troops—Case studies.   2. Leadership—Case studies.   3. Armed Forces—Officers—Biography.   4. Generals—Biography.   5. Military history, Modern—20th century.   I. Title.   II. Title: Principal officers behind history's great commanders.
UB210 .Z26 2008 vol. 2
355.0092'2—dc22

                                                                            2008003392

Printed in the United States of America on acid-free paper ∞
13 12 11 10 09 08   9 8 7 6 5 4 3 2
First printing

Photo Credits: Bayerlein, Speidel, Morgan, Bedell Smith, Gaffey, Sokolovsky, and Almond are courtesy of the National Archives and Records Administration. All others are public domain.

To my son, Jonathan T. Zabecki,

who is probably the only kid living in Freiburg, Germany,

whose great-uncle served in the U.S. Navy during World War II,

and whose great-great-great-great uncle served

in the Union Navy during the Civil War.

Discreet followers and servants help much to reputation.

Omnis fama a domesticis emanate. [All fame proceeds from servants.]

Francis Bacon
Essays
LV, "Of Honor and Reputation"

Contents

PART TWO. KOREA AND VIETNAM

Foreword

Professor Richard Holmes

I write this foreword with particular pleasure, because this is indeed one of those rare books genuinely meriting the term "long overdue." Shelves groan beneath the weight of books on commanders. Yet there is far too little recognition of the fact that military decisions are reached, and command is exercised, through a complex relationship in which the chief of staff generally plays a crucial role. However, in all but the most spectacular cases (with Napoleon and Berthier as perhaps the best example) these chiefs of staff are veiled from us by the mists of time. Sometimes this is because the powerful personality of their commander has obscured them as thoroughly in death as he did in life; sometimes it is because they themselves were perfectly content with anonymity; sometimes, like Maxime Weygand, they are remembered for subsequent success or failure as commanders than for their time on the staff; and sometimes we ourselves are too tempted to focus on "great men" at the expense of those who made their greatness possible.

But if we look at the evidence it is easy to see what a difference chiefs of staff made. It is hard to imagine that the errors of staff work that marked Napoleon's conduct of the culminating stages of the 1815 campaign would have occurred had the assiduous Berthier been at his side. Without the emollient de Guingand, Bernard Montgomery might well have been replaced in the autumn of 1944. Herbert Lawrence brought qualities to Douglas Haig's headquarters that had been absent when the bright but uncritical Launcelot Kiggell was his chief of staff.

Not least among the merits of this valuable book is the way it demonstrates how personality is even more important than process in determining the way that command relationships actually work. Of course it treats process very seriously, and the fact that almost half its subjects are German says much for the way that Germany led the way in the development of staff functions in general and the role of the chief of staff in particular. But it is striking to see just how much the interplay of personality, with all its variables, lay at the heart of command. Weygand, Ferdinand Foch's chief of staff, was described as like being "the marshal's second self." Although Hobart Gay and Hugh Gaffey, Patton's chiefs of staff, had very different personalities, each in his way not only ran Patton's headquarters but also served in practice as his assistant commander, with a great degree of devolved authority. It is soon evident that to see the commander as "the man outside" and the chief of staff as "the man inside" is too facile, for not all commanders are naturally outgoing nor all chiefs of staff naturally self-effacing. One experienced World War I British staff officer suggested that the "rule of differents" ought to apply, so that the commander and his chief of staff, between them, displayed a full range of aptitudes, though the balance might not be conventional.

The writers of this book's individual chapters make no attempt to be prescriptive, but their scholarship firmly underlines certain ageless qualities. If armies cannot hope to win without physical courage among their fighting men, they are scarcely less dependent on moral courage among their commanders and staff officers. It is never comfortable, on the one hand, for a chief of staff to advance a view he knows may displease his commander. Nor is it easy, on the other, for a commander to remember that not all who agree with him are right and not all who disagree with him are wrong. The way a commander deals with what we might term "loyal opposition" is one of the indices of his greatness.

For examples of real moral strength we need look no further than the moment when the relatively junior Fritz von Lossberg took over as chief of staff of the German Third Army in 1915, or for Siegfried Westphal's decision to order the crucial redeployments to meet the Anzio landing without waking his boss, the capable but testy Field Marshal Kesselring. Kesselring was nicknamed "Smiling Albert," but nobody crossed him twice. Some comfortable myths are soundly dispelled. Life on the staff was rarely "one long loaf." In World War I British officers who were used to the pressures of the front sometimes wilted beneath the burden imposed on them at GHQ. On a very good day Walter T. Kerwin, Westmoreland's chief of staff in Vietnam, managed four hours of sleep. Westphal affirmed that the troops deserved nothing less than the best from the staff that supported them, and imposed the highest standards on himself and others.

Although, as the introduction makes clear, staff procedures have evolved over time and vary somewhat between nations, successful chiefs of staff have provided the key link between a commander's intention and the purposeful activity that his subordinates must generate to achieve it. Sometimes they have done so by the promulgation of detailed orders. But, increasingly, it has become evident that clear understanding persists when detail might be overridden by rapidly changing circumstance, that commonality of thought and mutual trust weld together the links in any successful chain of command, and that the human spirit, with all its imponderables, lies at the heart of war. At one level this book provides historians with specialist studies that will illuminate their understanding. But at another it gives officers an invaluable insight into their profession at a time when stout hearts and cool heads, and moral no less than physical courage, are so fundamental to our future.

PROFESSOR RICHARD HOLMES
Defence Academy of the United Kingdom

Introduction

Volume 2 of *Chief of Staff* continues the examination of the history, development, and role of the military duty position of the chief of staff, the principal staff officer in almost all modern military units commanded by a general officer. There have been countless studies of history's great commanders and the art of command, but no study so far has analyzed in depth the position of the chief of staff—that key staff officer responsible for translating the ideas of the commander into practical plans that common soldiers can execute successfully on the battlefield. The exact nuances of that position vary from national army to national army, and even within a given army the exact nature of the position is often a function of personal and professional relationship between that particular chief and his commander. Thus it is often almost impossible to think of a certain great commander without also thinking of his chief of staff. Eisenhower and Bedell Smith and Montgomery and de Guingand are two of the more recent examples that come immediately to mind.

This book examines the role and functioning of the chief of staff primarily through profiles of the most important practitioners of the chief of staff's art. The focus is on the operational-level chiefs of staff—Morgan, von Mellenthin, Kerwin—rather than on the national-level chiefs of staff—Marshal, Allenbrook, Halder. In volume 1 we started with the nineteenth century and the beginning of the twentieth century through World War I. With volume 2 we examine the twentieth century primarily through the lens of World War II, but we also consider the Korean and Vietnam wars. In keeping with our operational-level focus, we concentrate on the chiefs at the army, army group, front, and theater echelons of command.

Each profile will examine a particular chief of staff's relationship with his commander; his relationship with subordinate, higher, and lateral commanders; and how he managed and ran the staff. Some of our subjects—Westphal and Dorman-Smith, for example—are known today almost exclusively for their work as a chief of staff. Others—like Speidel and Almond—are better known for a much wider range of activities. Some chiefs of staff were never

1

commanders themselves. Of those who were, some were successful, some were not. Patton's two excellent chiefs of staff are a perfect case in point. While Gaffey was fairly successful as a division and a corps commander, Gay had great difficulties as commander of the 1st Cavalry Division in Korea. Although Sokolovsky was an excellent chief of staff for Konev during the defense of Moscow, he later became a rather poor front commander.

The Duties and Role of the Chief of Staff

In almost all modern armies today the national-level chief of staff, or chief of the General Staff, has no direct command authority over the army he heads. The role of commander in chief is usually reserved for a civilian official, be it the head of state, head of government, or minister of defense. Up through World War I it was relatively common for the chief of the General Staff to also serve as the senior commander of the army in the field during wartime. Moltke (the Elder) and Hindenburg are two of the more prominent examples. But such command arrangements became increasingly rare after 1918. Today in most armies the national-level chief of staff is the head of the national military staff, coordinating strategy, policy, training, organization, and equipment development and procurement.

In operational military units the chief of staff is normally the senior staff officer at the divisional level and above. At the brigade, regimental, and battalion levels the coordination of the commander's staff is performed by the unit's executive officer or deputy commander in some armies, and by the operations officer in others. Armies still based on the Soviet model may have chiefs of staff at the brigade or regimental levels. The exact role of the operational chief of staff varies somewhat from army to army. Under the American, British, and French systems, he is the principal staff officer and the commander's closest advisor, but he has no direct command authority. Under the Russian/Soviet system, the chief of staff is actually a deputy commander. Under the pre-1945 German system, the chief of staff was almost a co-commander. Even under the post-1945 German system, the chief of staff has far more responsibility and authority than he does in most other armies.

The U.S. Army's *Field Manual 101-5, Staff Organization and Operations*, defines the roles and functions of an operational level chief of staff as follows:

The chief of staff is the commander's principal assistant for directing, coordinating, supervising, and training the staff, except in areas the commander reserves. The commander normally delegates executive management authority (equivalent to command of the staff) to the chief of staff. The chief of staff frees the commander from routine details and passes pertinent data, information, and insights from the staff to the commander and from the commander to the staff.

The value of a close and special relationship between the commander and the chief of staff cannot be overstated. The chief of staff must be able to anticipate battlefield events and share with the commander a near-identical battlefield vision of operations, events, and requirements. He must understand the commander's intent better than, or at least as well as, subordinate commanders. The chief of staff must understand the commander's personality, style, and instincts as they affect the commander's intentions.

The Development of the Modern Military Staff

Staff officers essentially are assistants to the commander. Although staff officers have no direct command authority, they procure information for the commander, prepare the details of his plans, translate his decisions into orders, transmit his orders to subordinate units, and supervise the execution to ensure the commander's intent. Commanders of large military organizations can have more than one staff. Under the American system, for example, the Coordinating Staff focuses on operations, intelligence, logistics, personnel, and communications. The Special Staff consists of functional specialists like the staff judge advocate, engineer, public affairs officer, and the chaplain. The commander's personal staff includes his aide-de-camp, his driver, and at higher levels his executive officer.

The chief of staff supervises the Coordinating and Special Staffs. The term "general staff" usually means the coordinating staff of a general officer commanding a division or larger organization. It also can mean the national-level military staff, and in some armies it refers to a specially trained and managed corps of officers.

Large staffs are a relatively modern development in military history. During the age of small armies and primitive line-of-sight weapons, military commanders did not need a large staff. They were able to control almost everything personally. As armies grew beyond the size and complexity of what one man could manage, the commander had to have help.

The first staff sections to emerge centered on the administrative and supply functions, which were more routine and predictable, and more easily reduced to set procedures. The more complex and situationally dependent functions of operations and intelligence evolved later. Up until the start of the modern era the operations function in smaller armies was exercised completely by the commander. In larger armies, a council of war among the commanders decided operational matters. Starting in the seventeenth century, the rise of permanently organized military forces was paralleled by the growth of special arms, such as artillery, signals, and engineers, which in turn increased the requirements for officers with special technical training. As discussed in the introduction to volume 1, all modern European staff systems trace their origins to the army of Gustavus Adolphus.

The French Staff System

During the latter part of the nineteenth century the French army adopted many of the features of the Prussian/German staff system. The French established a true General Staff headed by a chief, the Chef d'Etat-Major General de l'Armée. Candidates for the General Staff Corps attended the Ecole Militaire Supérieure, and rotated between staff and troop unit assignments. Around the turn of the century all French staffs were organized into three bureaus, and during World War I they added the 4th Bureau.

- 1st Bureau: Supply and administration
- 2nd Bureau: Intelligence
- 3rd Bureau: Operations
- 4th Bureau: Supply

When America entered World War I, Gen. John J. Pershing studied both the French and the British staff systems and opted to adopt the simpler and more straightforward four-bureau French model for the American Expeditionary Force (AEF). In American units from battalion to brigade, the four principal staff sections were identified with the letter S for Staff: S-1, S-2, S-3, and so on. At division and above, the staff sections were identified with the letter G for General Staff, for example, G-1, G-2. A general staff was always headed by a chief of staff. America entered World War II with basically the same system. When NATO was established following World War II, the American/French system of staff organization became the model for the staffs of NATO's combined military commands. Most of NATO's members, including Britain and Germany, eventually changed their own staff systems to mirror the NATO system. Thus, by the end of the twentieth century the basic staff organizational model pioneered by the French had been adopted by virtually all major Western armies.

The German Staff System

As described in the introduction to volume 1, the Prussian/German General Staff influenced the development of the military staff systems of almost all other countries. Many armies copied to greater or lesser degrees various aspects of the Prussian/German system, but no other country quite managed to make it work the same way.

In the nineteenth century the Prussian General Staff was organized into what were later called the Grossgeneralstab (Great General Staff) and the Truppengeneralstab (General Staff with Troops.) The Great General Staff was the national-level staff, and the General Staff with Troops provided qualified general staff officers to the field units. The same corps of general staff officers rotated between both elements. At the start of World War I, the chief of staff of a numbered field army supervised the unit's general staff, which dealt almost exclusively with operations. Each section of the general staff was headed by a qualified General Staff officer:

- Ia: Operations and Training
- Ib: Logistics and Movements
- Ic: Intelligence
- Id: Artillery and Infantry Ammunition Resupply

The remainder of the field army staff was supervised by an Oberquartiermeister, who himself was a qualified General Staff officer, although the staff section heads generally were not. Those sections included:

- II: Administrative and Personnel
- III: Judge Advocate General and Military Police.
- IV: Medical and Veterinary

At the corps level, generally only the chief of staff and the Ia and Ib were General Staff officers. The division was the lowest echelon to which General Staff officers were assigned, with the Ia usually being the sole representative. The Ia was normally a senior captain or a junior major. He did not supervise the other divisional staff officers and spent much of his time coordinating with the General Staff officers of the higher echelons. Over time, the role of the divisional Ia changed, and more General Staff officers were added to the divisional staff. By the late 1930s a division normally had only two fully qualified General Staff officers, the Ia and Ib, with the Ia "dual-hatted" as the chief of staff. Sometimes the Ic also was a qualified General Staff officer. The Ordonannz officers were senior staff officers, but not General Staff qualified. In some cases, they even might have completed the course of instruction at the Kriegsakademie, but yet failed to qualify for appointment at the end of their probationary period. The functional advisors—artillery, signal, engineer—in the Operations Division also had command authority over their respective units. German military staffs also had a number of civil servants (Beamter) in key positions. The senior of these was the Intendant, who was the head of the IVa section. (See table 1.)

The chief of staff was the key figure in the German staff system. He normally had the authority to make decisions in the commander's absence and to issue orders in the commander's name in all matters except legal and military justice proceedings. The commander always made the final decision, but he and his chief of staff discussed matters as almost equals until the final decision was made. Not being merely a rubber stamp or an echo chamber, the chief of staff was not only *permitted* to argue with his commander right up to the point of decision, he was *expected* to. It came close, but not quite, to being a system of dual command. This peculiar relationship between the commander and his chief of staff was unique to the German army. On purely operational matters, the chief of staff had the right to protest to the chief of staff of the next higher echelon any decisions of his commander with which he did not agree. That right, however, was exercised very rarely in the German army. Thus, the chief of staff was both the principal subordinate of his own commander and at the same time the High Command's liaison to that commander. He was not, however, an all-encompassing chief of staff, as in the American or French armies. A German chief of staff functioned more like a super operations officer, as did a British chief of the General Staff through the end of World War II. During the world wars it was common practice in the German army to replace the chief of staff, but not necessarily the commanding general, if a unit performed poorly in combat.

TABLE 1. German Divisional Staff, 1937–38

Operations Division	Supply Division	Administrative Division
Ia, Operations Section	**Ib, Supply Section**	**IIa, Personnel Section**
1st General Staff Officer	2nd General Staff Officer	Adjutant
1st Ordonnanz Officer	2nd Ordonnanz Officer	Assistant Adjutant[a]
Map Office	Infantry & Artillery	
	Equipment Officer	
	Ammunition Office	
	Supply Trains Commander	
	Baggage Train Commander	
	Postmaster	
Ic, Intelligence Section	**IVa, Administration Section**	**III, Legal Section**
Intelligence Officer	Intendant[a]	Judge Advocate[a]
3rd Ordonnanz Officer	Paymasters (2)[a]	Legal Document Clerk
Interpreters (2)[a]	Ration Office	
	Accounting Office	
Advisors	**IVb, Medical Section**	**V, Chaplain Section**
Artillery Commander	Division Surgeon	Catholic Chaplain
Engineer Commander	Assistant Surgeon	Protestant Chaplain
Signal Commander		
Antitank Commander		
Air Defense Commander[b]	**IVc, Veterinary Section**	**Headquarters Section**
	Veterinarian	HQ Commandant
	Assistant Veterinarian	HQ Guard Commander
		Motorcycle Messenger
		Platoon

[a]Beamter
[b]When attached

The German army in the nineteenth and early twentieth centuries pioneered innovative and flexible command and staff techniques that many other armies tried to copy, but almost none mastered. Weisungsführung (leadership by directive) was one such technique that granted wide latitude to higher-level commanders at the field army and, in some situations, at the corps levels. Rather than issuing detailed and rigid orders, the High Command issued a broad statement of its intentions and the general operational results to be achieved, which provided the subordinate commanders with the framework for independent initiative to achieve those results. Weisungsführung capitalized on the local commander's superior knowledge of the situation in his own sector, and it also compensated for the slow and primitive communications systems of the era. The system gave the German army the great advantage of being able to react faster to the rapidly changing situations of combat than its opponents could react.

Weisungsführung, of course, was the very antithesis of the rigid and hierarchical military structures of the period, not to mention the general nature of the broader German society. In order to make it work, German commanders and their staffs at all levels had to operate on the same set of principles and work through the tactical decisionmaking process with the same set of intellectual tools. The General Staff officers were the common linkage in that system at each echelon of command. Many critics over the years have dismissed the process as little more than "groupthink" on a huge scale; but such an assessment is far too simplistic and misses the main point entirely. The system did not produce the best possible solution every time, but it invariably produced a solution that would work, and it produced it fast.

Following World War I, the Germans pushed the concept of Weisungsführung farther down the chain of command, where it evolved into what is now known as Auftragstaktik. One of the most important military concepts of the twentieth century, the term can be translated loosely to "mission-type orders," but there is no real English equivalent that adequately conveys the full meaning. Auftragstaktik is based on the principle that a commander should tell his subordinates what to do and when to do it by, but not necessarily tell them how to do it. In accomplishing their missions, subordinate commanders are given a wide degree of latitude and are expected to exercise great initiative. Where Weisungsführung only entrusted commanders down to the army or sometimes the corps level with broad discretionary powers in the execution of their missions, Auftragstaktik extended that principle down to the lowest squad leader and even, when necessary, to the individual soldier.

For Auftragstaktik to work, a staff officer, a subordinate leader, or even a common soldier given a mission must fully understand his commander's intent (Absicht)—and in most cases, the intent of the next higher commander. This, of course, implies that the subordinate must understand "why." If he doesn't understand, he has the obligation to ask. Conversely, the superior issuing the order has the obligation to explain. Such a process is absolutely necessary for staffs to carry out the commander's intent, but it does not fit the popular stereotype of military organizations in general, nor especially is it characteristic of German society. Although traditional German deference to higher authority and preference for well-defined procedures are the very antithesis of Auftragstaktik, the German army made it work to a degree unsurpassed by any other army in history.

Another practice that was alien to most military hierarchies, and especially to class- and status-conscious German society, was the German army's concept that function overrode rank. The Germans routinely appointed officers to command and staff positions above their actual rank, in some cases, far above. Once in the position, however, the officer functioned with the full and unchallenged authority of the position, even though his functional subordinates may have held higher ranks and pay grades. German divisions in World War II were routinely commanded by anything from a colonel to a lieutenant general (the equivalent of a major general in the British and American armies.) In January 1944 the German Sixteenth Army was commanded by Field Marshal Ernst Busch, a five-star equivalent. But in September 1944 Army Group H was commanded by General of Panzer Troops Hermann Balck, a three-star equivalent. And Balck's chief of staff was Col. F. W. von Mellenthin, while most army group chiefs of staff were lieutenant generals (two-star equivalent).

Despite its strengths, the German General Staff had its share of institutional flaws. Herbert Rosinski and many other historians have pointed out that General Staff training was too narrowly focused, and the General Staff Corps suffered from overspecialization. General Staff officers were trained to be experts in operations to the exclusion of all else. The German officer education system and the General Staff system in particular were never designed to produce officers with broader political and strategic skills like George C. Marshall, Lord Alanbrook, or Colin Powell. This goes a long way to explaining why the Germans lost both world wars while simultaneously fielding some of the most tactically proficient soldiers and units that have ever been seen on a battlefield.

Following World War I the Versailles Treaty banned the Great General Staff but not the Truppengeneralstab. The postwar German army, now called the Reichswehr, was limited to a total officer corps of only 4,000. General Hans von Seeckt clandestinely revived a form of the Great General Staff, calling it the Truppenamt (Troop Office), with several major departments dispersed among various civil ministries. Seeckt also reinstituted a three-year General Staff officer-training course, starting with about seventy officers and producing between eight and ten General Staff officers at the end of the course.

After Hitler came to power and repudiated the Versailles Treaty and its restrictions, Gen. Ludwig Beck formally reestablished the Army General Staff. In reaction to the abuses of the chief system under Ludendorff, Beck received strong recommendations to issue an explicit directive stating that the commander alone was responsible for his command. Beck, however, was very reluctant to tamper with what had been a fairly successful system. When Gen. Franz Halder became chief of the Army General Staff, he finally eliminated the joint responsibility doctrine, which had never actually been codified in writing. The "Chiefs' Channel," though considerably restricted, continued to function during World War II to pass information up and down. Later in World War II, Hitler's operations chief, Gen. Alfred Jodl, wanted to restrict the influence of the chiefs of staff even further. Their position, he argued, was incompatible with the Nazi's Führerprinzip (Leader Principle).

Military command during the Third Reich became an overly complex process with a Byzantine structure. Unlike during World War I, where Oberste Heeresleitung (OHL) was clearly the central High Command, the World War II German military had multiple high commands. The Army High Command was Oberkommando des Heeres (OKH). The Navy High Command was Oberkommando der Kriegsmarine (OKM), and the Air Force High Command was Oberkommando der Luftwaffe (OKL). Superimposed over these high commands was an Armed Forces High Command created by Hitler, called the Oberkommando der Wehrmacht (OKW). The OKW never developed into a true joint staff. It remained dominated by the Army and grew to be a rough co-equal with OKH. The OKW ran operations in the West; OKH ran the war in Russia, under Hitler's direct command. Both staffs were drawn from the ranks of the General Staff Corps, and they increasingly became competing bodies.

In 1939 the Wehrmacht had about 25,000 officers, of whom 500 were General Staff officers. Throughout the course of the war, 166 General Staff officers were killed in action, and 143 were reported missing. A fair number of General Staff officers were active in the opposition to Hitler, with twenty-four being hanged by the Nazis, and another sixteen committing suicide. Among them was Beck, who resigned as army chief of staff in 1938, in protest over Hitler's aggressive plans toward Czechoslovakia. A key member of the opposition, Beck was implicated in the July 1944 assassination plot and committed suicide the night the coup failed. The most famous of the anti-Hitler plotters, Col. Claus Schenk Graf von Stauffenberg, was also a General Staff officer. It was his position as chief of staff of the Reserve Army that gave

Stauffenberg access to Hitler's bunker on 20 July 1944. Today Stauffenberg is considered to be the spiritual mentor of the General Staff officers of the Bundeswehr (German Federal Armed Forces).

Following World War II the German General Staff was tried at Nuremberg as a criminal organization. It was acquitted. Despite the fact that Winston Churchill wrote in his postwar memoirs, "If we arrest and shoot every general staff officer, we will have peace for the next 50 years," the basic foundations of the general staff system were retained with the establishment of the Bundeswehr in 1955.

The modern Bundeswehr has no General Staff officer branch or corps. There is no General Staff division within the Federal Ministry of Defense. The chief of staff of the Federal Armed Forces, the Generalinspekteur der Bundeswehr, is not a chief of the General Staff in the classical Prussian/German sense. He is the principal military advisor to the federal government, and he is not directly in the chain of command between the defense minister and the armed forces. The Bundeswehr staff and the service staffs of the army, navy, air force, and surgeon general's department are not involved in operational planning, which was the classic task of the former German General Staffs.

Nonetheless, when the Bundeswehr General Staff system was formed, the principles in the 1939 staff manual, *Handbuch für den Generalstabsdienst im Kriege* (Handbook for General Staff Service in War), were adopted almost unchanged. During the 1960s and early 1970s there was a major movement within Germany to abolish or greatly reduce the General Staff system. Many in the German government thought the system too opposed to the spirit of equal opportunity and too elitist, creating a modern caste system that weakened the authority of the commander and hurt cohesion in the overall officer corps. The Bundeswehr's General Staff system survived the proposed reforms almost unscathed.

All Bundeswehr officers reaching the rank of army or air force captain or navy lieutenant attend the three-and-a-half-month Field Grade Officer Selection and Qualification Course. After that course most then attend one of several functional staff officer courses of eight weeks duration. About 10 percent are selected to attend the two-year General and Admiral Staff Course of the Führungsakademie der Bundeswehr. Thus, the Bundeswehr actually has a somewhat higher percentage of General Staff officers than the old German or Prussian army. In the mid-1980s the Bundeswehr had about 1,500 General Staff officers. Forty of the Bundeswehr's 202 generals and admirals were not

General Staff officers, and 52 percent of the 1,087 army and air force colonels and navy captains were not General Staff officers. Officers in General Staff assignments in the grades of captain through colonel continue to use the traditional "i.G." (im Generalstab) after their ranks. General officers in General Staff positions do not use the i.G.

One major change is that the Bundeswehr now uses the staff section-numbering system first developed by France, adopted by the United States, and now used throughout NATO. A modern German General Staff officer still has the right and the obligation to provide advice to his commander, and the commander still is obligated to listen to him. This cultural quirk sometimes causes problems on NATO staffs, where Bundeswehr General Staff officers are sometimes seen as insubordinate by British and especially by American commanders.

A Bundeswehr division has five General Staff officers, the chief of staff, and the assistant chiefs of staff for personnel (G-1), intelligence (G-2), operations (G-3), and logistics (G-4). The division commander and assistant division commander may or may not be qualified General Staff officers, but their positions are not General Staff billets.

The lowest level of Bundeswehr General Staff assignment is a brigade operations officer, who usually is a captain and a newly qualified General Staff officer in his first assignment. But whereas the brigade's personnel, intelligence, and logistics officers are designated as the S-1, S-2, or S-4 respectively, the General Staff–qualified operations officer carries the designation of G-3. Although other officers on the staff may outrank him, the overall work of the brigade staff is synchronized and coordinated by the G-3. As it always has in the German army, function continues to override rank.

The Soviet Staff System

After the Bolshevik Revolution the Communists found it necessary to use many Tsarist officers, particularly General Staff officers. The 1914 staff regulations were adopted almost intact, and most of the staff operating principles carried over into the new Red Army. Trotsky and Stalin clashed over large-scale use of Tsarist officers, with Lenin reluctantly siding with Trotsky. As of 1920, there were over 48,000 former Tsarist officers in the Red Army. Many of those former Tsarist officers still on duty were jailed or murdered during Stalin

Purges of 1937, but former Tsarist officer Boris Shaposhnikov was the chief of the General Staff in the early days of World War II.

The Commissar system was the major Communist change to military staffs. Originally the political officers were created to detect and prevent any counterrevolutionary activities among former Tsarist officers. No operational order was valid until countersigned by the unit's commissar. This essentially made the commissar a co-commander. The commissar also was responsible for overseeing the unit's supply and counterintelligence functions. In 1934 the role was reduced to that of a political advisor and political training officer, but it returned to co-commander status after the 1937 purges. Following the Soviet debacle in Finland, the commissar once again was reduced to a political advisor and propagandist. Following the German invasion in June 1941, the position again was restored to co-commander status and downgraded to political advisor for the third time in October 1942. Oddly enough, at this point the commissars were given military rank.

In one of the great ironies of World War II, many of the senior commanders and staff officers received German military training in the interwar years because of the clandestine military cooperation that grew out of the 1922 Treaty of Rapallo. It was during this time period both the German and Soviet armies finally dropped the quartermaster general position from the staffs of field units. Soviet-German relations were severed only in 1935, but the 1936 *Red Army Field Regulations* bore the marks of heavy German influence. At the field-army level, the chief of staff was now firmly in charge of the General Staff, which had four main sections; Operations, Reconnaissance, Organization, and Signal. The staff of the Chief of Rear Services was the principal logistics planning agency, but it was not part of the General Staff proper. Hence, the disconnect between operations and logistics, first institutionalized in the Tsarist *Regulations for the Headquarters Staff* of 1903, continued to plague the Red Army.

Almost immediately after the German invasion, Stalin created the Stavka to function as his staff as the commander in chief. The Stavka coordinated and controlled both the Soviet navy and the Soviet army General Staff, which issued operational orders to the air force and to the fronts (as the Soviets called army groups). During the course of the war the Stavka formed a central pool of traveling command and staff teams, dispatched on order to assume command and control of various key operations. Although it was a very successful system, it also indicated a fundamental shortage of capable staff officers. Considering the 1937 purges, this is no surprise.

Following World War II the Soviets formed an armed forces General Staff, but it remained completely dominated by the Soviet army General Staff. The Soviets never did adopt a self-contained General Staff Corps like the Germans, but they did come to place great emphasis on formal military staff training. The Soviet Frunze Academy became the rough equivalent to U.S. Army Command and General Staff College, with the Voroshilov General Staff Academy equating to the U.S. Army War College. By the late Cold War Soviet divisional and corps staffs were organized along the following lines:

- Political Staff, under the Deputy Commander for Political Affairs
- Rear Staff, which included the staff of the:
     Deputy Commander for the Rear
     Deputy Commander for Technical Matters
     Deputy Commander for Armaments
- Divisional Staff, under the chief of staff
     1st Section, Operations
     2nd Section, Intelligence
     3rd Section, Communications
     4th Section, Personnel
     Topographic Section
     Cryptographic Section
     Administration and Finance Section
- Chiefs of Arms and Services, which actually answered to the chief of staff
     Rocket Troops and Artillery
     Reconnaissance Troops
     Signal Troops
     Air Defense Troops
     Engineer Troops
     Chemical Troops

Despite the numerous officers with the title of deputy commander, the chief of staff remained the real power after the commander in a Soviet division. The staff officers in charge of the 2nd and 3rd Sections also were "dual-hatted" as the chiefs of Reconnaissance Troops and Signal Troops, respectively. In none of the western armies does a divisional chief of staff exercise direct command over the supporting units, like artillery, air defense, and engineers.

The British Staff System

The British staff system changed little between the world wars. As initially evolved under first Marlborough and then Wellington, British staffs at divisional level and above were organized into three principal branches:

- General Staff (G Branch)
  Intelligence
  Planning
  Operations
- Adjutant General's Staff (A Branch)
  Personnel
  Administration
- Quartermaster General's Staff (Q Branch)
  Supply
  Transportation

As under the German system, the British chief of the General Staff was essentially a super operations officer. He did coordinate the work of the entire staff, but in collaboration with the chief administrative officer, who directly supervised both the A and Q branches. The chief administrative officer still had direct access to the commander. The British army never really had an all-encompassing chief of staff until Montgomery started using Francis de Guingand in that role, following the American model. British General Staff officers during the period of both the world wars held a variety of job titles that were confusing to outsiders, as were the abbreviations for those positions:

- General Staff Officer 1 (GSO1), the head of G Branch
- General Staff Officer 2 (GSO2), the head of a staff division, intelligence, operations, and so on
- General Staff Officer 3 (GSO3), an assistant division chief
- Brigade Major, the GSO1 of a brigade
- Brigadier, General Staff (BGS), the senior G officer on corps staff
- Major General, General Staff (MGGS), the senior G officer on army staff
- Assistant Adjutant General or Assistant Quartermaster General (AAG or AQMG), lieutenant colonels, or in some cases colonels, heading sections of the A or Q Branch

- Deputy Assistant Adjutant General or Deputy Assistant Quartermaster General (DAAG or DAQMG), majors as assistant section heads of the A or Q Branch
- Staff Captain A or Q (SCA or SCQ), captains assigned to the A or Q Branches

During World War II the British and the Americans broke new ground in coalition warfare when they established the binational Combined Chiefs of Staff following the Arcadia Conference in 1942. The combined staff model eventually extended down to the highest level of operational headquarters. (In today's parlance, "joint" means more than one service, "combined" means more than one country.)

Eisenhower's two staffs, Allied Forces Headquarters (AFHQ) in North Africa, and later, Supreme Headquarters Allied Expeditionary Force (SHAEF) in Europe, were hybrid organizations that basically followed the French/American model. The primary addition was the creation of a G-5 for civil affairs. Under Eisenhower's staff at SHAEF, the G-1, G-3, and G-4 were American officers and the G-2 and G-5 were British. Each staff principal had an assistant from the opposite army. The chief of staff, Lt. Gen. Walter Bedell Smith, had three British deputies: one for air; one for operations and intelligence; and one for the adjutant general and quartermaster general functions. Following World War II, the British also adopted the French/American staff organization, which also became the basis for all NATO military staffs.

In 1923 the British formed a rudimentary joint staff with the establishment of the Chiefs of Staff Committee. The committee was made up of the three service chiefs: the Chief of the Imperial General Staff, the Chief of the Air Staff, and the First Sea Lord. Today the British military is headed by a joint Defence Staff headed by a Chief of the Defence Staff (CDS) and the three service chiefs: the Chief of the General Staff, the Chief of the Air Staff, and the Chief of the Naval Staff and First Sea Lord. In 1996 the British established a Permanent Joint Headquarters (PJHQ).

The American Staff System

As previously noted, Pershing in 1917 adopted the French staff organizational structure for the American Expeditionary Force. Lower-command echelons, however, only had three staff sections, eliminating logistics (S-4). But at the

General Headquarters (GHQ) level, the Americans added a fifth principal staff section for training, which reflected the realities of having to train a massively expanded mobilization army in the shortest time possible. To provide crash training for 500 General Staff officers, the AEF established a staff college at Langres, France.

When Pershing became the chief of staff of the U.S. Army in 1921, he established a staff reorganization board under his former AEF chief of staff, Maj. Gen. James Harbord. The result was a reorganization of the War Department staff along the same lines as AEF. Under the chief of staff of the Army the new General Staff had five divisions:

- G-1, Personnel and Administration
- G-2, Intelligence
- G-3, Operations and Training
- G-4, Logistics
- War Plans Division

During World War II the War Plans Division became the Operations Division. The four G-sections dealt with policy, while the Operations Division oversaw operations worldwide. In 1942 President Roosevelt established the Joint Chiefs of Staff (JCS), as an informal coordinating body to synchronize the war effort across the services. That prototype JCS consisted of the chief of staff of the Army, the chief of Naval Operations, and the commanding general of the Army Air Forces—even through the air service was still technically part of the Army. Presiding over the group was chief of staff to the president, Adm. William D. Lahey. In 1942 the British and Americans also established the Combined Chiefs of Staff, with its base of operations in Washington.

Following World War II the National Security Act of 1947 merged America's military forces for the first time, establishing the Department of Defense (DOD) and creating the U.S. Air Force as a separate service. The JCS also was established as a formalized body, supported by a joint staff, called the "J-Staff." The Joint Staff was organized along the same lines as the Army Staff, but the designation for each staff section started with the letter J. In 1949 the position of Chairman of the Joint Chiefs of Staff (CJCS) was established, with Gen. Omar Bradley the first officer to hold that position.

Perhaps the most significant feature of the new national military architecture was the grouping of most American military forces under a series of joint "unified commands." The service staffs also were removed from the management of direct military operations. Essentially, the military services became force providers to the commanders in chief (CinC) of the unified commands, with the Joint Chiefs of Staff planning and coordinating American military operations worldwide. The JCS, however, was not in the direct operational chain of command, which ran from the warfighting CinC directly to the secretary of defense and the president—collectively called the National Command Authority (NCA). The Joint Chiefs collectively were the military advisors to the secretary of defense and the president.

In 1952 the commandant of the Marine Corps became a member of the JCS, for Marine Corps matters only. In 1978 the Marine commandant became a JCS full member. The sweeping 1986 Goldwater-Nichols DOD Reorganization Act established the position of Vice Chairman of the Joint Chiefs of Staff, and significantly strengthened the position of the chairman by designating that officer as the primary military advisor to the president and the secretary of defense. The national-level Joint Staff is limited to 1,627 military and civilian personnel. Presided over by the director of the Joint Staff, it is organized into eight principal directorates:

- J-1, Manpower and Personnel
- J-2, Intelligence
- J-3, Operations
- J-4, Logistics
- J-5, Strategic Plans and Policy
- J-6, Command, Control, Communications, and Computer Systems
- J-7, Operational Plans and Interoperability
- J-8, Force Structure, Resources, and Assessment

At the level of the unified commands, each CinC is supported by a J-Staff organized similarly to the Joint Staff, but presided over by a chief of staff. In late 2002 Secretary of Defense Donald Rumsfeld directed that only the president of the United States held the title of Commander in Chief, and henceforth the commanders of the unified commands simply would be called commanding generals, or combatant commanders.

Below the national level, the staffs of current-day U.S. Army units commanded by a general officer are organized into three primary groupings. The heart of the staff is the Coordinating Staff Group, which generally is uniform in its composition from unit to unit. Also called the "G-Staff," the coordinating staff consists of the G-1, G-2, G-3, G-4, and so on. The senior officer in charge

of each of these sections normally has the title of Assistant Chief of Staff for
_____, or Deputy Chief of Staff for _____. The Special Staff Group varies
from unit to unit, but generally includes the command's surgeon, provost
marshal, engineer, safety officer, chemical officer, fire-support coordinator, and
the headquarters commandant. The chief of staff directly supervises both the
Coordinating and the Special Staff groups. The Personal Staff Group consists
of those staff members who report directly to the commander, including the
command sergeant major, inspector general, staff judge advocate, chaplain,
and the aides-de-camp. Commanders, however, do have considerable latitude
to modify the reporting arrangements within their staffs. In some organizations,
for example, the public affairs officer might be a part of the Personal Staff
Group, while in others he might be part of the Special Staff Group. In other
units, the fire-support coordinator and chemical officer might be detailed to
work directly under the G-3. Every staff, then, has its unique characteristics
that reflect how the commander and the chief of staff want it to operate.

Summary

Each of the subjects presented in this study operated within the framework
of his own army and its command and staff system of the time. Hence, the
purpose of this introduction is to provide the background for the profiles that
follow. Volume 1 of this study focused on the significant practitioners of the
chief of staff's art from Napoleon through World War I. This volume focuses
primarily on World War II and the Korea and Vietnam wars. Although we
focus on the operational-level chiefs of staff, this introduction provided an
overview of the major national-level staff systems from which they came and
under which they operated. In most cases, the national- and field-level staff
systems evolved together, and staff structures of the field units are smaller
versions of the national systems.

All armies also developed sets of abbreviations, acronyms, and symbols as
a method of shorthand for more efficient communications. The operations
officer of a World War II corps may have been the G-3 in the U.S. Army,
the GSO1 in the British army, and the Ia in the German army. In the
divisions and corps of those armies today, however, that same officer is now
uniformly called the G-3. This introduction provides the reader with a guide
to understanding those various systems, and a general understanding of how
they evolved to where they are today.

Selected Bibliography

Armed Forces Staff College. *The Joint Staff Officer's Guide 1995*. AFSC Pub 1. Washington, D.C.: Government Printing Office, 1995.

Cole, David M. *The Red Army*. London: Rich and Cowan, 1943.

Creveld, Martin van. *Command in War*. Cambridge: Harvard University Press, 1985.

Görlitz, Walter. *History of the German General Staff, 1657–1945*. New York: Praeger, 1953.

Handbuch für den Generalstabsdienst im Kriege, H.Dv.92. Berlin: German Army, 1939.

Heyman, Charles. *The Armed Forces of the United Kingdom: 1999–2000*. Barnsley, England: Pen and Sword Books, 1998.

Hittle, J. D. *The Military Staff: Its History and Development*. Harrisburg, Pa.: Military Service Publishing, 1949.

Megargee, Geoffrey. *Inside Hitler's High Command*. Lawrence: University Press of Kansas, 2000.

Militärgeschichtliches Forschungsamt. *Die Generalstäbe in Deutschland 1871–1945*. Stuttgart: Deutsche Verlagsanstalt, 1962.

Millotat, Christian O. E. *Das Preussisch-deutsche Generalstabssystem: Wurzeln— Entwicklung—Fortwirken*. Zurich: vdf Hochschulverlag AG an der ETH, 2000.

——. *Understanding the Prussian-German General Staff System*. Carlisle Barracks, Pa.: U.S. Army War College, 1992.

Rosinski, Herbert. *The German Army*. Washington, D.C.: The Infantry Journal, 1944.

U.S. Department of the Army. *FM 101-5: Staff Organization and Operations*. Washington, D.C.: Government Printing Office, 1997.

U.S. Department of the Army. *FM 100-2-1: The Soviet Army: Operations and Tactics*. Washington, D.C.: Government Printing Office, 1984.

Warlimont, Walter. *Inside Hitler's Headquarters, 1939–45*. New York: Praeger, 1964.

Wilkinson, Spenser. *The Brain of an Army*. London: Constable and Co., 1891.

Zabecki, David T., and Bruce Condell. *On the German Art of War: Truppenführung*. Boulder, Colo.: Lynne Rienner, 2001.

Great Commanders

Commander	Chief of Staff	Volume
Creighton Abrams	Walter T. Kerwin Jr.	2
Friedrich Sixt von Armin	Fritz von Lossberg	1
Claude Auchinleck	Eric Dorman-Smith	2
Hermann Balck	Friedrich-Wilhelm von Mellenthin	2
Fritz von Below	Fritz von Lossberg	1
Gebhardt von Blücher	August Neithardt von Gneisenau	1
Hans von Boehn	Fritz von Lossberg	1
Napoleon Bonaparte	Louis-Alexandre Berthier	1
Karl von Einem	Fritz von Lossberg	1
Dwight D. Eisenhower	Frederick Morgan	2
	Walter Bedell Smith	2
Erich von Falkenhayn	Fritz von Lossberg	1
Ferdinand Foch	Maxime Weygand	1
Ulysses S. Grant	John A. Rawlins	1
Friedrich Karl, Prince of Prussia	Helmuth von Moltke (the Elder)	1
Douglas Haig	Launcelot Kiggell	1
	Herbert Lawrence	1
Paul von Hindenburg	Carl Adolf Maximilian Hoffmann	1
	Erich Ludendorff	1
Albert Kesselring	Siegfried Westphal	2
Alexander Kluck	Hermann von Kuhl	1
Ivan Konev	Vasily D. Sokolovsky	2
Leopold, Prince of Bavaria	Carl Adolf Maximilian Hoffmann	1
Douglas MacArthur	Edward M. Almond	2
George B. McClellan	Randolph B. Marcy	1
August von Mackensen	Hans von Seeckt	1

Commander	Chief of Staff	Volume
Giovanni di Messe	Fritz Bayerlein	2
Bernard Law Montgomery	Francis de Guingand	2
George S. Patton	Hobart R. Gay	2
	Hugh J. Gaffey	2
John J. Pershing	James Guthrie Harbord	1
Erwin Rommel	Fritz Bayerlein	2
	Hans Speidel	2
	Siegfried Westphal	2
Gerd von Rundstedt	Siegfried Westphal	2
Rupprecht, Crown Prince of Bavaria	Hermann von Kuhl	1
Josef Stalin	Aleksey I. Antonov	2
Joachim von Stülpnagel	Hans Speidel	2
Walton H. Walker	Eugene M. Landrum	2
William C. Westmoreland	Walter T. Kerwin Jr.	2
Wilhelm, Crown Prince of Germany	Konstantin Schmidt von Knobelsdorf	1

Part One
World War II

CHRONOLOGY OF FRITZ BAYERLEIN

14 Jan 1899	Born, Würzburg, Germany.
5 Jun 1917	Appointed Fahnenjunker, 9th Bavarian Infantry Regiment.
28 May 1919	Accepted into the Reichswehr, 45th Infantry Regiment.
24 Jun 1919	Promoted to Fähnrich.
1 Jan 1921	Promoted to Oberfähnrich, 21st Infantry Regiment.
1 Jan 1921	Promoted to lieutenant.
1 Jan 1927	Promoted to senior lieutenant.
1 Oct 1930	Assigned as adjutant, 1st Battalion, 21st Infantry Regiment.
1 Oct 1932	Appointed to the staff of the 2nd Division as a General Staff candidate.
1 Mar 1934	Promoted to captain.
15 Oct 1935	Assigned to the staff of the 15th Division as a General Staff candidate.
15 Apr 1936	Assigned to the General Staff of the 15th Division.
12 Oct 1937	Appointed company commander, 6th Machine Gun Battalion.
1 Jun 1938	Promoted to major.
10 Nov 1938	Assigned to General Staff, XV Corps.
1 Apr 1939	Assigned as Ia, 10th Panzer Division.
24 Feb 1940	Assigned as Ia, XIX Panzer Corps.
1 Jun 1940	Assigned as Ia, Panzer Group Guderian.
1 Sep 1940	Promoted to lieutenant colonel.
16 Nov 1940	Assigned as Ia, 2nd Panzer Army.
30 Aug 1940	Assigned to the Führer Reserve.
5 Oct 1941	Assigned as Chief of the General Staff, Afrika Korps.
26 Dec 1941	Awarded Knight's Cross of the Iron Cross.
1 Apr 1942	Promoted to colonel.
7 Dec 1942	Assigned as chief of the General Staff, Panzer Army Afrika.
1 Mar 1943	Promoted to major general and assigned as chief of the General Staff, Italian First Army.
7 May 1943	Assigned to the Führer Reserve.
6 Jul 1943	Awarded Oak Leaves to the Knight's Cross.

15 Dec 1943	Assigned as commander, 3rd Panzer Division.
5 Jan 1944	Assigned to the Führer Reserve.
10 Jan 1944	Assigned as commander, Panzer-Lehr Division.
1 May 1944	Promoted to lieutenant general.
20 Jul 1944	Awarded Swords to the Knight's Cross.
20 Jan 1945	Assigned to the Führer Reserve.
29 Mar 1945	Assigned as commander, LIII Panzer Corps.
8 May 1945– 1947	Prisoner of war.
30 Jan 1970	Died, Würzburg, Germany.

Fritz Bayerlein

Julius A. Menzoff

In 1940 Axis forces achieved spectacular success and suffered remarkable failures. German arms triumphed in Belgium and Holland, and defeated France with stunning rapidity. Adolf Hitler was poised to invade Britain, and ordered the German General Staff to begin preparing plans to invade Russia. Italy, Germany's ally, fared less well. Italy's fascist dictator, Benito Mussolini, had become extremely jealous of Nazi Germany's Adolf Hitler's ascendancy both politically and militarily. Mussolini was determined to have his own conquests, as he boasted, "A new Roman Empire." On 10 June 1940 Italy declared war on France after its fate was sealed by Germany's Panzer divisions. The same day Italy formally entered the war against Britain. Mussolini ordered operations against the British in the Middle East, but he also hungered for a successful Italian venture in Europe. His targets were Greece and, later, the Balkans. This would give Italy control of both shores of the Mediterranean.

On 28 October 1940 Italy gave Greece an ultimatum to allow occupation of certain strategic points to "guarantee Greek neutrality."[1] The Greek rebuff of Mussolini's demand gave the Italian dictator the excuse he had been waiting for. Italy had occupied Albania in 1939 and from there Italian troops crossed the Greek frontier.[2] The ably led and well-motivated Greek forces, lacking almost every implement of modern war, handed the Italians a stunning defeat in the difficult mountainous terrain. Prime Minister Winston Churchill and his advisors decided that either a "friendly neutral" or allied Greece was in Britain's best interests. A force, constituted from North African assets of British, Australian, and New Zealand troops and under the command of Lt. Gen. Sir Henry M. Wilson, deployed to Greece and commenced joint operations with the Greeks against the Germans and Italians. A small Royal Air Force detachment was included to aid the hopelessly obsolete Greek air force.

At sea the Royal Navy's Mediterranean Fleet commanded by Sir Andrew Cunningham quickly moved to neutralize Italy's fleet. On 11 November 1940 aircraft of the fleet air arm sunk three Italian battleships at Taranto. This effectively kept the rest of Italy's navy in port and out of the war. Britain was able to maintain the flow of supplies to and from the Middle East and exert control over the Mediterranean. Italy's campaigns in North Africa were disastrous. Outnumbered British and Commonwealth forces pushed the Italians westward across the Libyan desert with relative ease, inflicting on them horrific losses. Early in 1941 British victories in North Africa at Benghazi (6 February) and Bedda Fromm (7 February) threatened to force the Italians to capitulate in North Africa. A distraught Mussolini considered the possibility of a separate peace with Britain, but instead appealed to Germany for help.

Hitler, now forced to secure his southern flank against the British presence in southern Europe and politically bolster Mussolini's sagging fortunes, decided that German forces must take an active role. Throughout 1939 and 1940, the German General Staff considered the possibility that they might be embroiled in southern Europe, but they were extremely reluctant. Germany's primary interests were in northern and central Europe and Russia. In 1939 Hamburg University's Tropical Institute was commissioned to develop tropical uniforms and individual equipment for German forces that might be deployed to those regions. By 1940, large stocks of tropical equipment had been manufactured and stored in depots.[3]

On 6 December 1940 the German X Fliegerkorps was deployed, with Italian consent, to bases in southern Italy and Sicily. Their mission was to begin attacks on Allied shipping and secure air superiority over the Mediterranean with their allies. In January 1941 Hitler issued Führer Directive Number 22, which stated Germany's political interests in the Mediterranean and paved the way for complete military intervention.[4] Throughout mid-1941 German forces drove the British from Greece, conquered the Balkans, and captured the island of Crete with the first airborne invasion in history. On 12–14 February 1941 German troops landed in North Africa at Tripoli and assumed the offensive against the British.

On 6 February 1941 Hitler appointed Gen. Erwin Rommel to command German ground forces deployed to Africa. Rommel had commanded the 7th Panzer Division in the Battle of France and was a Pour le Mérite holder from

World War I. He was not the first choice of the General Staff, but having made a favorable impression on Hitler in 1934, and with his masterful command of the 7th Panzer, he was given the African command. Rommel was abrasive toward his own superiors, and he and Luftwaffe Field Marshal Albert Kesselring would evolve into bitter enemies.[5] He was firmly anti-general staff and held the Prussian nobility in contempt. This attitude was one of the features that endeared him to the Führer.

Rommel, while loved by his soldiers, was caustic toward his officers and often made scapegoats of them for his mistakes. This tendency to blame his subordinates was often the cause of conflict with his corps commanders. He also detested the Italians, both personally and professionally. He had served on the Italian front in World War I and his prejudices were rooted in that experience. Kesselring, the consummate gentleman and product of the German staff system, was formally appointed overall commander of the German Southern Theater in November 1941. Rommel and the Afrika Korps, however, were not under his direct control.

The Axis command system was fundamentally flawed. Success against the Allies would depend not only on internal cooperation between Kesselring and Rommel but equally on the ability of the Germans and Italians to cooperate. Italian Field Marshal Italo Gariboldi was designated as supreme commander of forces in North Africa. He was a cautious commander, but he competed with considerable political in-fighting among the Italian General Staff in Rome for Mussolini's favor. Rommel disregarded Gariboldi's instructions to build up German forces slowly. Instead, on 24 March 1941, he launched a quick strike against the British with elements of the German 5th Light Division at El Agheila. This changed the course of the war in the Mediterranean by clearly announcing that the Germans were in charge of the desert campaign.

The German army forces were designated the Deutsches Afrika Korp (DAK) by the German High Command. The first forces dispatched were the 5th Light Division (later redesignated the 21st Panzer Division) and the 15th Panzer Division with support troops. Luftwaffe general Stefan Frolich's three fighter- (two Bf-109 and one Bf-110) and two fighter-bomber (Ju-87 Stuka) squadrons provided tactical air support. The Luftwaffe, however, under Reichsmarshall Hermann Göring, operated autonomously. Rommel's requests for close air support were processed through Frolich. Any disagreements regarding the use of air assets between army and air force, if not resolved by the commanders in Africa, were forwarded to Kesselring, and if necessary to Göring. Interestingly, the antiaircraft batteries or Flak Batterie (88mm) were detached from the Luftwaffe and assigned to the army.[6] These units became the backbone of Rommel's antitank forces. A small German naval force arrived at North African ports with the missions of conducting escort and reconnaissance duties for convoys bound to Africa from Italy.

The internal command structure of the Afrika Korps was equally confusing. Rommel was commander of German forces in Africa, yet the tactical command of the corps was given initially to Gen. Ludwig Crüwell. Rommel's immediate chief of staff was Col. Alfred Gause. It was his responsibility to administer Rommel's overall headquarters. Lieutenant Colonel Siegfried Westphal was operations officer and Lt. Col. Friedrich-Wilhelm von Mellenthin the intelligence officer.[7] Crüwell, as nominal tactical commander, was authorized his own staff. This arrangement led to much in-fighting between Crüwell and Rommel. Lieutenant Colonel Fritz Bayerlein arrived in Africa in September of 1941 after service with Guderian's panzer group in Russia. He was appointed chief of staff of the DAK.

Bayerlein was born to an upper-middle-class family in Würzburg on 14 January 1899. He served in World War I as an officer cadet with the 2nd Jäger Battalion, 9th Bavarian Infantry Regiment from 1917 to 1918. He joined the Reichswehr in 1919 and in 1921 was promoted to lieutenant and assigned to the 21st Infantry Regiment. He progressed through the ranks and as a major was assigned to the General Staff. In 1939 Bayerlein was assigned as operations officer to the newly organized 10th Panzer Division. His talents as a tactician and organizer caught the eye of Gen. Heinz Guderian, creator of the Panzer force. Bayerlein served as the operations officer of Guderian's corps during the French campaign in 1940. In recognition of his talents he was promoted to lieutenant colonel in September 1940. After brief service in Russia, he joined the desert army.[8]

Rommel and Bayerlein seemed to establish an immediate personal rapport upon their initial meeting in October 1941.[9] And later, Crüwell too seems to have placed great faith in Bayerlein as his chief of staff. Although not shy about voicing an opinion if asked, Bayerlein showed a remarkable diplomacy in successfully arbitrating conflicts between his own and Rommel's staffs. Bayerlein was extremely loyal to Crüwell and served him well as his primary staff officer.

In January 1942 the Afrika Korps was upgraded to a Panzerarmee (Panzer army) under Rommel, and this seems to have resolved the command problem. Rommel was now an army commander and Crüwell a corps commander. In addition to the administrative reorganization, German reinforcements consisting of two divisions plus support troops arrived in Africa. Additionally three Italian corps were placed under the overall command of the Panzerarmee.

In Hitler's view, Africa had gone from a "side show" to a major theater of the war. In spite of the epic struggle in Russia, the German dictator was determined to fulfill the promises made to Italy.

Alfred Gause was promoted to major general and formally titled army chief of staff. On 29 March 1942 General Crüwell was shot down while flying in a light reconnaissance aircraft and was taken prisoner by the British. On 31 May, near Bir Hachim, Gause was wounded, forcing his evacuation to Europe. As a result, Bayerlein on 7 December was appointed as Panzerarmee Afrika's acting chief of staff. General Georg Stumme was sent by the German High Command to take over Crüwell's post.

Rommel demanded that the chief of staff stay at the commander's right hand. He ordered the entire primary staff to be mobile, in small cells, fighting the immediate battle. The mobile war in the African desert over great distances made it necessary for commanders and staff officers to conduct extensive personal reconnaissance. Rommel, Crüwell, and other general and field-grade officers routinely used the light Storch aircraft for this purpose.[10] Bayerlein routinely conducted air and ground observations, usually without escort troops or even moderate numbers of staff officers and specialists. On one occasion in November 1941, this penchant to range the forward edge of the battle line almost led to his capture by New Zealand troops.[11]

Rommel, despite his reputation for invincibility trumpeted by the German propaganda apparatus, had a habit of indecision and confusion at critical times. Bayerlein, a tough, resolute field soldier, often stiffened Rommel's vacillation during periods of crisis. He never appeared at odds with his commander, however, and insisted that the staff carry out its doctrinal functions. Bayerlein subordinated his personal feelings in loyalty to Rommel and to Panzerarmee Afrika.

The war in the desert was going to be decided not only on the battlefield, but by logistics as well. Rommel, who preferred to fight divisions in combat, rarely showed concern for his supply lines until shortages in such items as fuel became the deciding influence upon the immediate combat. Rommel's relations with his theater commander were strained at best, and openly hostile at worst. Despite Kesselring's and Mussolini's best efforts to keep sea lanes and air corridors open from Italy, the British stranglehold on the Mediterranean and an ever-increasing Allied air presence virtually shut off the German forces from fuel, ammunition, clothing, spare parts, and medical supplies for long periods of time. The side that could maintain the balance of forward supply bases and a strong logistical base would be the victor in North Africa. The introduction of American forces into North Africa, coupled with the

British confidence in Sir Harold Alexander and Gen. Bernard Montgomery, would tip the scales in favor of the Allies.

The main German ports of supply were Tripoli and Benghazi. Rommel and Bayerlein failed to establish a formal headquarters there with sufficient staff to coordinate their logistical effort. Rommel's emphasis on fighting the current battle with his entire staff instead of constituting a battle staff and allowing his primary staff to function at the operational level put Panzerarmee Afrika at a great disadvantage. It is not clear if these issues were discussed between Rommel and his chief of staff, but if they were, Rommel's penchant for commanding in combat won out. The lack of an established headquarters made German-Italian relations more difficult and, worse, caused many confused signals between Rommel and Kesselring. By 1942 the rift between the two was beyond repair.

In August 1942 the Panzerarmee Afrika was at its zenith. Through the efforts of Kesselring and his staff in Italy and Rommel's staff in Africa, Italian forces, with acquiescence of the Italian High Command in Rome, were combined into cohesive combat commands.[12] On 21 June 1942 Tobruk finally fell. The British fortress and port in Libya long had been a thorn in the side of the Desert Fox. Hitler promoted Rommel to general field marshal and authorized pursuit of British forces into Egypt. His objective became the Suez Canal and the destruction of the British presence in Egypt. During this period Rommel's health began to fail drastically and Bayerlein was forced to assume more of a command than a staff function. During the tactical standoff at Alam Halfa on 30 August–1 September 1942, it was Bayerlein's strength of character and leadership that saved Rommel from complete disaster.[13]

The decisive battle of the North African war occurred between 23 October and 4 November 1942 at El Alamein. Rommel's health had so deteriorated that he spent from 23 September to 23 October in Germany on sick leave. During that period, Gen. Wilhelm von Thoma commanded the Panzerarmee in the initial stages of the battle at Alamein. On 4 November Rommel conceded the field and began a withdrawal across the desert. On 8 November 1942 American and British forces landed in Algeria and began the pincer movement that eventually would end the North African campaign.

After the loss at Alamein Rommel's star began to decline. Hitler chastised him, and Kesselring, with Göring's assistance, began to assert himself as commander of the southern flank. Kesselring's ability to placate and work with Mussolini and the Italian general staff was instrumental in his success. Rommel finally was relegated to the role of Kesselring's subordinate. Facing the Allies on two fronts in North Africa, Kesselring began to give priority of supplies and equipment to Gen. Hans-Jürgen von Arnim in Tunisia to strengthen the western sector and protect its vital ports and air bases. This was done over Rommel's objections.[14]

During the retreat from Alamein, Bayerlein began to experience serious differences with Rommel over the conduct of the campaign and the state of the Afrika Korps.[15] Rommel was a shell of his former self, the pressures of the North African war having taken their toll physically and emotionally. Bayerlein's role as chief of staff was more complex, attempting to produce staff work that would ensure Rommel's ever-conflicting directives were executed.

The rift between Rommel and Bayerlein reached the point to where Lt. Col. Siegfried Westphal had to arbitrate their differences. When Gen. Walter Nehring was wounded, Bayerlein assumed temporary command of the Afrika Korps. Westphal, one of Bayerlein's closest comrades on the staff, left to assume temporary command of the 164th Infantry Division. Rommel had wanted to make Westphal his chief of staff, but he eventually allowed Westphal to take his new command.[16]

In January 1943 the situation in the Mediterranean reached the point where the issue was not if but when Axis forces were going to lose North Africa. Panzerarmee Afrika still remained a viable fighting unit, but it was forced to conduct strictly defensive operations with ever-dwindling resources, hemmed in on both sides in Tunisia. That same month Hitler and Mussolini came to an agreement that gave Kesselring complete command of the southern front. In February 1943 the last major reorganization of Panzerarmee Afrika took place. Rommel was installed as the commander of Army Group Afrika, and German and Italian units were formed as the Italian First Army under Gen. Giovanni di Messe, with Bayerlein as chief of staff. Bayerlein was given authority for direct consultation with Kesselring to insure German interests and troops were cared for.[17] Bayerlein's posting as Rommel's chief of staff was ended.

Bayerlein was wounded and evacuated from Africa before the surrender of German and Italian forces on 13 May 1943. In December 1943 he was appointed to command the 3rd Panzer Division and in January 1944 he assumed command of the Panzer-Lehr Division. Under his leadership, that division fought well in Normandy and in the central and southern French campaigns.[18] Bayerlein finished the war as commander of the LIII Panzer Corps. He retired after the war and died in Würzburg in 1970.

A chief of staff must fill many roles. He must create both a professional and a personal bond with his commander if he is to be effective. He must anticipate the needs of the commander and be able to translate the commander's intent into orders. He is the officer who is responsible for the multifaceted work the staff must accomplish to support the line units. The chief of staff must focus on all matters that pertain to personnel, intelligence, operational planning, and logistics. He must keep the force commander advised of these issues and be prepared to assist the primary staff officers in problem resolution. In many cases, the position of chief of staff calls for diplomacy and the ability to resolve conflicts within the command, and to represent the commander's views to higher headquarters.

Fritz Bayerlein executed these roles with effectiveness. In attempting to assess objectively his performance as Panzerarmee Afrika chief of staff, one must realize the many constraints that affected his daily performances. As Crüwell's chief, he managed to resolve conflicts with Rommel and his staff, and still carry out the directions of his immediate commander. As Panzerarmee Afrika chief of staff, he was dependent upon two higher echelons for support.

The climate and terrain of North Africa certainly had a dramatic impact upon how the Afrika Korps and Panzerarmee Afrika were forced to operate. The desert war was based upon mobility. Rommel's demand that his staff operate in the forward battle areas in small groups certainly diminished their ability to coordinate the overall logistical effort of the operational campaign. With the primary staff officers—the chief, operations officer, and intelligence officer—committed to the current tactical battle, the overall operational planning certainly suffered. These staff officers suffered a high casualty rate, causing frequent shifting of critical personnel from line units to the staff. The record shows that the considerable "tail" of the German force in Africa was often left to its own devices in supporting the "teeth." In his efforts to stabilize the staff environment upon his assumption as Rommel's immediate chief of staff, Bayerlein was unsuccessful.

Bayerlein became an assistant commander rather than a staff officer. He was an outstanding combat commander, and this is how Rommel employed him. To Bayerlein's credit, for the better part of his tenure as chief of staff he was able to establish working relationships with his higher and subordinate headquarters, the Italian command and troop units, and placate Rommel's monumental ego. Perhaps his greatest achievement as Rommel's chief of staff was the diplomatic skill that kept relations between German and Italian units on fairly good terms so that Panzerarmee Afrika functioned as an effective fighting force.

Bayerlein, however, must bear the responsibility for failing to be Rommel's "voice of reason" within the upper levels of Panzerarmee Afrika. As chief of staff he might have been more forceful in presenting staff estimates and planning. An illustrative example of this was the almost personal obsession Rommel had with Tobruk. After its capture Bayerlein should have been the primary voice for the staff and insist that Panzerarmee Afrika reorganize, resupply, and request the Luftwaffe move to forward airfields prior to undertaking the push into Egypt.

Despite the many personal and professional differences that arose between Rommel and Bayerlein, the two shared a deep and mutual respect for each other. Bayerlein edited the first account of the winter campaign of 1941–42 for Liddell Hart's compilation of Rommel's documents in *The Rommel Papers*. Bayerlein certainly was Rommel's staunchest advocate and defender during the North African campaign. To his death, Bayerlein's personal and professional pride in his, and his comrades' accomplishments while part of Panzerarmee Afrika, never diminished.

After the Afrika Korps and Panzerarmee Afrika passed into history in 1943, Fritz Bayerlein became a successful and decorated combat commander in his own right. Learning the lessons of the desert war, like the effectiveness of allied close air support, he insisted that his division and later his corps take the camouflage of personnel, vehicles, and equipment to unheard-of levels in the German army. Bayerlein understood the role of the chief of staff and gave the full measure of devotion to duty in service in North Africa to the Desert Fox.

Notes

1. Ronald H. Bailey, *Partisans and Guerrillas* (Alexandria, Va.: Time-Life Books, 1978), 16.
2. For a detailed account of Italy's campaign in Greece see Mario Cervi, *The Hollow Legions: Mussolini's Blunder in Greece 1940–1941* (New York: Doubleday, 1971).
3. Gordon Williamson, *The Afrikakorps 1941–43* (London: Osprey, 1991), 28–29.
4. Paul Carell, *The Foxes of the Desert* (New York: Bantam Books, 1967), 6–7.
5. Kenneth Macksey, *Rommel: Battles and Campaigns* (New York: Da Capo Press, 1997), chaps. 4–7.
6. Williamson, *Afrikakorps*, 13.
7. Macksey, *Rommel*, 71.
8. Trevor N. Dupuy, Curt Johnson, and David L. Bongard, eds., *The Harper Encyclopedia of Military Biography* (Edison, N.J.: Castle Books, 1992), 72.
9. David Irving, *The Trail of the Fox* (New York: E. P. Dutton, 1977), 117–18.
10. The Storch was similar to the U.S. Piper Cub but bigger and more powerful. It was very similar in configuration to the British Lyslander light aircraft. Its primary roles were reconnaissance, artillery spotting, and limited transport.
11. Carell, *Foxes of the Desert*, 73–74.

12. Williamson, *Afrikakorps,* 14–15.

13. Macksey, *Rommel,* 135.

14. Ibid., 164–65.

15. Ibid., 167.

16. Ibid.

17. Ibid., 169.

18. The Panzer-Lehr Division was constituted from numerous German armored training centers with the most experienced officers and NCOs. It was initially equipped with the latest types of tanks and armored vehicles. It would be the same if the U.S. Army's Armor School were to take all its instructor cadre and form an active division.

CHRONOLOGY OF SIEGFRIED WESTPHAL

18 Mar 1902	Born, Leipzig, Germany.
10 Nov 1918	Fahnenjunker, 12th Grenadier Regiment.
1 Jan 1919	Promoted to Fähnrich, 6th Cavalry Regiment.
15 Jun 1920	Assigned to 7th Cavalry Regiment.
1 Nov 1922	Promoted to Oberfähnrich, 11th Cavalry Regiment.
1 Dec 1922	Promoted to lieutenant.
1926	Assigned to 16th Cavalry Regiment.
1 Nov 1927	Promoted to senior lieutenant.
1 Nov 1932	Student officer, Berlin.
1 Nov 1933	Student, Kriegsakademie.
1 May 1934	Promoted to Rittmeister (captain).
1 Aug 1935	Assigned to Great General Staff, Operations Division.
20 Jan 1937	Full acceptance to the General Staff.
10 Nov 1938	Assigned as squadron commander, 13th Cavalry Regiment.
13 Jan 1939	Promoted to major.
26 Aug 1939	Assigned as Ia, 58th Infantry Division.
5 Mar 1940	Assigned as Ia, XXVI Corps.
1 Aug 1940	Attached to French-German Armistice Commission.
30 Jan 1941	Promoted to lieutenant colonel.
15 Jun 1941	Assigned as Ia, Panzer Group Afrika.
Jun 1942	Badly wounded by artillery fire.
1 Aug 1942	Promoted to colonel.
6 Oct 1942	Assigned as chief of staff, German-Italian Panzer Army.
29 Nov 1942	Awarded Knight's Cross of the Iron Cross.
1 Feb 1943	Chief, Leadership Division, OB-Süd.
1 Mar 1943	Promoted to major general.
15 Jun 1943	Assigned as chief of staff, OB-Süd.
21 Nov 1943	Chief of staff, OB-Südwest (Army Group C).
1 Apr 1944	Promoted to lieutenant general.

9 Jun 1944	Assigned to the Führer Reserve.
9 Sep 1944	Assigned as chief of staff, OB-West.
1 Feb 1945	Promoted to general of cavalry.
May 1945	Captured.
2 Jul 1982	Died, Celle, Germany.

Siegfried Westphal

Geoffrey P. Megargee

I n mid-August 1942 Col. Siegfried Westphal returned to the headquarters of the Panzerarmee Afrika from Germany, where he had been recovering from wounds he received at the beginning of June. Field Marshal Erwin Rommel, who was not known for his effusiveness, welcomed him with the words, "Your return, Westphal, is worth two divisions to me."[1] Such praise was not uncommon in Westphal's career. "One of the best horses in the stable," wrote one commander who worked with him.[2] Another superior, upon receiving the Knight's Cross, remarked, "Three arms of this belong to Westphal."[3] And Field Marshal Albert Kesselring, Westphal's commander in Italy in 1943 and 1944, wrote of him in his memoirs, "I could not have wished for a better Chief of Staff."[4]

There is little doubt that Westphal was a brilliant staff officer, one of the best that the German army produced during World War II. That fact brings with it a degree of risk for this study, for the best of anything often provides but a poor way to understand the whole. Additionally, any examination of Westphal suffers from the paucity and one-sidedness of the sources that deal with him.[5] Westphal, however, retains his usefulness as an ideal type, one of those men who came closest to personifying the qualities that the German army tried so hard, and with such consistent success, to bring out through its General Staff training and education programs. Through an examination of his career one can see the ways in which the German staff system combined both practical and intangible, moral elements.[6] Those elements played a significant role in the Germans' early victories in 1939–41 and the tenacious defense over the course of the following four years; but they also played a role in the Third Reich's ultimate defeat.

The "Bible" for the German General Staff was Army Regulation 92, *Handbook for General Staff Duty in War.*[7] This regulation laid out the moral principles and working methods that governed the General Staff's activities. It represented, in one small volume, the distilled wisdom of over a century of institutional development. In its instructions for chiefs of staff, especially, the handbook reflected the partnership that had developed between the bureaucratic and moral parts of the General Staff's culture.[8] The chief of staff was the quintessential General Staff officer; his was the role through which the staff had established its position as the bearer of military expertise in the nineteenth century. The German command system demanded of the chief that he be both a consummate bureaucrat and an inspired leader and tactician. Westphal's ability to meet that demand, to be a commander's administrative assistant and partner at the same time, was the reason for his success.

The 1939 edition of the handbook, which remained in force throughout World War II, placed obvious emphasis on the intangible aspects of the relationship between the commander and the chief of staff, starting with the personal attributes that a staff officer had to possess. It opened with a famous quote from Schlieffen: "Achieve much, but do not stand out; be more than you seem: every General Staff officer must take this as his motto."[9] It went on from there to call upon every staff officer to demonstrate strength of character and tact; clear, creative thinking; untiring working power and strictness with himself; and physical health. Of these, Westphal neglected only that last; he suffered from recurring health problems, most of them due to overwork. That flaw, however, was not one that interfered much with the excellent relationships he maintained with his commanders.

Those relationships—with Rommel in 1941 and 1942, Kesselring in 1943 and early 1944, and later with Field Marshal Gerd von Rundstedt—were, naturally, the focus of his career. From the beginning of his training as a General Staff officer, their importance had been drummed into him. The chief of staff "is the primary advisor to the commander in all spheres," stated the handbook. "A close relationship of trust between them both is essential, as the basis for the successful functioning of the command."[10] In part that trust came about because of the common background the men shared. Gone were the days when a professional staff officer had to manage an amateur commander. In World War II the General Staff dominated the officer corps (for example, only one field marshal—Rommel—was not a General Staff officer). To a large extent, that fact gave commanders and chiefs of staff the same attitudes and a common conceptual framework from which to approach operational and tactical problems.

The handbook went on to define, inasmuch as was possible, the nature of the communication that had to take place between a commander and his chief, as well as the limits of their respective spheres of authority:

> Before making operational and tactical decisions, as long as it is not necessary to issue orders immediately, the commander has to hear the chief of staff out. The latter has the right and the duty to present his views and to make suggestions. The decision and responsibility lie with the senior leader alone. The chief of staff has to show complete commitment in the execution of his superior's will, even when the superior's views and decisions differ from his own.[11]

That second passage marked something of a departure from traditional practice in the General Staff. In the nineteenth century, and as late as World War I, Prussian (and later German) staff officers had shared responsibility for the orders they issued, and staff officers had been able to contest decisions with which they disagreed by appealing to the chief of staff at the next higher headquarters. With the increasing professionalization of the officer corps, however, this practice had become increasingly anachronistic, and the 1939 handbook confirmed its official abandonment.

In reality, of course, no manual can reduce the complexity of such a relationship to simple terms, and the handbook's clauses left a good deal of negotiating room. If the chiefs of staff no longer shared official responsibility for orders with their commanders, in no sense did they take on a merely instrumental role. The nature of the relationship between a commander and his chief, when it worked well, was much like a partnership, in which the chief felt free to act in the commander's name or to speak out strongly for or against a particular course of action. Certainly Westphal did not hesitate to do either. One example comes from January 1942, when he was acting as Rommel's chief of staff while Col. Alfred Gause was in Germany trying to squeeze more supplies out of the High Command. The Axis had just completed a withdrawal across all of Cyrenaica, but Westphal persuaded Rommel, over the latter's initial doubts, to launch a counteroffensive against the British, who were temporarily overextended. (The resulting "raid" retook all of Cyrenaica in seventeen days.) Likewise, two years later, in the early morning hours of 22 January 1944, Westphal set defensive measures in train at Anzio without bothering to wake his commander, Kesselring. The field marshal was distinctly unhappy at this, but Westphal pointed out that he had done all there was to do at that point, while Kesselring had needed the rest.

Yet another series of events in November 1941 provide perhaps the most powerful example of a German staff officer's authority. Westphal was then a lieutenant colonel and Rommel's operations officer (the so-called Ia on a German staff); Gause was on the scene as chief. On 23 November the Germans and Italians had gained an advantage over the British at Sidi Rezegh, southeast of Tobruk, which the Axis forces were besieging. Rommel decided to launch a daring thrust the next day into the British rear areas on the Egyptian frontier. He took Gause with him to lead the attack, leaving Westphal at the headquarters to watch over operations at Tobruk. In the course of the next two days the situation there became ever more critical, but Rommel and Gause ignored Westphal's warnings. On the night of 26–27 November the British broke through the besiegers and established a link with the city. Repeated attempts to contact Rommel failed, and so Westphal, on his own authority, called the German forces back from the frontier and warned them to ignore any orders to the contrary. When Rommel heard of the order he went into a rage and threatened to have Westphal court-martialed, but upon his return to the headquarters on 28 November he had to admit that his Ia had made the right decision.[12] One should note that Westphal did not have true command authority. Officially, his order came from the Panzerarmee headquarters, not from him personally. Still, he clearly exercised a level of authority that staff officers in other armies have rarely enjoyed.

The ability to take advantage of such authority depended, of course, not just upon an officer's skill as an operator and tactician, but also upon the fuel that drives any staff—information. Westphal, like other chiefs, obtained his from several sources. His consultations with his commander and the staff officers under him gave him much of what he needed, but he was careful not to depend upon them too much. Westphal also visited the front personally on a frequent basis, often in the company of his commander. As the handbook enjoined, he wanted to be able to "feel the pulse of the troops, in order to be able to evaluate correctly their capabilities."[13] (Such a visit was, in fact, the occasion of his wounding in June 1942.) And finally, Westphal kept in close personal contact with other chiefs and commanders in headquarters above and below his; in this way he could supplement the contacts that his commander made.

At times in Westphal's career his work with other headquarters was the trickiest of his responsibilities. This was especially true in Africa, where both the command organization and Rommel's personality created difficulties. The former was a problem in that it was extraordinarily complicated. Panzerarmee Afrika had to deal simultaneously with the Italian command in Africa; the

Comando Supremo in Rome; the German theater commander (Kesselring); the German Army High Command (Oberkommando des Heeres or OKH); and the German Armed Forces High Command (Oberkommando der Wehrmacht or OKW), headed personally by Hitler. Not only did this create confusion and extra work, but it gave Rommel the opportunity to circumvent orders with which he did not agree, as was his wont in any case. His staff then had to deal with the consequences. In one case Kesselring even appealed directly to Gause and Westphal to restrain their errant commander, without success.[14] Generally speaking though, Westphal's relationships with other headquarters serve to further illustrate his independence. In February 1942, for instance, Westphal debated the objectives for the drive through Cyrenaica with the Italian theater and supreme commands. The points he made plainly agreed with Rommel's intentions, and he signed his communications "for the Army Command, Chief of Staff, Acting," but the fact remains that he was the Panzerarmee's official representative.[15]

As the war went on, the link with higher headquarters would become the source of increasing burdens, as Hitler exerted more and more personal control over operational and even tactical decisions. Whereas a chief's relationship with his commander was one of independence built on trust, Hitler often showed little interest in staff officers' opinions and allowed them no latitude in executing his orders. Even when he was open to suggestions, the headquarters on the spot lost precious time consulting with him and his staff. On 27 January 1944, for example, Westphal received orders from Hitler and his principal staff officer, Col. Gen. Alfred Jodl, on the details of a counterattack against the new Allied bridgehead at Anzio. These orders were at odds with the counterattack plans that Westphal and Kesselring had already developed, and Westphal had to go through the effort of explaining why his plan would be more effective. In the end he won out, but he certainly could have put his time to better use.[16] This was no isolated incident; the OKW War Diary shows a constant stream of orders, instructions, reports, and explanations flowing between the two headquarters, most of them at a level of detail that was wholly unnecessary. Perhaps the worst aspect of this pattern, moreover, is that it tended to spread throughout the system. As the war went on, more and more commanders and staff officers were willing to interfere in business that was properly the sphere of their subordinate commands, and this fact had implications for every staff's internal working methods.

As one might expect, the chief of staff was the focal point for those methods. According to the handbook, the chief was to proof all drafts before they went to the commander for signature, and he himself could sign any orders that were not fundamental in nature. Obviously the potential existed for the chief to exercise a great deal of flexibility, depending on the definition of "fundamental" that he and the commander agreed upon. Westphal wrote of his time under Rundstedt that the field marshal allowed him a lot of freedom and limited himself to the most important matters; thus the day-to-day management of operations often lay in the chief's hands. Further, Westphal wrote all important orders himself, so his stamp lay upon even those documents that bore his commander's signature.

No matter how skilled and knowledgeable a chief was, however, he could not hope to do everything himself. As his title implied, one of his tasks—perhaps the most important in the end—was to regulate the work of the staff officers under him. They were formally subordinate to him, and the handbook laid down the principles by which they and he were to work together:

> Simplicity and tautness in the leadership of the staff, sharp delineation of the spheres of work with one another, and close collaboration are necessary. That staff works best in which the Chief of Staff elicits and maintains a joy of work, a sense of responsibility, foresight and independence in his subordinates.[17]

The emphasis here on responsibility and independence is especially important. German staffs were small in comparison to their Allied counterparts. Even an army group headquarters would contain no more than ten or twelve officers and a number of supporting enlisted personnel. (When Westphal first went to Africa, he and one junior officer comprised the entire operations section for the Panzerarmee headquarters.) Thus the chief of staff had only a small group with which to work, and his best interest lay in seeing that each officer could act on his own within a collaborative framework. Westphal encouraged independence in even his youngest officers. He would, for example, have a junior officer read his drafts over before he submitted them to the commander, in an effort to find any points that could be misinterpreted. He laid great value, he wrote later, on the fact that every colleague, no matter how junior, could express his opinions to him without timidity.[18]

One should certainly not imply from this that Westphal was an easy man for whom to work. By his own admission he was a hard taskmaster. He drove himself hard, and he expected the same from his subordinates. His workdays stretched from 6:00 in the morning until 2:00 the following morning with only a brief midday break. The idea that he was able to engage in "clear, creative thinking" during all those hours of work stretches credibility, and yet that was precisely Westphal's hallmark, and he had difficulty tolerating those who could not match his energy, his attention to detail, or his intellect. "Westphal has only one flaw," said one of his superiors, "that he cannot understand that most officers think somewhat more slowly than he, and that he has no patience for that."[19] He rarely had to threaten anyone on his staff with disciplinary measures, but he once put a young staff officer under house arrest because the officer had failed, on three consecutive days, to produce a report that Westphal wanted.[20]

Westphal justified his strictness quite simply: the troops deserved nothing less than the very best performance from the staffs that supported them. He reminded his subordinates in Italy that, in contrast to the soldiers in the frontlines, they would usually have hot meals and could sleep in peace. In return, he expected them to answer requests from the front on the same day whenever humanly possible, and not to overburden the frontline commanders with questions and demands for reports. That second point proved to be a particular bone of contention at times; in Italy he found that every company and battery commander faced more than thirty standing deadlines every month, not including special queries. Those reports had to make their way upward, along with the normal situation reports, through battalion, regiment, division, corps, and army headquarters. Westphal wrote—hyperbolically, one hopes—that he nearly had to use force to achieve any significant deletions.[21]

Granted, many of the reports that a headquarters received were of critical importance; here again one must remember that only with sufficient information could a staff perform its duties. Most upper-level staffs counted on a series of daily reports for their knowledge of developments at the front. Thrice-daily situation reports gave the status of friendly ground units. Enemy situation reports gave the corresponding picture of the foe's activities. Supply and communications reports rounded out the staffs' understanding of their subordinate units' capabilities. And special reports from higher headquarters supplemented the intelligence picture. Westphal had special praise in his memoirs for his supply officer in Italy, Colonel Fähndrich, who would present an overview of the entire army group's supply situation every morning. It allowed Westphal to see at a glance what supplies were on hand at the front and the various rear echelons, including munitions, food, fodder, fuel, and engineering materials. It also told him what was underway from Germany. When front commanders and staff officers justified setbacks to Kesselring as having been the result of supply shortages, Westphal was often able to use

Fähndrich's report to demonstrate that they were uninformed as to their own situations. "I could only conclude," he later wrote, "that the gentlemen did not have mastery of the tools of their trade."[22]

Actually such conflicts mirrored a much deeper set of problems within the German command system. The small size of German staffs allowed for close collaboration and quick decisionmaking on questions of operational maneuver but created real weaknesses in some supporting functions, especially logistics and intelligence, in which complex problems of coordination and analysis outstripped the abilities of the small groups that had to solve them. In part this weakness reflected a broad prejudice on the part of German officers against support functions. The problem was a subtle one, one that does not jump out from the available sources. In fact the handbook devotes a good deal of space to the roles of the intelligence (Ic) and supply (Ib) officers. In practice, however, the Germans maintained the superiority of the maneuver plan over other considerations. "According to our opinion," wrote Franz Halder, chief of the General Staff from 1938 to 1942, "the material has to serve the spiritual. Accordingly, our quartermaster service may never hamper the operational concept."[23] So, while supply issues were never far from the chiefs' minds, the message they communicated to their supply officers was: "Supply is critically important; now make it work!" Similarly, the handbook enjoined the intelligence officer to do his work in light of the information he received from the operations officer, not the reverse.

Whatever the deeper flaws in their approach to war, the Germans did at least have an organized decisionmaking system. Each officer knew his special tasks, the steps that he carried out in the process of generating decisions and orders. The main event in that process was the daily briefing (or briefings) for the commander. The chief was responsible for organizing and leading them, as the handbook specified:

> The Chief of Staff regulates the briefings for the commander. He may participate in them. All important matters must be briefed to the commander at the right time, in a concise form that singles out the most important elements and so facilitates decision-making, and without a one-sided presentation that tends toward a predetermined opinion.[24]

This approach may seem obvious, but one wonders if the Germans saw the battle against human nature that it entailed. Given the opportunity, most staff officers will gladly brief the commander on whatever they deem important, whether or not the subject matter is crucial to the operations at hand. They know that this is the quickest way to get the commander's attention and to bypass any resistance that their colleagues or superiors within the staff might raise. Moreover, too many commanders enjoy an elaborate and lengthy briefing put on for their benefit, in which they can feel that they have control over every detail of the headquarters' activities.

Westphal encountered this problem with Kesselring. Under Westphal's predecessor the daily brief, which took place in the evening, had become—to use a modern American military phrase—a "dog and pony show." The number of briefers was large and included many specialists who presented material of no great importance. Even the field marshal's dinner guests were invited. Westphal saw little use in such display. With Kesselring's reluctant approval he switched the briefing to the morning and cut the number of briefers to a minimum. Only the principal General or Admiralty Staff officers made presentations, along with the meteorologist. Other specialists appeared only as the situation demanded, and guests were no longer invited. The changes shortened and simplified the decisionmaking process and so allowed both Kesselring and Westphal to save time and energy.[25]

After the war, Albert Kesselring summed up the qualities that made Siegfried Westphal such an outstanding chief of staff:

> He had my full trust, full freedom in the expression of his views, had the staff firmly in hand, was highly capable organizationally and untiring in the fulfillment of his responsible position. . . . Above-average tactical knowledge and like technique in issuing orders distinguished him.[26]

These were, in fact, exactly the qualities that the Germans identified in the *Handbook for General Staff Duty in War* as being most critical to a chief of staff's effectiveness. Westphal managed to combine the moral, intangible, personal characteristics that made up a staff officer with a mastery of the specialized knowledge and practices that the General Staff inculcated in its officers. Where the practice was undefined, or in those inevitably chaotic situations that define warfare, Westphal's personal attributes often bridged the gap between failure and success. Of course one must temper this view of the man and the system with the certainty that we do not have a complete picture of either. Westphal's failings and those of the General Staff remain partly hidden from view by the inadequacy of the sources and the scope of this examination. Still, some broad conclusions do stand out.

The position of chief of staff in the Wehrmacht was one that entailed great responsibility, as it did in all armies. The unique culture of the German General Staff dictated, however, that the position would depend more on tactical and operational skill for its impact than it would on attention to logistics, intelligence, or the other support functions. Also, that culture mandated small staffs, which could make and implement tactical and operational decisions quickly; they were great at considered improvisation. On the other hand, the officers in those staffs were under incredible stress, and they often lacked the ability to carry out the more manpower-intensive staff functions as thoroughly as their Allied counterparts. Westphal, as a representative of Germany's ideal chief of staff, embodied both the strengths and weaknesses of the system that produced him. Thus, for all his skills, he could not prevent the cataclysm that eventually engulfed his service and his state.

Notes

1. Franz Kurowski, *Das Vermächtnis. Siegfried Westphal: Als Generalstabschef dreier Feldmarschälle im Krieg 1939-1945* (Bochum: Heinrich Pöppinghaus Verlag, 1982), 73.
2. Fridolin von Senger und Etterlin, quoted in Richard Brett-Smith, *Hitler's Generals* (San Rafael, Calif.: Presidio Press, 1977), 180.
3. Albert Wodrig, quoted in Kurowski, *Das Vermächtnis*, 25.
4. Albert Kesselring, *Kesselring: A Soldier's Record* (New York: William Morrow, 1954), 306.
5. Most secondary sources, including the biographies of Westphal's commanders, mention him only briefly. His memoirs (*Erinnerungen*, [Mainz: Hase and Koehler Verlag, 1975]) are predictably positive, and the only biography of him, Kurowski's *Das Vermächtnis* (*The Legacy*), is an exercise in hero-worship and lacks any citations.
6. I am using the word "moral" here not as an indication of right conduct, but in the sense that some principles of German staff work focused on the mind, feelings, will, or character rather than being simply practical rules for staff work.
7. Germany, Heer, Heeresdienstvorschrift 92 (H.Dv. 92), *Handbuch für den Generalstabsdienst im Kriege*, Teil I, II, abgeschlossen am 1.8.1939 (Berlin: der Reichsdruckerei, 1939). Note that the term "General Staff" denoted both a central command element within the Army High Command and, as used here, a broader corps of trained staff officers who held key positions at division and above.
8. For more on the development of this culture, see Geoffrey P. Megargee, "Triumph of the Null: The War Within the German High Command, 1933–1945," Ph.D. diss., Ohio State University, Columbus, 1998), chap. 1.
9. *Handbuch*, 2.
10. Ibid., 14-15.

11. Ibid., 14.
12. On this incident, see Kurowski, *Das Vermächtnis*, 34-47; also David Fraser, *Knight's Cross: A Life of Field Marshal Erwin Rommel* (New York: HarperCollins, 1993), 289.
13. *Handbuch*, 2.
14. Samuel W. Mitcham, *Rommel's Greatest Victory: The Desert Fox and the Fall of Tobruk, Spring 1942* (Novato, Calif.: Presidio Press, 1998), 95–96.
15. Percy Ernst Schramm, ed., *Kriegstagebuch des Oberkommandos der Wehrmacht (Wehrmachtführungsstab)* (München: Verlagsgesellschaft mbH, 1982), 2:287–88. The negotiation was taking place at this point in part because Rommel and Westphal had carefully kept the attack a secret from their erstwhile allies until after it started.
16. Ibid., 4:134–35. See also Kurowski, *Das Vermächtnis*, 100–101.
17. *Handbuch*, 16.
18. Westphal, *Erinnerungen*, 245.
19. Kurowski, *Das Vermächtnis*, 25.
20. Westphal, *Erinnerungen*, 245.
21. Ibid., 243–44.
22. Ibid., 240.
23. Peter Bor, *Gespräche mit Halder* (Wiesbaden: Limes Verlag, 1950), 85–86.
24. *Handbuch*, 17.
25. Westphal, *Erinnerungen*, 246.
26. Kesselring, *Kesselring*, 306.

CHRONOLOGY OF HANS SPEIDEL

28 Oct 1897	Born in Metzingen, Würtemburg, Germany.
30 Nov 1914	Appointed Fahnenjunker in the 123rd Guard Grenadier Regiment.
19 Nov 1915	Promoted to second lieutenant and platoon commander, Argonne.
1916	Assigned as company commander, Battle of the Somme.
9 Aug 1916	Assigned as battalion adjutant, 123rd Guard Grenadier Regiment.
18 Dec 1918	Assigned as regimental adjutant, 123rd Guard Grenadier Regiment.
1919	Assigned as aide-de-camp, Infantry Command 13, Stuttgart. Student at Technical University Stuttgart.
1 Oct 1919	Assigned to the Reichswehr, 26th Regiment.
1 Oct 1921	Assigned to the 18th Cavalry Regiment.
Feb 1925	Received Ph.D.
1 Aug 1925	Promoted to senior lieutenant.
1 Oct 1929	Assigned to the staff of the 16th Cavalry Regiment as a General Staff candidate.
1930	Language study in France.
1 Oct 1930	Assigned as General Staff officer, Foreign Armies West.
1 Feb 1932	Promoted to captain.
1 Oct 1933	Assigned as assistant military attaché, Paris.
1 Oct 1936	Promoted to major and assigned as company commander, 56th Infantry Regiment.
1 Oct 1937	Assigned as Ia, 33rd Infantry Division.
1 Jan 1939	Promoted to lieutenant colonel.
1 Oct 1939	Assigned as Ia, IX Corps on the West Wall.
10 May 1940	Participated in the western campaign on the staff of Sixth Army.
31 May 1940	Assigned to Army Group B staff to prepare assault on Paris.
15 Jun 1940	Assigned as chief of staff to the military governor of Paris.
1 Aug 1940	Chief of staff to military governor of France.

1 Feb 1941	Promoted to colonel.
25 Mar 1942	Assigned as chief of staff, V Corps, eastern front.
1 Jan 1943	Promoted to major general.
5 Jan 1943	Assigned as chief of staff to the German liaison element attached to the Italian Eighth Army.
5 Feb 1943	Assigned as chief of staff, Army Detachment Lanz (later Kempf), Army Group South, eastern front.
15 Aug 1943	Assigned as chief of staff, German Eighth Army.
1 Jan 1944	Promoted to lieutenant general.
15 Apr 1944	Assigned as chief of staff, Army Group B, France.
7 Sep 1944	Arrested by the Gestapo.
29 Apr 1945	Freed by advancing French troops.
1946–47	Wrote studies for the U.S. Army Historical Division.
Mid–1948	Defense adviser to Bavarian premier.
Late 1948	Served as defense adviser to federal chancellor.
Feb 1949	Lecturer, Tübingen University.
22 Oct 1954	Served as a negotiator for German entry into NATO.
10 Oct 1955	Assigned as a lieutenant general in the Bundeswehr.
22 Nov 1955	Assigned as chief of Department for Combined Forces at Federal Ministry of Defense in Bonn.
2 Apr 1957	Appointed commander in chief, NATO Land Forces, Central Europe.
5 Apr 1957	Promoted to general.
30 Sep 1963	Retired as commander, NATO Land Forces, Central Europe.
28 Nov 1984	Died, Bad Honnef, Germany.

Hans Speidel

Russell Hart

Born into a nonmilitary middle-class civil service family in Württemberg on 28 October 1897, Hans Speidel grew up in the relatively liberal cities of Metzingen and Stuttgart. He completed a classical gymnasium education where he displayed particular interest in history and philosophy and exceptional literary skills. In late November 1914, at the age of seventeen he volunteered as an officer cadet for service in the elite 123rd Karl König von Württemberg Guard Grenadier Regiment of the Royal Army Württemberg based at Ulm. After enlisting he completed an officer training course at the Döberitz proving grounds and received his commission as a second lieutenant in November 1915. Speidel first saw action as a platoon commander in the Battle of the Argonne in late 1915 on the western front. It was here that Speidel had his first contact with Erwin Rommel, another young, aspiring infantry commander.[1]

During the latter half of 1916 Speidel commanded an infantry company in the bloody Battle of the Somme. At the end of that protracted battle he was promoted to battalion adjutant in his home regiment, in recognition of his good organizational and administrative abilities. By 1918 he had risen to the position of regimental adjutant and he had in the meantime been personally awarded the Iron Cross by Kaiser Wilhelm II. As the war turned against Germany, Speidel participated in the general German retreat on the western front back toward Germany, where he experienced the bitterness of defeat that accompanied the gradual disintegration of Germany's ground forces. After Germany requested—and the Entente Powers agreed to—an armistice on 11 November 1918, Speidel marched back to Ulm with his regiment, where the formation disbanded.

Central to understanding Speidel's military thought as well as his sub-sequent career and actions is that Speidel was not a product of the prewar Prussian military tradition. Instead, like Rommel, his worldview was forged by the terrible battles of attrition that dominated the warfare on the western front during World War I.[2] Also, like many other decorated and talented young German officers, Speidel found himself retained in the provisional Reichswehr, the intermediate armed forces maintained by the new Weimar Republic, the Western-style democratic regime imposed by the victorious Entente Powers. But suitable appointments were in very short supply amid the tiny 1920s German officer corps allowed by the Treaty of Versailles.

Speidel therefore found opportunity to study warfare and history, his favorite high school subjects. In 1919 he was appointed as aide-de-camp to the commander of the 13th Infantry Command in Stuttgart and he began studies at the nearby Technical University of Stuttgart. Between 1920 and 1922 he undertook the disguised and abbreviated General Staff training course offered by the Reichswehr and served until 1922 as a platoon commander in the 13th Infantry Regiment that was subordinated to the Stuttgart command. Ultimately completing his studies at the University of Stuttgart in the late 1920s, Speidel became one of only a handful of German staff officers who received a doctorate of philosophy in the field of history during the interwar period, completing a dissertation on a historiographical theme. This learning—and particularly his understanding of European history—gave Speidel a broader and more sophisticated worldview than that held by most of his officer counterparts. Moreover, it was the breadth and depth of his education that contributed to Speidel's relatively rapid disillusionment with Hitlerian Germany.

Consequently, Speidel already demonstrated a more realistic worldview than was typical of the German General Staff, which he formally entered in 1930. That same year he completed a linguistics course in France, and with his historical background he was an obvious candidate for an intelligence posting. Thus in October 1930 he joined the Foreign Armies Section of the General Staff, which was tasked with gathering information concerning the military capabilities of Germany's neighbors and potential future enemies.

It was during this intelligence assignment that Speidel gained a good appreciation of both the lack of will to confront Germany and the very limited military capabilities of Hitler's intended enemies. He therefore enthusiastically supported Hitler's platform of rearmament and the reunification of all Germans in a "Greater Germany." From October 1933 Speidel served a two-year tour as the assistant to the German military attaché in Paris. In 1936 he served briefly as the chief of the Foreign Armies West section. But the desperate need for experienced officers amid the massively expanding German army led to his recall to field command as he was made a company commander in the 56th Infantry Regiment. In 1937, in recognition of his organizational skills, he was promoted to major and became the operations officer (Ia) of the 33rd Infantry Division.

At the start of World War II in September 1939, Speidel had risen to the rank of lieutenant colonel, as he benefited directly from the rapid promotion possible during the years of unprecedented and massive military expansion of the late 1930s. During the early months of the war he served in a General Staff appointment as the operations officer of the IX Army Corps, which was deployed defensively on Germany's western frontier. Here his knowledge of France and French military capabilities was again put to good use as he undertook the detailed staff work organizing a viable defense with the meager forces at his disposal, as Hitler threw the bulk of the German military into an all-out offensive against Poland. Speidel made his defensive preparations in accordance with the doctrine of delaying defense, developed by Gen. Hans von Seeckt during the interwar period, in which numerically inferior German forces would conduct a fighting withdrawal inflicting maximum damage on the enemy while preserving their own strength.[3] But France, the reluctant enemy, failed to take advantage of German weakness in the west during the so-called Sitzkrieg ("Sitting War") of the fall of 1939, and the French launched only half-hearted offensive operations that rapidly petered out. Consequently, Speidel's defensive preparations were never really tested.

During the summer of 1940 Speidel participated in the German offensive operations that overran France and the Low Countries, serving on the headquarters staff of the Sixth Army, which advanced across the Maas River. Speidel was directly responsible for the army staff's plan for an assault on Paris. Speidel planned a classic Prussian Kesselschlacht encirclement battle, with a pincer envelopment of the city. But disintegrating French resistance ensured that his blueprint never needed to be enacted, as the Germans motored into Paris brushing aside only slight resistance. After the French capitulation in June 1940, Speidel remained as the chief of staff to the military governor of France, where he was involved primarily in the administrative problems of occupation policy and garrison duty. His direct superior as military governor was Joachim von Stülpnagel, cousin to Karl-Heinrich von Stülpnagel, two men who had already become disillusioned with Hitler and Nazism.[4]

It was in trying to restore law and order and to affect a logical and coherent occupation policy in France that Speidel first came to understand Hitler's deliberate policy of "divide and rule," and his uncompromising and virtually limitless territorial and political ambitions. Thus, it was here in France in 1940 that Speidel first actively began to oppose the encroachment of the Nazi Party into what he considered as purely German military affairs.

During 1940 a cell of opponents of the regime known as the "George Group" began to gather around Speidel in Paris. Speidel tried, but failed, to prevent the growing German retaliation and repression of the French resistance movement, though he was apparently able to scale down to a small degree Nazi reprisals, especially the killing of hostages. Speidel, with his knowledge of history and the French, realized how counterproductive the harsh and uncompromising German occupation policy was. He understood that mass reprisals in particular would only fuel and solidify opposition to Nazi rule.

In February 1942, and now a colonel, Speidel left the occupation problems of France behind him as he transferred to the eastern front, following the flurry of dismissals that occasioned the serious German defeats over the winter of 1941–42. He was apparently at first relieved by the transfer, as he, like most Germans, firmly believed in the ideological threat that Nazi propaganda claimed Communism presented to the survival of the "Thousand Year Reich" and the Aryan Volk.

Speidel served as the chief of staff of the V Army Corps. In Russia Speidel was confronted for the first time with the bitter racist violence that pervaded the struggle in the east.[5] Speidel's previous conclusions about the counterproductive and self-defeating consequences of Nazi terror were thus reconfirmed and reinforced. In January 1943 he was promoted to brigadier general and became the chief of staff to the German liaison headquarters attached to the Italian Eighth Army that served alongside the Nazis on the eastern front. There, he witnessed anew the detrimental consequences of Nazi racism—this time directed at Germany's "inferior" Axis ally, Italy.

In the aftermath of the Stalingrad debacle Speidel joined the improvised Army Detachment Lanz (later Kempf) and made a contribution to the ultimate stabilization of the southern sector of the eastern front during late spring 1943, which is usually associated with the generalship of Field Marshal Erich von Manstein.[6] Indeed, Speidel oversaw the detailed administrative, and particularly logistic, preparations that underpinned German counteroffensive successes that recaptured Kharkov and stabilized the southern sector of the eastern front. In reward he became the chief of staff of the German Eighth

Army and was promoted to lieutenant general in January 1944. For his dedicated service on the eastern front he was awarded the Knight's Cross of the Iron Cross during the spring of 1944.

However, it was on the eastern front that Speidel developed a growing aversion to the corruption, violence, and inhumanity of Nazism. It was his first-hand experience of Hitler's disastrous interference in military operations and his experience working alongside the Italians that finally persuaded Speidel that Germany's political and military future was grim. He gradually became convinced during 1943 that the war could not be won and that Hitler's leadership would ultimately destroy Germany. At some point during that year Speidel became convinced of the necessity of ousting Hitler.

During the spring of 1944 Erwin Rommel personally selected Speidel as his chief of staff for the new appointment he assumed as the commander of Army Group B deployed in northern France. Rommel apparently had several motivations for selecting Speidel. Not only did Speidel have a reputation as a brilliant staff officer, but also both were Swabians by birth. Moreover, the two had previously met during World War I and the two had served together for a short time in the same infantry regiment during the interwar period. Rommel's "lead from the front" style meant that he required in a chief of staff an independently minded and intuitive subordinate with strength of character. Rommel believed that only Speidel of those staff officers currently available fit that bill.

Thus on 15 April 1944, Hans Speidel flew to Versailles and then drove onto the eleventh-century Norman castle of La Roche Guyon, between Mantes and Vernon, the former residence of the duke de la Rochefoucauld, to assume his duties. His appointment provided Speidel with a historic chance to win over the most popular German general to the anti-Hitler conspiracy.

No sooner had Speidel arrived than he apparently entered into discussions with Rommel about political issues. He also joined an established group of activists led by Karl-Heinrich von Stülpnagel, now the military governor of France, who was complicit in the widening military conspiracy that aimed at deposing Hitler. Speidel's increasing political activities occurred against a backdrop of frenetic activity, as Rommel characteristically threw himself into his new job with his typical energy and vigor. Involved in lengthy, daily visits to the troops, Rommel frequently left Speidel unsupervised for long periods of time, during which Speidel often acted as the de facto army group commander, issuing orders in the commander in chief's name with Rommel's full support.

Rommel and Speidel quickly fell into a regular routine. Rommel's staff rose before 0600 hours. Thereafter, Rommel and Speidel routinely ate breakfast alone, which provided an opportunity for Speidel to talk privately with Rommel about political issues. Rommel would then remain busy all day, frequently away from La Roche Guyon, with a short stop for lunch, until evening when he returned to his headquarters. Rommel and Speidel dined late each evening, usually with a group of ten to twelve officers of the staff. A friendship of sorts quickly developed between the pair, as they discovered that they had many commonalities. Neither was more than a light social drinker, neither was an ideologically committed Nazi, and both doubted that Germany could win the war. Rommel was accustomed to taking a late evening stroll in the grounds of the castle, usually with Speidel and Vice Adm. Friedrich Ruge, and it was on these walks that again their private conversations apparently often drifted toward discussion of Germany's future.

The day he took up his new appointment, Speidel gave Rommel an exceptionally frank appraisal of the war, in which he drew particular attention to the disastrous consequences of the racial war of extermination that Nazi Germany was waging on the eastern front. The clarity and farsightedness of Speidel's erudition had a great impact on Rommel, who having spent most of his time in the Mediterranean theater, apparently remained unaware of the true extent and ramifications of Nazi racism and terror in the east.

Speidel was a bespectacled, reserved, intellectual of great organizational skill and efficiency. He was cultured and loved the arts, qualities that the more down-to-earth Rommel appreciated and admired. Speidel was also rather egotistical and somewhat vain, and sometimes came across to others as self-centered. Nevertheless, Rommel recognized his great talents and glossed over his weaknesses because Speidel was the kind of chief of staff who was temperamentally suited to his own personal command style. Rommel's energetic and individual leadership style left considerable freedom of action for Speidel, who undertook responsibilities not normally associated with a chief of staff. Rommel remained personally friendly toward Speidel and admired his unflappable dependency.

By June 1944 Speidel, the educated intellectual, had become disillusioned with the Nazi regime. Never a Nazi ideologically—he was too educated and cultured to fall sway to the brash, crass, ahistoric, and racist propaganda in which National Socialism was rooted—Speidel had become convinced that Hitler was leading Germany toward national suicide. He apparently found in Rommel a German war hero who shared his doubts and uncertainties. However, both Rommel and Speidel remained loyal German officers, infused with the Prussian tradition of political neutrality and absolute obedience, and neither was prepared to act either decisively or on his own.

Nonetheless, it was Speidel who reintroduced Rommel to Karl-Heinrich von Stülpnagel, the latter two having served together as instructors at the Dresden War Academy. The three struck up a rapport and slowly Speidel and Stülpnagel drew Rommel into the conspiracy. In late May 1944 Rommel sent Speidel to Germany to make contact with other opposition leaders, while a procession of conspirators made their way to La Roche Guyon to consult with Rommel.

Indeed, unlike the dynamic war hero Klaus von Stauffenberg, Speidel, the calculating intellectual, was not temperamentally disposed toward rash and risky behavior. He thus had at best a peripheral involvement in the 20 July plot to assassinate Hitler—and much less than the central role he portrayed for himself in the postwar era that helped him to rehabilitate his military career.[7]

Speidel's postwar claim's that he had repeatedly and with some success managed to win over an evidently increasingly disillusioned Rommel to his cause of the conspirators remains inconclusive and probably will never be clarified. With the death of Rommel and the other conspirators, there is little evidence to corroborate or repudiate Speidel's version of events. The lack of documentary evidence and reliable testimony thus precludes a definitive determination of the extent to which Speidel won over Field Marshal Rommel to the conspiracy, and it therefore remains a matter of controversy. A close reading of Speidel's postwar recollections, and he was after all the only survivor of the inner circle of conspirators, shows them to be sometimes contradictory and often ambiguous. More recent claims that Speidel influenced the deployment of Army Group B's armored reserves in the Pas de Calais in order to have reliable troops at his disposal for an attempted coup d'état is based upon Speidel's own exaggerated role in the conspiracy and superficial evidence. There is no contemporary documentary evidence that supports this contention, and it is not on its face credible. Indeed, German deployments were wholly consistent with German perceptions of the Allies' capabilities and intentions.[8]

Moreover, Speidel in his memoirs clearly had the objective of elevating the status of the fallen Rommel to that of a German national hero. Thus, he probably exaggerated both his and Rommel's involvement in the 20 July bomb plot. Careful evaluation of the available evidence, however, suggests that Speidel failed in his objective of totally winning over Rommel. While Speidel succeeded in hardening Rommel's attitude against Hitler, the field marshal apparently remained ambivalent toward either a military coup or the assassination of Hitler. At best, Rommel appeared to have toyed with the possibility of arranging a separate capitulation in the west, as he came to realize by late June 1944 that his forces could not in the long run defeat the Allied Normandy invasion.

On D-day, 6 June 1944, with Rommel away in Germany celebrating his wife's fiftieth birthday, it was Speidel at La Roche Guyon who along with many of the other senior officers at subordinate commands dismissed a mounting tide of intelligence clues pointing to an impending invasion, which in retrospect seems an enormous oversight. Such omission has only fueled the conspiracy-theorists' belief in Speidel's central involvement in the anti-Hitler coalition. But with German forces on high alert, with continuous, nocturnal Allied bombing operations, and with repeated false alarms, German reactions inevitably had been dulled. That Speidel did not contact Rommel until the early hours of the morning thus hardly appears exceptional. Indeed, there is no substance whatsoever to the allegations that Speidel deliberately prevaricated to aid the Allied landings. For there weighed on Speidel's shoulders the heavy responsibility of the possibility that the Normandy landings were a diversion designed to draw off German reserves prior to a major landing in the Pas de Calais. Consequently, Speidel—like his superior the Commander-in-Chief West, Field Marshal Gerd von Rundstedt—did not order up the Army Group B reserves in Rommel's absence.

Speidel continued to act as Rommel's chief of staff as the army group commander first attempted to cobble together a substantial armored force for a counterattack to the coast to split the Allied bridgehead. This counteroffensive never really got off the ground, as the arriving armored reserves, disrupted by Allied tactical air strikes, straggled into Normandy and were quickly sucked into bitter defensive fighting against Allied forces seeking to expand and consolidate their bridgehead. On 10 June Rommel abandoned hope of driving the Allies back into the sea with his available forces, and he set about constructing an unyielding defense to pin the Allies to a narrow and shallow bridgehead while he awaited the arrival of fresh armored reserves withdrawn from the eastern front. Speidel was at the center of planning for this offensive, which aimed to break through to the coast and divide the Allied lodgment in two. The long-planned counteroffensive spearheaded by the II SS Panzer Corps, recalled from the eastern front, commenced on 28 June. Despite Speidel's detailed staff work and preparations, it quickly fizzled because of the great Allied strength on the ground, aerial mastery, defensive naval fire, and inadequate German strength and supplies. Rommel had no choice but to resume the defensive and surrender the initiative to the Allies. Convinced the main enemy effort would come from the Anglo-Canadian sector of the front at Caen, Rommel and Speidel improvised an extensive defense in depth southeast of Caen.

Speidel remained chief of staff of Army Group B after Rommel was seriously wounded by an Allied fighter-bomber attack on 17 July at, ironically, St. Foy de Montgomery. He served under Rommel's successor, Field Marshal Günther von Kluge, until he in turn unfairly fell under suspicion of treachery and took his own life in late August after being recalled to Berlin by Hitler. In the meantime, Speidel was completely passive on 20 July 1944 after Count Klaus von Stauffenberg's bomb narrowly failed to assassinate Hitler. While other members of the conspiracy made frantic last-minute and ultimately abortive efforts to induce von Kluge to join the conspiracy, Speidel remained utterly neutral, to such an extent that active plotters on that day in the west were unaware of his involvement in the conspiracy.

In his defense, Speidel was very busy trying to orchestrate the successful defense against the British Operation Goodwood offensive that had ripped open the German defenses south of Caen. In particular, he was preoccupied with the desperate need to resupply the German forces engaged via an utterly inadequate logistic system.[9] Such was Speidel's passivity that even von Kluge apparently had no suspicions whatsoever about the loyalty of his chief of staff. Thus, Speidel continued to serve under von Kluge's successor, Field Marshal Walther Model, until 7 September 1944 when Speidel was suddenly arrested by the Gestapo for his alleged involvement in the 20 July plot. It transpired that several of the conspirators had divulged his name under terrible torture. Going against the grain of the contemporary and extremely thorough Gestapo witch-hunt for conspirators, Speidel was cleared of complicity in the plot against Hitler by an army court of inquiry, which saved him from almost-certain execution. This fact provides the strongest evidence that Speidel greatly exaggerated his involvement in the plot in the postwar period. Nonetheless, he remained in custody—clearly the Gestapo considered him suspect—until liberated by French troops on 29 April 1945.

Though he was guilty of complicity and Hitler was convinced of it, Speidel had covered his tracks well and his passivity on 20 July helped to save his skin. For his supposed participation in the anti-Hitler resistance, however, Hans Speidel was able to rehabilitate his public image in the postwar era. He resumed his historical studies, became a well-known historian specializing in military history at the University of Tübingen, and in 1955 became a lieutenant general in the newly created Bundeswehr. In 1957 he became the commander of NATO Land Forces, Central Europe, and a full general. He published his memoirs and recollections of the Normandy campaign, and he became one of the highest-ranking generals of the new Bundeswehr before his retirement.[10] He died in 1984 at the age of eighty-eight.

Notes

1. For the best, brief description of Speidel's military career see Klaus-Jürgen Müller, "Witzleben, Stuelpnagel and Speidel," in *Hitler's Generals*, ed. Corelli Barnett (New York: Grove Weidenfeld, 1989), 43–74. Speidel published his own autobiography: Hans Speidel, *Aus unserer Zeit: Erinnerungen* (Berlin: Propyläen, 1977).
2. Good insight into the Prussian military worldview may be found in Jehuda Wallach's *The Dogma of the Battle of Annihilation: The Theories of Clausewitz and Schlieffen and Their Impact on the German Conduct of Two World Wars* (Westport, Conn.: Greenwood Press, 1986).
3. James Corum, *The Roots of Blitzkrieg: Hans von Seeckt and German Military Reform* (Lawrence: University of Kansas Press, 1992).
4. Müller. "Witzleben, Stuelpnagel and Speidel," 43–74.
5. On Nazi racist violence and atrocities on the eastern front see Hannes Heer and Klaus Naumann, *Vernichtungskrieg: Verbrechen der Wehrmacht, 1941–1944* (Hamburg: Hamburger Edition, 1995); Omer Bartov, *The Eastern Front, 1941–45, German Troops and the Barbarisation of Warfare* (New York: St. Martin's Press, 1988); and *Hitler's Army: Soldiers, Nazis, and the Third Reich* (Oxford: Oxford University Press, 1991).
6. Eberhard Schwarz, *Die Stabilisierung der Ostfront nach Stalingrad: Mansteins gegenschlag zwischen Dontez und Dnirpr im Frühjahr 1943* (Göttingen: Hansen-Schmidt, 1985).
7. Hans Speidel, *Invasion 1944: Ein beitrag zu Rommels und des Reiches Schicksal* (Tübingen: Rainer Wunderlich Verlag Hermann Leins, 1949), pt. 4, chap. 2.
8. Russell A. Hart, *Clash of Arms: How the Allies Won in Normandy, June–August 1944* (Boulder, Colo.: Lynne Rienner, 2001), chap. 10.
9. Russell A. Hart, "Feeding Mars: The Role of Logistics in the German Defeat in Normandy, 1944," *War in History*, no. 4 (Fall 1996): 418–35.
10. Speidel, *Aus unserer Zeit*.

CHRONOLOGY OF FRIEDRICH-WILHELM VON MELLENTHIN

30 Aug 1904	Born in Breslau, Germany.
1 Apr 1924	Appointed Fahnenjunker, 7th Cavalry Regiment.
1 Sep 1926	Promoted to Fähnrich.
1 Aug 1927	Promoted to Oberfähnrich.
1 Feb 1928	Promoted to lieutenant.
1 Apr 1931	Promoted to first lieutenant.
1 Oct 1934	Assigned to Breslau Cavalry Regiment.
1 Aug 1935	Promoted to captain.
1 Oct 1935	Assigned to Kriegsakademie.
1 Aug 1937	Assigned to III Army Corps staff and candidate to the General Staff.
1 Apr 1939	Assigned as Ic, III Army Corps General Staff.
5 Jan 1940	Assigned as Ia, 197th Infantry Division.
1 Aug 1940	Assigned as Ic, First Army General Staff.
1 Dec 1940	Promoted to major.
29 Apr 1941	Assigned as Ic, Second Army General Staff.
15 Jun 1941	Assigned as Ic, Afrika Korps General Staff.
15 Aug 1941	Assigned as Ic, Panzerarmee Afrika General Staff.
1 Jun 1941	Promoted to lieutenant colonel.
12 Sep 1942	Assigned to Führer Reserve.
26 Nov 1942	Attached to the General Staff, XLVIII Panzer Corps.
1 Jan 1943	Assigned as chief of the General Staff, XLVIII Panzer Corps.
1 May 1943	Promoted to colonel.
20 Aug 1944	Assigned as chief of the General Staff, Fourth Panzer Army.
20 Sep 1944	Assigned as chief of the General Staff, Army Group G.
30 Nov 1944	Assigned to Führer Reserve.
1 Dec 1944	Promoted to major general.
28 Dec 1944	Assigned as regimental commander, 9th Panzer Division.
5 Mar 1945	Assigned as chief of the General Staff, Fifth Panzer Army.
28 June 1997	Died, Johannesburg, South Africa.

Friedrich-Wilhelm von Mellenthin

David T. Zabecki

Friedrich-Wilhelm von Mellenthin was a German General Staff officer whose career read like a map trace of the great armored campaigns of World War II. He was born in the garrison town of Breslau in 1904 to a Pomeranian Junker family. His father, Paul Henning von Mellenthin, was an artillery officer who was killed in action on the western front in June 1918. His mother, Orlinda von Waldenburg, was the great-granddaughter of Prince August of Prussia. Mellenthin's older brother Horst also served as an artillery officer in World War I. During World War II he commanded two divisions and then two corps, finishing the war as a General der Artillerie. After the war Horst von Mellenthin became a key figure in first the Gehlen Organization, and then the Bundesnachrichtdienst, the West German equivalent of the CIA.

F.-W., as he preferred to be called, enlisted in the 7th Cavalry Regiment as an officer candidate in April 1924. A life-long passionate horseman, he became a master of dressage, the most demanding and sophisticated of the equestrian sports. He continued to ride in and win competitions until he was well into his eighties.[1] Mellenthin received his commission in 1928, becoming one of only 4,000 officers allowed in the German army under the restrictions of the Versailles Treaty. For the first several years of his career he served as a regimental officer.

In 1935 von Mellenthin, along with approximately 1,000 other officers, took the entrance examination for the prestigious Kriegsakademie, the first step to becoming a General Staff officer. Only 150 of the applicants were

---

Major Friedrich-Wilhelm von Mellenthin standing on the right.

accepted for admission, with von Mellenthin placing in the top 10 percent.[2] He started the two-year course that October.

In the fall of 1937 Mellenthin was posted to the staff of III Corps as a General Staff candidate. The commanding general of III Corps at that time was Gen. Erwin von Witzleben, who later became a field marshal. Implicated in the July 1944 plot to kill Hitler, von Witzleben was hanged by the Gestapo. Mellenthin worked for a brief time in counterintelligence in the Berlin Military District, where in the summer of 1938 he had his first encounter with Erwin Rommel. The future commander of the Afrika Korps had just been appointed the supervisor of military training for the Hitler Youth in the Berlin area, and he dropped in to von Mellenthin's office to discuss some administrative matters.[3] In less than three years, von Mellenthin would be a key member of Rommel's staff in the desert.

In April 1939 von Mellenthin became the Ic (intelligence) of III Corps. The following October von Mellenthin was scheduled to report to the 5th Panzer Regiment for a year of cross-training. The Polish campaign hit first, and von Mellenthin remained as the Ic of III Corps, part of the Eighth Army that cut across the Polish Corridor from Pomerania to the Vistula. On 11 September 1939 III Corps came under the Eighth Army and started moving west of the Vistula. During a liaison visit to Eighth Army headquarters near Lodz, the light plane von Mellenthin was riding in suffered engine trouble and had to make a forced landing. The Storch landed near a group of troops in strange green uniforms that both von Mellenthin and the pilot assumed were Polish. On the verge of opening fire, they finally realized the strangely dressed troops were really from Organisation Todt, the German paramilitary construction organization.[4]

Immediately following the Polish campaign, von Mellenthin became the Ia (operations officer and chief of staff) of the 197th Infantry Division. During the French campaign, the 197th was part of the First Army. On 14 June the 197th attacked the Maginot Line near Puttlinger, south of Saarbrücken. Immediately following the surrender of France, von Mellenthin was posted to the First Army as the Ic. He was still only a captain at that point. He spent almost a year in Lorraine, giving him a great advantage in familiarity with the territory when he returned late in the summer of 1944.

In April 1941 von Mellenthin, now a major, transferred to the Second Army, again as the Ic. At the time, the Second Army was in southern Austria, assembling for the Balkans Campaign. On 14 April the headquarters of the Second Army moved into Belgrade. When Dusan Simovic resigned and the new Yugoslav government appealed for an armistice, von Mellenthin was given the task of drafting the document. On June 15, von Mellenthin became the head of the German liaison staff with the Italian Second Army at Fiume. He spent time on maneuvers with the Italians and was surprised by their obsolete equipment and the low level of training of their junior officers. During a trip to Venice he shocked the Italian officers at a hotel by eating at the same table as his driver. Writing about the event fifteen years later, von Mellenthin noted; "In contrast to 1918, the inner knowledge that officers and men belonged together was never shaken, and even in 1945 there were no signs of rot in the German Army."[5]

On August 15, 1941 von Mellenthin reported to Munich to become the Ic of a new staff being formed for Panzergruppe Afrika. There he met Lt. Col. Siegfried Westphal, who was designated to become the Ia (operations). Moving by rail to Rome, they linked up with Maj. Gen. Alfred Gause, the chief of staff. The new staff landed in Africa in mid-June. Not a General Staff officer himself, Rommel at first was extremely skeptical. He was only too aware of the dual reporting system, where General Staff officers reported not only to their commander but also to the chief of staff at the next higher level. Gause apparently had orders from Oberkommando der Wehrmacht (OKW) not to place himself under Rommel's command, but he did so after Rommel made it clear that he had command of all German forces in Africa.[6]

Rommel's methods of operating often ran counter to standard General Staff practices. He involved himself in planning details that normally would have been handled by the chief of staff. He often took his chief of staff with him on his visits to the frontline, leaving the Ia to run the headquarters for days at a time. During the Operation Crusader battle in 1941, Westphal and von Mellenthin, a lieutenant colonel and a major, were completely in charge of Rommel's headquarters from 23 to 28 November. Mellenthin later wrote:

> It is in periods such as this that sound staff training proves its value. The officers of the German General Staff were not mere clerks or mouthpieces of their commanders, but were trained to accept responsibility for grave decisions and were respected accordingly. In contrast, the British fighting commanders tend to look down on the staff, and the British show a curious reluctance to appoint capable staff officers to operational commands.[7]

Despite their differing backgrounds—the nobleman General Staff officer and the commoner line officer—von Mellenthin was intensely loyal to his commander, even though he could be a most difficult boss. In a 1987 interview von Mellenthin recalled that the Desert Fox could be abrupt and even rude with his staff officers, but never with his soldiers and his POWs. Mellenthin remembered:

He was the toughest taskmaster I've ever known. He spared no one, least of all himself. He was never as nice or polite as James Mason portrayed him [in the movie]. To work for him you had to have an iron constitution and even stronger nerves. He would arrive from the field covered with dust and grime, burst into the command post, and gruffly demand, "Wie is die Lage?" [What is the situation?] which Westphal and I would instantly respond with a crisp 5-minute summary.[8]

During the Gazala battle in May 1942, von Mellenthin was detached temporarily to become the Ia of a battle group under Gen. Ludwig Crüwell. When Crüwell was shot down and captured, von Mellenthin was left in temporary command of the group. Field Marshall Albert Kesselring, the theater commander, later arrived at the group headquarters on a command visit. Mellenthin asked him to assume direct command of the group for the remainder of the battle, but Kesselring initially refused. As a field marshal, he was not about to place himself even temporarily under the command of Rommel, a colonel general at the time. There was always a great deal of personal friction between Kesselring and Rommel. Kesselring finally relented when von Mellenthin pointed out that the only other alternative was for one of the Italian generals to assume command of Group Crüwell.[9]

Westphal was wounded on 1 June 1942, and von Mellenthin had to take over temporarily as Ia of Panzerarmee Afrika. On 21 June von Mellenthin was present at a meeting between Rommel and Kesselring in Rommel's command vehicle. Near the end of April Hitler and Mussolini had agreed that after the fall of Tobruk, Panzerarmee Afrika would go over to the defensive along the Egyptian border while all Axis air and naval forces in the area concentrated on taking Malta. The island fortress was the pivot point of British power in the Mediterranean. Now, however, Rommel was arguing that he had to exploit his recent successes against the British immediately, driving for the Suez Canal without waiting for Malta to fall.

Kesselring, a far better strategist than Rommel, knew better. He understood that as long as the British held Malta, the Germans would never have secure lines of communications to Africa. He made it clear to Rommel that he intended to withdraw the majority of the Luftwaffe units to Sicily, whether Rommel agreed or not. Rommel did not. But following his victories at Gazala and Tobruk, Rommel had been promoted to field marshal, which gave him direct access to Hitler. Rommel took his case to the Führer and carried the day, despite stiff opposition from the Italian General Staff, the German naval staff, and Kesselring. It was one of Germany's bigger strategic blunders of World War II. Writing after the war, von Mellenthin recognized the error, but ever loyal to his old commander, he placed the blame on Hitler and the German supreme command.[10]

Mellenthin served as Rommel's acting Ia through the battles of Mersa Metruh, Ruweisat Ridge, and Alam Halfa. During the Ruweisat Ridge battle, von Mellenthin personally organized and led a scratch force he pulled together to stop a British counterattack. Rommel later credited his acting Ia with stopping the British.[11] By the time Westphal returned to duty, von Mellenthin had been suffering from amoebic dysentery for months. He was medically evacuated back to Germany in September 1942, realizing full well what the future held in store for the German forces in Africa. As he left, Rommel handed him an estimate of the situation and a request for more supplies, to be delivered personally to the chief of the German General Staff.

Mellenthin spent two months in a military hospital in Garmisch in the Bavarian Alps. At the end of November he received orders to report to the newly formed XLVIII Panzer Corps, then part of the Romanian Third Army in Russia. The corps was positioned at the great bend in the Don River, near its confluence with the Chir River. The XLVIII Panzer Corps was designated to play a key role in supporting the upcoming attack of the German Fourth Panzer Army to relieve the encircled Sixth Army at Stalingrad. But in late November the XLVIII Panzer Corps itself had been attacked and encircled. Both the commander and the chief of staff were relieved, and Lieutenant Colonel von Mellenthin was thrown in as the new chief of staff.

Mellenthin arrived at the corps headquarters on 29 November, just days after it fought its way out of the encirclement. Both the old commander and chief of staff were gone and the Ia was holding things together. The XLVIII Panzer Corps held a small bridgehead on the left bank of the Don at Nizhna Chirskaya, only some twenty-five miles from the closest Sixth Army troops at Marianowka. Mellenthin immediately set out visiting units and positions to assess the situation. General Hans Cramer—who later was captured in Tunisia as the last commander of the Afrika Korps—assumed temporary command of the XLVIII.

Before the Fourth Panzer Army could attack, the Soviets attacked first. In early December Gen. P. L. Romanenko's Fifth Tank Army launched heavy attacks across the Don at various points. The XLVIII Panzer Corps was detached from the Romanian Third Army and committed to counter the Soviet attacks. Moving to Nizhna Chirskaya, the corps assumed command of the 11th Panzer and 336th Infantry Divisions, and a Luftwaffe Field Division. General Otto von Knobelsdorf also assumed command of the corps.

The main striking force of the XLVIII Panzer Corps was the 11th Panzer Division, commanded by Maj. Gen. Hermann Balck. Working closely with the corps chief of staff, Balck conducted one of the most brilliant series of divisional counterattack battles in military history. Between 6 and 22 December, some 700 Soviet tanks were knocked out along the Chir River in the XLVIII sector. On 22 December, XLVIII Panzer Corps was ordered to move to Tatsinskaya, 150 kilometers to the west. There, attacking with the 6th and 11th Panzer Divisions, the XLVIII Panzer Corps wiped out a Soviet guards tank corps.[12]

During lulls in the action during the early months of 1943, von Mellenthin took the time to learn how to drive the PzKpfw-VI Tiger tank and fire its 88mm main gun. During a short leave in early April, von Mellenthin visited the new chief of the General Staff, Gen. Kurt Zeitzler. While at army headquarters, von Mellenthin learned of the initial plans for what would become Operation Citadel, the German attack at Kursk. Initially supportive of the idea, von Mellenthin told Zeitzler that the attack should be made immediately, that any delay would favor the Soviets.[13]

Hitler, of course, continually delayed the attack to build up a more decisive force. By the time the attack finally was launched on 4 July 1943, the window of opportunity had long since passed and almost all of Hitler's military advisors were against it. The XLVIII Panzer Corps formed the left half of the Fourth Panzer Army's main effort, attacking into the salient from the south. Mellenthin's corps had the 3rd and 11th Panzer Divisions and the Grossdeutschland Division, with a total of sixty assault guns and more than 300 tanks. By 23 July, however, the Fourth Panzer Army had been thrown back to its lines of departure.

In early November 1944, Balck assumed command of the XLVIII Panzer Corps. Mellenthin remained as the chief of staff, starting one of military history's most remarkable partnerships between a commander and his chief of staff. It was another interesting relationship between a noble General Staff officer and a line officer from a commoner—although militarily distinguished—family. Mellenthin later wrote that he considered Balck to be Germany's finest battlefield commander of World War II. He also wrote: "Between him and myself there was that ideal cooperation, based on unlimited mutual faith—a state of things which could not be improved upon between a commander and his chief of staff."[14] And: "Balck never interfered in the details of staff work; for such work his chief of staff was required to take sole responsibility."[15] In Balck's own memoirs he wrote:

> An extraordinarily happy partnership began with this outstanding staff officer. On the Chir we had already got to understand one another quickly and with a few words. Now, a brief discussion every morning, often simply a short indication of something on the map, was enough to keep us synchronized for the entire day. We also agreed that one should get things done with as little staff work as possible. We never loaded the units with unnecessary paperwork.[16]

During the German counterattack against the Kiev salient in late 1943, the XLVIII Panzer Corps commanded six Panzer and one infantry division. Balck and von Mellenthin planned a deep thrust into the Soviet rear, but Col. Gen. Erhard Raus, commander of the Fourth Panzer Army, vetoed the plan as too risky. The result was a more conventional frontal attack that merely pushed the Soviet forces back but did not destroy them.[17] Around Christmas 1943, Soviet forces broke through the line of the XXIV Panzer Corps and started pouring through the gap. The XLVIII Panzer Corps, which now was being called the fire brigade of the eastern front, was thrown in to close the gap and restore the situation. Another lull set in following that battle. With von Mellenthin's dysentery still bothering him, Balck sent his chief of staff back to Germany on medical leave.

Mellenthin reported back to the front in April 1944. The XLVIII Panzer Corps was now part of the First Panzer Army, under Field Marshal Walther Model's Army Group South (renamed Army Group North Ukraine). Although von Mellenthin had a great deal of professional respect for the army group commander, he believed that Model interfered in details too much, and was too prone to tell his corps and army commanders how to deploy their units.[18] During a visit to XLVIII Panzer Corps, Balck and Model had "a terrible row" in private over the field marshal's somewhat chaotic leadership style. After that, Model never again visited XLVIII Panzer Corps, but Model always was the first to send congratulations whenever Balck received a new appointment.[19]

On 14 July the Soviets launched a major attack against Army Group North Ukraine. The next day the XLVIII Panzer Corps launched a counterattack with the 1st and 8th Panzer Divisions. Despite the excellent plan of attack, the commander of the 8th Panzer Division moved his division along an open road, rather than through the woods, as Balck had instructed. Soviet aircraft caught them in the open, the division suffered heavy losses, and the corps attack stalled. Balck relieved the division commander and put von Mellenthin in temporary command.

With another coordinated attack planned for 18 July, von Mellenthin placed his frontline infantry units under the commander of the division's Panzer regiment, to ensure unity of command. Just before dawn on the morning of the attack, von Mellenthin and his divisional artillery commander were headed for the front when they ran into the infantry units in the process of withdrawing—even though they were supposed to attack in less than a half hour. When von Mellenthin finally found the Panzer regiment commander, he said that he had wanted to regroup the forces before the attack. Mellenthin relieved him on the spot, but the Soviets established new minefields before the attack could be reorganized. Mellenthin had no choice but to cancel the attack.[20]

The Soviets captured Lublin in eastern Poland on 1 August 1944. The Fourth Panzer Army was driven back across the Vistula River, and the First Panzer Army with the XLVIII Panzer Corps was forced into the Carpathian Mountains. With disaster looming for the Germans, Balck was appointed commander of the Fourth Panzer Army. Mellenthin followed two weeks later as his chief of staff. With his army positioned at the great bend of the Vistula where it joins the River San, Balck organized a masterful defense that stopped the Soviets cold and stabilized that sector of the front for the next four months.[21]

In September 1944 Balck was summoned to Hitler's headquarters and told he was being appointed commander of Army Group G on the western front. Mellenthin was to go with him as chief of staff. Hitler also informed Balck about the planned German counteroffensive into the Ardennes. The mission of Army Group G, to the south of the Ardennes, was to hold Alsace and Lorraine at all costs; buy time for the German buildup; and avoid the development of any situation that would divert forces to Army Group G. Balck and von Mellenthin were the only officers in Army Group G who knew of the overall plan.

They arrived at Army Group G headquarters on 20 September, relieving Col. Gen. Johannes Blaskowitz and his chief of staff. Blaskowitz had been fired as the result of one of the political intrigues of SS chief Heinrich Himmler. That same fate awaited Balck in the not-too-distant future. Initially, Field Marshal Gerd von Rundstedt, the German Commander-in-Chief West, was opposed to Balck's appointment of the basis of his lack of experience in fighting the Western Allies. Rundstedt's chief of staff was Mellenthin's old friend Siegfried Westphal, and in short order, the two chiefs of staff managed to smooth over any differences between their commanders.[22]

Balck's army group initially consisted of the First and Nineteenth Armies, and the Fifth Panzer Army under Gen. Hasso von Manteuffel. Balck immediately launched a large-scale attack to stop the advance of U.S. XII Corps. The Germans, however, were hit by Allied fighter-bombers, far harder than anything Balck and von Mellenthin had experienced in the East. As von Mellenthin later put it, "the normal principles of armored warfare did not apply in this theater."[23] From that point on, Army Group G started training in night operations to counter the Allies' advantage in air power.

Unknown to the Germans at the time, Supreme Allied Commander General Dwight Eisenhower simplified Army Group G's problems by ordering Gen. George S. Patton's U.S. Third Army to go over to the defensive on 22 September because of theater-wide logistics problems. Balck and von Mellenthin both knew of Patton's reputation, and they couldn't understand his actions. Standing in front of their situation map, Balck often commented to von Mellenthin, "Patton is helping us; he failed to exploit another success."[24]

By the beginning of November Army Group G was down to only about 140 tanks. They had plenty of artillery pieces, but they were mostly captured guns with little or no ammunition. Sometime in November Gen. Heinz Guderian, now the chief of the German General Staff, sent a personal emissary to Lorraine to advise Balck and von Mellenthin how to deploy their useless artillery. Mellenthin had no time for such nonsense and virtually ignored the representative.

When the word got back to Guderian, he summoned von Mellenthin back to Berlin, relieved him, and placed him under house arrest. He also took the unusually draconian step of dismissing von Mellenthin from the General Staff.[25] Balck wrote in his diary:

> Today my chief of staff Mellenthin has been relieved. The reason is obvious. Mellenthin committed himself very forcefully and with all his powers of argument in favor of all our decisions. The withdrawal of unusable elements from Alsace and the evacuation of the Belfort pocket were his work. He battled hard for our latest decision. To me he was a chief of staff and a supporter such as one seldom finds. For two years we have stood together firmly in the most difficult crises and we mastered every situation.[26]

Less than two weeks later the Nineteenth Army was taken away from Army Group G and placed under Himmler, a man with absolutely no military knowledge or experience. Balck too was relieved, but Guderian quickly managed to get him assigned as commander of the reformed Sixth Army in Hungary.

Oddly enough, the day after von Mellenthin was relieved and transferred to the Führer Reserve he was promoted to major general. For the first time since the war started, he was able to spend Christmas with his family. He used the time to move his family from eastern Germany to north of Berlin, out of the path of the advancing Soviet army. The day after Christmas von Mellenthin received orders to report to the 9th Panzer Division as a regimental commander. The 9th Panzer Division was fighting in the Ardennes. By the time von Mellenthin reached his new unit on 29 December, the German advance already had ground to a halt. During the Allied counterattacks that followed, the 9th Panzer Division was the rearguard of the Fifth Panzer Army.

Mellenthin did not remain a line officer for long. At that point in the war the Germans were desperate for trained and experienced General Staff officers. By the end of February 1945 he was functioning as von Manteuffel's chief of staff at Fifth Panzer Army. On 1 April the U.S. First and Ninth Armies linked-up inside Germany to form the Ruhr Pocket. Trapped inside was most of Model's Army Group B, including the Fifth Panzer Army. Mellenthin had a great deal of close contact with Model during that period. They actually discussed whether or not Model should initiate negotiations with the Allies. They both decided against the move.[27]

On 17 April Model offered discharges to most of the soldiers of Army Group B. Four days later he committed suicide in the Ruhr Pocket. Refusing to surrender, von Mellenthin and a small group of officers managed to evade until captured by American troops on 3 May near Höxter, on the Wesel River. As a member of the General Staff, von Mellenthin remained a prisoner for two and a half years. Following that, he was a homeless refugee in West Germany for three more years. His family had managed to avoid capture by the Soviets, but they lost all their estates and property in eastern Germany. They finally were able to immigrate to South Africa after von Mellenthin's wife received an inheritance from her grandfather, who had immigrated to South Africa himself years before.[28]

After he moved to South Africa, von Mellenthin started a local airline, which soon grew to handle much of Lufthansa's business in that part of the world. Eventually, Lufthansa made him their regional director. In the late 1970s and early 1980, both Balck and his old chief of staff participated in a series of interview and seminar programs for the U.S. Army. Their views and opinions were sought eagerly by the American military leaders who were then developing the new AirLand Battle doctrine, which itself was deeply rooted in World War II German tactical doctrine. Commenting on Auftragstaktik, the German concept of "mission orders" which the U.S. military has struggled to apply for the last sixty years, von Mellenthin said:

> To follow a command or an order requires that it is thought through on the level from which the order was given. The following through of an order requires that the person to whom it was given thinks at least one level above the one at which the order was given. The mission requires one to be able to think, or to penetrate by thought, the functions of the higher commander.[29]

A few years after von Mellenthin made that comment, the concepts of mission orders and the commander's intent became standard elements of U.S. military doctrine.[30]

Notes

Note: The source for the chronology is Bundesarchiv-Miliärarchiv, "Chronologies of German General Officers" (Freiburg, Germany), File MSg 109/10849.

1. Verner R. Carlson, "Portrait of a German General Staff Officer," *Military Review* (April 1990): 69–70.
2. Ibid., 71.
3. F. W. von Mellenthin, *German Generals of World War II as I Saw Them* (Norman: University of Oklahoma Press, 1977), 57.
4. F. W. von Mellenthin, *Panzer Battles: A Study of Employment of Armor in the Second World War* (Norman: University of Oklahoma Press, 1956), 8.
5. Mellenthin, *Panzer Battles*, 46.
6. Erwin Rommel, *The Rommel Papers*, ed. Basil H. Liddell Hart (New York: Harcourt Brace, 1953).
7. Mellenthin, *Panzer Battles*, 90.
8. Carlson, "Portrait of a German General Staff Officer," 74–75.
9. Albert Kesselring, *Kesselring: A Soldier's Record* (New York: William Morrow, 1954), 145–46.
10. Mellenthin, *Panzer Battles*, 151–52.
11. Rommel, *Rommel Papers*, 253.
12. Bundesarchiv-Miliärarchiv, "Kriegstagebuch Nr.6 der 11.Panzer Division. Einsatz Russland in der Zeit vom 1.11.1942 bis 31.12.1942," (Freiburg, Germany), Files RH27-11/53 and RH27-11/55-59; Hermann Balck, *Ordnung im Chaos: Erinnerungen 1893–1948* (Osnabrück: Biblio Verlag, 1981), 399–408; Mellenthin, *Panzer Battles*, 211–20.
13. Mellenthin, *Panzer Battles*, 261–65.
14. Ibid., 304.
15. Ibid., 305.

16. Balck, *Ordnung im Chaos*, 467.
17. Ibid., 488–90.
18. Mellenthin, *Panzer Battles*, 336.
19. Battelle Columbus Laboratories, "Translation of a Taped Conversation with General Hermann Balck, 13 April 1979," Columbus, Ohio, July 1979, 28.
20. Balck, *Ordnung im Chaos*, 527.
21. Heinz Guderian, *Panzer Leader* (New York: Ballantine Books, 1957), 374; Balck, *Ordnung im Chaos*, 542.
22. Mellenthin, *Panzer Battles*, 372–406.
23. Ibid., 380; BDM Corporation, "Generals Balck and von Mellenthin on Tactics: Implications for NATO Military Doctrine," U.S. Army War College Art of War Colloquium, Carlisle Barracks, Pa., April 1983, 51.
24. Battelle Columbus Laboratories, "Translation of a Taped Conversation"; "Military Doctrine," U.S. Army War College Art of War Colloquium, Carlisle Barracks, Pa., April 1983, 51.
25. Carlson, "Portrait of a German General Staff Officer," 78–79.
26. Balck, *Ordnung im Chaos*, 590.
27. Mellenthin, *German Generals*, 157.
28. Carlson, "Portrait of a German General Staff Officer," 69–70.
29. BDM Corporation, "Generals Balck and von Mellenthin on Tactics," 22.
30. U.S. Army, *FM 100-5 Operations* (Washington, D.C.: Government Printing Office, May 1986), 15, 21.

CHRONOLOGY OF ERIC DORMAN-SMITH

24 Jul 1895	Born, County Cavan (now in the Republic of Ireland).
1910–13	Attended Uppingham School.
1913–14	Attended Royal Military College, Sandhurst.
25 Feb 1914	Commissioned, Northumberland Fusiliers.
1914–17	Served in France and Belgium during World War I, wounded three times.
1916	Awarded Military Cross.
26 Nov 1917	Transferred to Italy.
9 Apr 1918	Assigned as adjutant, 12th Battalion, Durham Light Infantry.
28 Jan 1918	Assistant military landing officer, Italy.
12 Jun 1921	Adjutant, Northumberland Fusiliers, occupation duty in Germany and anti-IRA duties in Northern Ireland.
28 Aug 1924	Assigned as an instructor at Sandhurst.
1927–28	Attended the Staff College, Camberley. Passed out in the top four and with A grade.
15 Jan 1929	Assigned as an instructor in tactics at Royal Engineer School, Chatham (the first infantry officer to hold this post).
11 Jul 1931	Appointed as brigade major of the 6th (Experimental) Infantry Brigade at Aldershot, under Brig. Archibald Wavell.
Jul 1933	Assigned to 2nd Battalion, Northumberland Fusiliers.
16 Jan 1934	Appointed as a General Staff officer (GSO2) in the War Office, London, in the department dealing with development and annual estimates. Met Liddell Hart and was influenced by his views.
1 Jan 1936	Assigned as an instructor at the Staff College, Camberley.
26 Apr 1937	Appointed as commanding officer, 1st Battalion, Northumberland Fusiliers, Egypt. Converted the unit from line to a mechanized machine-gun battalion.
10 May 1938	Promoted to temporary brigadier. Appointed director, Military Training, India. Responsible for training one-half million Indian and British soldiers. Served as member of Gen. Sir Claude Auchinleck's Modernization Committee.
1 Jul 1938	Promoted to colonel.

1940	Served as commandant of the new Middle East Staff College set up by Wavell at Haifa, Palestine.
19 Sep 1940	Chief Staff Officer to Gen. Sir Richard O'Connor during the first British offensive in Western Desert.
May 1942	Assigned as deputy chief of the General Staff to Auchinleck, as commander in chief, Middle East.
Jun–Aug 1942	Acted as Auchinleck's chief of staff at the battle of Ruweisat Ridge when the latter assumed direct command of the Eighth Army.
16 Jun 1942	Promoted to acting major-general.
6 Aug 1942	Auchinleck and Dorman-Smith both dismissed by Winston Churchill after their victory.
17 Sep 1942	Assigned as commander, 160th Infantry Brigade in southern England.
27 Apr 1944	Assumed command of the 3rd Infantry Brigade at Anzio.
14 Aug 1944	Dismissed when it was alleged his battalion commanders found it impossible to serve under him.
14 Dec 1944	Retired as substantive colonel, honorary brigadier.
1950–54	Served as military advisor to the Irish Republican Army during its Border Campaign in Northern Ireland.
11 May 1969	Died, County Cavan, Republic of Ireland.

Eric Dorman-Smith

Phillip Green

Eric Dorman-Smith was one of the most controversial and enigmatic personalities produced by the British army in World War II. Though he lived for seventy-four years, thirty of them in the army, he was chief of staff for a mere six weeks of that time, when in June 1942 Gen. Sir Claude Auchinleck took personal command of the Eighth Army at a moment of desperate crisis and pressed Dorman-Smith into service as his chief of staff. Together they rallied and reorganized the Eighth Army, defeated Rommel in the battle of Ruweisat Ridge (sometimes called the first battle of El Alamein) and laid the firm foundations for Lt. Gen. Bernard Law Montgomery's victory in the second battle in October that year.

Yet within a few weeks both had been dismissed on Prime Minister Winston S. Churchill's insistence and Dorman-Smith's career was virtually at an end. It is as if fate had decreed that the whole of his life's work should be compressed into those six dramatic weeks when Britain's position in the Middle East hung in the balance, as if all his previous life was simply a preparation for this trial, and all his subsequent years but a sad anticlimax. "Tremendous achievement followed by tragic waste," was Correlli Barnett's verdict on this affair. This "tremendous achievement" was overshadowed for almost twenty years by the glamour of Montgomery's victory at El Alamein, and it was not until Barnett produced the book *The Desert Generals* that Auchinleck and Dorman-Smith eventually received the recognition due to them.

Dorman-Smith was born in Ireland in 1895. Somewhat unusually he was raised a Catholic while his two younger brothers (one of whom was governor of Burma when the Japanese invaded) were raised as Protestants. He was educated at Uppingham and Sandhurst. Brian Horrocks, one of Montgomery's corps commanders in the desert and northwest Europe, was Dorman-Smith's contemporary at both establishments. Dorman-Smith was commissioned into the Royal Northumberland Fusiliers in 1914. He soon received the nickname "Chink" from his likeness to the regimental mascot, a Chinkara antelope, and this was to stay with him for the rest of his life. From 1914 until 1939 his career was a continuous success story in both war and peace.

Dorman-Smith served in Flanders and Italy for most of World War I. He was awarded the Military Cross and two Mentions in Dispatches and was wounded three times, and he commanded a battalion at Passchendaele at the age of twenty-three. In Italy he became friendly with Ernest Hemingway, who was serving there in the American Red Cross. Through Hemingway Dorman-Smith met such literary people as Gertrude Stein, James Joyce, and Ezra Pound in the early 1920s. This was an unusual circle of friends for a British army officer of that period, but one with which he was happy intellectually. It is probable that Hemingway based some of his characters on Dorman-Smith, most noticeably Robert Cantwell in *Across the River and Into the Trees*.

Between the wars Dorman-Smith rose from captain to brigadier in ten years with the help of well-earned brevet promotions. He was a firm disciple of Sir Basil H. Liddell Hart's theories and a strong believer in the need to reform the army to meet the needs of modern war: not just its equipment, but its tactics, organization, and method of thinking as well. Not surprisingly he made many enemies, especially among those who could not match his quick and analytical brain.

In 1938 he was promoted to major and appointed director of military training, India. It was here that he first met Auchinleck, then Deputy Chief of Staff, India, and they developed an excellent personal and professional relationship that was to prove invaluable in 1942. "We discussed war and training . . . and I found him very valuable to talk to," wrote Auchinleck later. "Very imaginative. Not popular, because he was a little bit inclined to state his opinions very openly, and the less intelligent didn't like him much. But I had a very great opinion of him." Dorman-Smith was a member of Auchinleck's four-man modernization committee that just in time began to prepare the Indian army, an enormous but rather old-fashioned part of the British empire's military assets, for the trials ahead. The excellent performance of Indian divisions in the Middle East is a testimony to the efficiency and military acumen of Dorman-Smith and his colleagues.

With hindsight it is obvious that Auchinleck should have dismissed Gen. Neil M. Ritchie and taken command of the Eighth Army long before he did on 30 June 1942, and as Churchill had urged. There were two good reasons for his reluctance. One was the enormous area for which he was responsible as Commander in Chief (CinC) Middle East; not just the Eighth Army and the Western Desert, but East Africa, the Levant, the Balkans, Persia, and Iraq as well. A particular concern was that further Soviet defeats in the Caucasus would make it possible for the Germans to invade Persia and Iraq, and he did not have enough troops to meet this possible new threat. The other reason was that he was loathe to dismiss Ritchie so soon after appointing him in Cunningham's place. By the time Auchinleck did take personal command, Tobruk had fallen and Gen. Erwin Rommel had advanced 400 miles in thirty-six days. The bewildered Eighth Army was in danger of disintegrating, not so much out-fought as out-generaled. Italian premier Benito Mussolini certainly thought the campaign was over, having flown to Derna complete with a white horse on which he proposed to lead the victory parade through Cairo. On 1 July *The Times* emphasized the danger of the situation: "This is the most serious moment for the Middle East since the beginning of the war, and unless we can hold Rommel's forces for a few more days there is no knowing what may happen."

In fact we do know with a fair degree of certainty what would have happened if Auchinleck and Dorman-Smith had failed to hold Rommel's forces. Had he been able to continue his advance to Alexandria and Cairo, it would have been a strategic disaster for the Allies. The way to the oilfields of Persia and Iraq, on which the empire depended, would have been opened; the Allied supply route to the Soviet Union through those countries would have been cut; India would have been threatened by the Germans from the northwest as well as by the Japanese from the northeast; the British Fleet would have been forced out of the Mediterranean; and Turkey may have been tempted to join the Axis. But Auchinleck, with the indispensable help and advice of Dorman-Smith, did not fail.

He took Dorman-Smith, who was at the time deputy chief of the general staff at his Middle East headquarters, with him because of his "fertile, active and very good brain. . . . He was a man I could talk to—a fresh mind." And though Dorman-Smith had so far spent the war in either Haifa or Cairo, away from the fighting, he had visited the desert three times on behalf of the two CinCs—first Gen. Archibald Wavell, then Auchinleck. In 1940 Dorman-Smith was sent to Lt. Gen. Richard O'Connor's headquarters to advise him on the plan for the attack on Sidi Barrani. It was on Dorman-Smith's suggestion that the assault, the most successful British land operation of the war till then, was launched on the unsuspecting Italians from the west and without prior artillery registration. At the end of the campaign Wavell sent him again to produce a report on the lessons learned. In early 1942 Dorman-Smith visited the Eighth Army on Auchinleck's behalf to assess its command procedures.

These visits had given him a feel for the Western Desert and its peculiar tactical and logistical problems. He must also have appreciated the contrasting reasons for O'Connor's success and Ritchie's failure, and in particular the difference between fighting the Italians and the Germans. Above all, on his third trip he saw at first hand the faults that had crept into the Eighth Army's tactics and organization.

Strictly speaking, Dorman-Smith was not chief of staff at Eighth Army headquarters, as there was officially no such post in the British army until Montgomery was permitted to appoint Francis de Guingand later that year. Moreover, J. F. M. Whitely, as Brigadier General Staff, the nearest to a chief of staff that then existed, remained in that post after Dorman-Smith's arrival. But he was a very tired man and after a few days Auchinleck decided to issue all orders through Dorman-Smith, in effect using him as chief of staff, unofficial though this may have been. In any case he had already said, "Shall use Dorman-Smith as my chief of staff," in his signal to the chief of the Imperial General Staff, reporting his intention to assume command. Correlli Barnett is thus right to call him the first one in the British army. Dorman-Smith believed that in this new (to the British) role he should be interdependent with the commander, indeed almost his equal; he thought such a relationship to have been the key to the success of the Ludendorff-Hindenburg partnership in World War I. Auchinleck certainly accepted the interdependence—why otherwise had he chosen him for the job?—but it is hard to imagine such a robust and doughty leader accepting the idea of virtual equality with any subordinate, however highly he valued his intelligence and support.

The first problem to confront the new command team was to find out what was going on. Ritchie's headquarters was too far back, and communications and the chain of command had broken down. The tactical headquarters was immediately moved forward to a position just behind the Ruweisat Ridge, a feature that was to play a vital part in the battle. Arguably this was dangerously far forward, but from there Auchinleck never lost control of the battle. Tactical headquarters lived a Spartan life, a complete contrast to the luxury the "gilded staff" was supposed to have enjoyed in 1914–18. Dorman-Smith and Auchinleck slept in blankets on the ground alongside the commander's operations caravan. These conditions, quite normal to the hardened Indian army campaigner Auchinleck, were not entirely to the liking of his more fastidious chief of staff, who complained in a letter to his future second wife about the hard blankets, poor food, flies, and shortage of water for washing. There is, though, not the slightest evidence that he allowed his distaste to affect his performance.

They rose at 0600 hours and worked through the day until supper at 1930 hours. Dorman-Smith's first task each morning was to look at the overnight situation reports and make as many decisions based on them as he could, leaving only the most important matters for his commander to deal with. The day ended with the evening conference (or "prayer meeting" as it is irreverently called in the British army), attended by Auchinleck, Dorman-Smith, the heads of the operations, intelligence, and logistics staffs, and the artillery commander. Dorman-Smith regarded it as his job to get the outline plan from Auchinleck at the prayer meeting (this usually being the fruit of their discussions throughout the day) and pass it on to subordinate staff officers with sufficient added detail to enable them to issue clear and concise orders to the various parts of the army. These, of course, are the standard duties of any chief of staff in any army. But it was the ideas that the imaginative and quick-thinking Dorman-Smith fed to Auchinleck that comprised his main contribution to the British victory. During the day the two spent much of the time closeted together discussing possible courses of action, with almost all the original thought coming from Dorman-Smith. To enable him to think logically and clearly, he needed to get away from Auchinleck from time to time and be alone, routinely after the prayer meeting and, if he could, during the day as well when Auchinleck was visiting forward formations.

We have already seen that Auchinleck chose Dorman-Smith for this mission because of his "fertile and active brain." He obviously regarded him as his ideas man. It is interesting to see what Dorman-Smith in turn thought of his master. "He is a commander and a fighter but definitely not a deep thinker, though he has the power to grasp a new idea and the energy to put it into practice," he wrote. Later he turned to a story of two Roman officers in Kipling's *Puck of Pook's Hill* to describe their working relationship. He equated himself with Parnesius, "who saw very clearly what needed to be done," and Auchinleck with Pertinax "who realized that things had to be done through men and knew how to manage that."

This aptly describes how the two men complemented each other: each had abilities and talents the other lacked, but together they possessed the skills and qualities of character needed to command the Eighth Army in the perilous situation they inherited. And, just as important, both understood the other's strengths and weaknesses. Not that under the stress of battle all was sweetness and light. Dorman-Smith complained in another letter of the abuse he often received from the commander; "Whenever I suggest a new thing his first instinct is to force me to justify it by oaths. He usually says no and then goes off and does it."

The course of the fight at Ruweisat Ridge is as confusing as any other battle in the Western Desert, but essentially it fell into three phases. In the first the British fell back on El Alamein, covered by a series of rearguards and in as orderly a manner as they could achieve in the circumstances. There they sorted themselves out and received welcome reinforcements. Had Rommel been able to mount a properly organized attack at this stage it is unlikely that the British could have resisted it, but his army was almost as disorganized and weakened by pursuit as the British were by headlong retreat. Moreover Rommel's 1,000-mile supply line from Tripoli was under constant attack, first by British special forces using the open desert flank to excellent effect, then by the Royal Air Force's Desert Air Force, which, operating from permanent bases in Egypt, maintained constant air superiority over the battlefield.

After a short pause the Germans attacked. Though they made a number of penetrations these were always repulsed by counterthrusts, on some occasions coming close to being cut off. The great advantage the British had was, of course, the Alamein position itself. With the impassable Quattara Depression some forty miles inland it was one of the few places in the theater with a secure southern flank. Three ridges, very low but nonetheless dominating features in that flat terrain—Miteirya, Ruweisat, and Alam Halfa—gave depth to the position. With his troops worn out and his supplies running short, especially fuel for his armor, Rommel was forced to abandon his attack.

The Eighth Army, though scarcely strong enough to do so, and against Auchinleck's judgment, launched a counteroffensive under pressure from London. This fared no better, and on 27 July, a month after Dorman-Smith and Auchinleck had taken over, the two exhausted armies settled into defensive positions to regroup and await reinforcements. Egypt and the Middle East had been saved. Auchinleck was the victor, but his chief of staff's ideas were crucial and their influence can be seen in the way Auchinleck handled the battle and in many of his key decisions.

Though the advantages of the Alamein position were obvious it was Dorman-Smith who saw the tactical significance of the Alam Halfa ridge and advised Auchinleck how to use it. Running east-west, it lay behind the left center of the British line. There were not enough troops to man the whole forty miles from the sea to the depression effectively. Making a virtue out of necessity, the Eighth Army left the southern ten to fifteen miles lightly covered, and turned Alam Halfa into a strongly held refused left flank. The aim was to tempt Rommel to outflank the main British position using the open inland flank, a standard desert tactic. If he then turned north to get behind the British he would run onto the Alam Halfa defenses. If he continued east on the inland axis, his supply lines would be vulnerable to a counterthrust from the ridge. Rommel fell into the trap and Alam Halfa played a large part in the British victory.

On his visit to Ritchie's headquarters earlier in the year, Dorman-Smith had seen at first hand the faults that had developed in the Eighth Army's tactics. Stated briefly these were an overreliance on static defensive "boxes," the armor's disastrous habit of acting alone, and the failure to concentrate artillery fire. The boxes were usually manned by static infantry and sited too far apart for mutual support. As a result, far too often they were either bypassed by more mobile forces or destroyed by stronger ones. The armor's habit of acting alone was, paradoxically, partly the product of tradition with recently mechanized regiments harking back to the days of their elite cavalry predecessors, and partly that of ultramodern thinking that saw the tank as the unchallengeable lord of the land battle. The Germans were guilty of none of these mistakes. Dorman-Smith also had seen how Ritchie constantly allowed Rommel the initiative, always reacting to his opponent's moves as if, in Dorman-Smith's opinion, they were acts of God. All this Auchinleck, acting on his chief of staff's advice, the value of which he willingly admitted, had to put right. There was no time or opportunity for leisurely conferences or training in secure areas; it had to be achieved during the course of the battle.

At the root of the problem was the organization of divisions into either armored or infantry. (This was exacerbated by the fact that in this imperial army most of the armor was British, most of the infantry from India or the Dominions; whenever the armor failed to arrive in time to help a hard-pressed infantry box an element of "tribal" friction was likely to arise.) Dorman-Smith and others had concluded from the evidence of the campaign so far that divisions should be mixed, with a proper balance of the two arms, and in the fluid, not to say disorganized, state the Eighth Army arrived at Alamein it was possible to partially reorganize on these lines. The result was a number of brigade groups, each containing armor and infantry, though not in a standard mix, and still coming under a divisional headquarters. The accusation was later made that breaking up established formations at a critical time was a wrong move that was likely to damage morale. The answer must be that the old system had not worked when faced by the more flexible Germans; that Dorman-Smith's sharp brain had seen it as one of the fundamental causes of failure; and, above all, that the new system brought success at Ruweisat Ridge.

Closely linked to this was the avoidance of static boxes. Though the word was still used to denote a defensive position, "boxes" now became bases from which counterattacks by mobile infantry supported by armor could be launched, and this tactic of fluid and mobile defense was one of the keys to success. Many times the Germans penetrated the British line—not a difficult thing to do in the wide-open desert spaces—but each time they were counterattacked, usually in the flank, and forced to beat a hasty withdrawal before they were cut off.

Churchill said that fame awaited the commander who restored the artillery to its proper place on the battlefield. Montgomery claimed that fame, but it properly belongs to Auchinleck, acting on his chief of staff's advice. For the first time since O'Connor defeated the Italians two years earlier, the artillery, the one arm in which the British were undoubtedly superior to the Germans in both equipment and training, was controlled centrally at army level. Batteries were deployed so that they could support not only their own divisions and corps, but neighboring ones as well. The result was a series of powerful concentrations of fire (one of which fortuitously pinned down Rommel and one of his corps commanders for two hours and prevented them exercising command at a vital time), the likes of which the Germans and Italians had not experienced before in the desert. At a number of critical moments these concentrations proved decisive, especially against troops who were disheartened by the unexpected stiffening of British resistance and by now becoming extremely tired.

The last major piece of advice Dorman-Smith gave enabled Auchinleck to wrest the initiative from Rommel. By the end of the battle Rommel was dancing to their tune, and he admitted as much. Dorman-Smith identified the Italians, who comprised half the Axis forces, as the weak link and he advised his commander to attack them whenever possible. He had known them as allies in 1917–18 and as O'Connor's enemies in 1940. He had a low opinion of their fighting quality: "I thought the Wop would behave badly once we got him out in the open, especially now the vision of juicy brothels in Alexandria has faded and been replaced by the gleam of bayonets," he wrote in his diary on 1 July. Helped by Ultra intercepts, which often pinpointed the location of Italian formations, the Eighth Army launched a series of violent attacks on them. Each time Rommel was forced to abandon his own plans and divert German divisions to save the situation. His opinion about his allies, though expressed rather more politely, was the same as Dorman-Smith's: "Every time I was on the point of forcing a breakthrough . . . they launched an attack on the Italians elsewhere and on each occasion I was forced . . . to hurry to the help of the threatened sector. . . . We were forced to conclude that the Italians were no longer capable of holding their line."

The Desert War was the most mobile and mechanized campaign the British army had ever fought, and it is remarkable that it took two officers from old-fashioned infantry regiments—Auchinleck of the Punjabis and Dorman-Smith of the Royal Northumberland Fusiliers—to impose belatedly the correct tactics on the armor-heavy Eighth Army. Their predecessors had become so mesmerized by the strange desert conditions that they developed tactical concepts that contradicted basic military principles. In complete contrast Auchinleck and Dorman-Smith (and also Rommel) adapted orthodox principles to the conditions they faced. For this Dorman-Smith must take the major credit.

It seems unreasonable that Auchinleck and Dorman-Smith were dismissed immediately after their victory, but Churchill was looking at the whole Middle Eastern Command over a longer period. (It would have been poor consolation to them to have learned that Fritz Bayerlein, Rommel's chief of staff, was amazed that they were given no credit by their own side for their achievement.) The prime minister could never understand why so few of the hundreds of thousands of British troops in the theater were actually in contact with the enemy. He was angered by the fall of Tobruk and the shambles leading up to Ruweisat Ridge, for which as CinC Auchinleck was ultimately responsible, and concluded that he was tired after bearing such heavy burdens for too long. The loyal Auchinleck did not disagree with this judgment. It also was alleged that Dorman-Smith was a malign influence in the headquarters—ironic, when it was the benign influence of his ideas that finally got the Eighth Army operating efficiently. But he had made many enemies over the years by his bluntness and abrasiveness to men of lesser intelligence, and this undoubtedly contributed to his downfall. So, probably, did the fact that he was having an affair with another officer's wife.

His abrupt and ungenerous dismissal cannot hide the part he played as chief of staff in this important battle. His personality was such that he could never have held high command himself. As Liddell Hart said, he lacked the necessary qualities to organize and train men. But equally it is doubtful if Auchinleck, the robust and determined leader, would have halted Rommel without his imaginative chief of staff by his side. Dorman-Smith's critics claimed that he was merely a dreamer whose ideas would never work in practice. But when put to the supreme test, and with Auchinleck to put them into practice, they defeated Rommel. Anyone in doubt about the quality of Dorman-Smith's military thinking should read the "Appreciation of the Situation in the Western Desert" he produced on 27 July 1942 to guide his commander on the way ahead after the successful conclusion of Ruweisat Ridge. It is reproduced in full in *The Desert Generals* and in *Chink, a Biography* and is a model of analytical thinking and clear expression.

The rest of Dorman-Smith's life can be told very briefly. In 1944 he commanded an infantry brigade at Anzio, but soon after the capture of Rome he was again dismissed, this time because it was alleged that his battalion commanders found him impossible to serve under. He then left the army and retired to his family estate in Ireland. He never again found an outlet for his talents. He stood for the British and Irish Parliaments, both times unsuccessfully. He was more fortunate in his dealings with Churchill and Montgomery, challenging them both over the way they covered the events leading up to his dismissal in their war memoirs. Under threat of libel proceedings both backed down. Bizarrely for a man who had served the British Crown loyally for thirty years he embraced Irish nationalism, changing his name to Dorman-O'Gowan (the name of his remote Irish ancestors) and even flirting with the Irish Republican Army. The imagination boggles at the thought of IRA men, whose normal ambition is to blow innocent civilians to bits, listening to a lecture by a retired British general on Liddell Hart's theory of the indirect approach to war delivered in a Sandhurst accent—but his biographer claims this did happen! Whether he was genuine in his newfound beliefs, or acting in this way in response to what he saw as the unfair way he had been treated, must be a matter for conjecture.

Dorman-O'Gowan died of cancer in 1969. It is appropriate to end with words written by Auchinleck on hearing of his death: "I owed him more than I could ever repay. . . . He was tragically mistreated and betrayed in the end. Envy and malice pursued him but he never gave in."

Selected Bibliography

Barnett, Correlli. *The Desert Generals*. London: William Kimber, 1960.

Bidwell, Shelford. *Gunners at War: A Tactical Study of the Royal Artillery in the Twentieth Century*. London: Arms and Armour, 1970.

Churchill, Winston S. *The Second World War*. 6 vols. London: Cassell, 1959.

Greacen, Lavinia. *Chink, a Biography*. London: Macmillan, 1989.

Greenwood, Alexander. *Field-Marshal Auchinleck: A Biography of Field-Marshal Sir Claude Auchinleck*. Durham, UK: Pentland Press Ltd, 1991.

Montgomery, Bernard L. *Memoirs*. London: Collins, 1958.

CHRONOLOGY OF FRANCIS DE GUINGAND

28 Feb 1900	Born at Acton, West London.
1918	Accepted as gentleman cadet, Royal Military College, Sandhurst.
17 Dec 1919	Commissioned into West Yorkshire Regiment.
22 Apr 1926	Seconded to King's African Rifles.
1930	Assigned as officer commanding troops, Nyasaland.
1 Jul 1932	Adjutant, 1st Battalion, West Yorkshire Regiment.
1935	Completed Army Staff Course, Camberley.
15 Feb 1938	Assigned as brigade-major, Small Arms Wing, Netheravon.
15 Jul 1939	Assigned as military assistant to secretary of state for war Leslie Hore-Belisha, MP.
25 Feb 1940	Assigned as instructor, Middle East Staff College, Haifa.
26 Feb 1942	Assigned as director of military intelligence (Middle East).
25 Aug 1942	Assigned as chief of staff, Eighth Army.
1 Jan 1944	Assigned as chief of staff, 21st Army Group.
19 Sep 1945	Assigned as director of military intelligence, the War Office.
6 Feb 1947	Retired from the army.
1949–70	Served as director of Tube Investments, South Africa.
1959–71	Served as founding president, the South Africa Federation.
1972	Retired at Cannes, France.
29 Jun 1979	Died at Cannes, France.

Francis de Guingand

Stephen Hart

Francis Wilfred de Guingand was born in February 1900 at Acton, West London, the son of a Roman Catholic couple with French blood in the paternal line. In 1918 he applied to join the Royal Navy but was turned down on medical grounds—he was found to be color-blind. As a second choice, de Guingand attended the Royal Military College at Sandhurst as a gentleman cadet, where his French surname earned him the sobriquet "Freddie" from his fellow cadets after the popular cartoon of the time, "Freddie the Frog."

After an unimpressive performance at Sandhurst, the intellectually bright but fun-loving de Guingand received his commission into the West Yorkshire Regiment. After service in India, de Guingand deployed to Ireland during the "Troubles," during which one Brevet-Major Bernard Law Montgomery befriended him. Next de Guingand saw service with the King's African Rifles, before returning to England in 1935 to attend the Army Staff College at Camberley. His fine mind got him through the course without much effort or any diminution of his fun-loving lifestyle.

Subsequently, de Guingand obtained his first staff appointment as brigade-major at the Small Arms Wing, Netheravon, from 1938 to 1939. He then became military assistant to the secretary of state for war, Leslie Hore-Belisha. In early 1940 de Guingand went to the new Middle East Staff College at Haifa as an instructor. In 1942 he was appointed director, military intelligence (DMI) in the Middle East. In July 1942 he assumed the job of brigadier general staff (operations) (BGS[Ops]) to the Eighth Army in North Africa, just a few weeks before Montgomery assumed command of that formation.

From Montgomery's August 1942 arrival in North Africa until May 1945 de Guingand served as his chief of staff, first in the Eighth Army and then, from January 1944, in the 21st Army Group. After VE-Day, de Guingand went on sick leave, but returned to duty in September 1945 as acting DMI at the War Office in preparation for the key job of vice-chief of the imperial general staff (Vice-CIGS), which Montgomery had promised him. In January 1946, however—after hearing of de Guingand's continuing ill health and the objections of the outgoing CIGS, Lord Alan Brooke, Montgomery, with unbelievable insensitivity, casually informed him that he was not going to appoint his loyal chief of staff as Vice-CIGS. A heartbroken de Guingand realized that now there was no job for him in the peacetime British army, yet he could not even afford to retire, as his substantive rank was still only that of colonel, insufficient to support his family. It took Gen. Dwight Eisenhower's intervention—Montgomery declined to become involved—to get de Guingand promoted to substantive major-general so that he could consider retirement. In February 1947 de Guingand retired from the army and moved to South Africa where he became a successful businessman. Yet during his years in Africa, de Guingand never entirely overcame his sense that the superior he had served so faithfully throughout the war had betrayed him. In June 1979, at the age of seventy-nine, de Guingand died at Cannes, southern France.[1]

De Guingand possessed a character very different from his cold and arrogant superior, whom he called his "Chief." He was a lively, humorous, charming, and easy-to-befriend officer who liked dining and entertaining. His main leisure-time interests included associating with pretty women, gambling, fishing, hunting, country walks, and traveling the world.[2] He was oft said to possess good foresight, and his well-known diplomatic qualities were regularly called upon owing to the tactlessness of his superior.[3] Yet the poor health that dogged de Guingand's career formed another key aspect of his relationship with Montgomery. As early as 1920 de Guingand fell ill with gallstone problems, and this ailment reoccurred periodically throughout his military career. Notably, his illness resurfaced in December 1942, after the pressures associated with El Alamein, and Montgomery sent de Guingand off on three months' sick leave, only to recall him after just four weeks. He again fell ill during the high-pressure planning for the D-Day landings, and again during autumn and winter 1944, when the depression he experienced over the ineffective cooperation between the Allies exacerbated his condition, and yet again during the last weeks of the war. Nonetheless, Montgomery preferred a not fully fit de Guingand to any alternative, even though, in de Guingand's absence, Brig. David Belchem, the 21st Army Group's BGS(Ops), deputized for him effectively.[4]

Unlike some famous chiefs of staff, like Hugh Gaffey, who were effective higher field commanders in their own right, de Guingand had neither the experience nor the temperament to be a successful field commander. De Guingand himself knew this only too well, and hence was amazed when he learned from Gen. Walter Bedell Smith long after the war that the Americans had suggested him in autumn 1944 as a possible successor to Montgomery. De Guingand's response to this news was that he could not have replaced his Chief because he recognized that there was a vast difference between being an effective chief of staff and being a successful commander.[5]

When Montgomery arrived to assume command of the Eighth Army in August 1942, he immediately implemented his personal—and unofficial— Continental-style chief of staff system by appointing the formation's recently arrived BGS(Ops), Freddie de Guingand, as his chief of staff with full powers. Montgomery issued all his orders through the authority of his chief of staff and delegated to de Guingand the daily running of his army (and later his army group) main headquarters. To all intents and purposes, de Guingand was Montgomery's deputy commander in all but name. Once Montgomery had made clear his decision or outline plan, he let de Guingand get on without interference with the task of supervising the staff as they implemented the details of their commander's intent.[6] Yet in those first days during August 1942, Montgomery made it clear that de Guingand—despite his wide powers—was on trial, and also hinted that he intended in the near future to bring out an officer from England to be his chief of staff. De Guingand assumed this officer to be Brig. Frank Simpson. But the replacement never materialized. Instead de Guingand and his commander forged a highly effective working relationship that lasted from August 1942 through until victory in Europe in May 1945. The main constraint on this partnership, however, was Montgomery's habit, first implemented at El Alamein, of commanding from a Tactical Headquarters (Tac HQ) sited well forward.

In addition to his normal duties during the 1942–43 North African campaign supervising the operational and administrative work of the Eighth Army headquarters, de Guingand became heavily involved in several particular roles. First, he personally coordinated army-air cooperation arrangements, and stood in for his Chief as the main point of contact with Air Marshal Arthur "Maori" Coningham.[7] In addition, as a former DMI, de Guingand monitored closely the intelligence gathered by his G(Int) Staff. During these months de Guingand learned how to handle his difficult, forceful, and arrogant master. He recognized that Montgomery disliked paperwork and detail, and soon realized, given his Chief's need to be seen to be in control, that it was pointless to argue with his superior. He soon learned that the best way to influence the general was to subtly float an idea past Montgomery during a one-on-one private discussion, and then not mention it for a while, until it had time to germinate in his Chief's mind. Some while later, Montgomery often came back to de Guingand with the very same idea that he now seemed to think was the product of his own thought.[8]

During 1944–45, as chief of staff 21st Army Group, de Guingand assumed wider responsibilities that ranged from operational and administrative matters across the spectrum to civil affairs. In the winter of 1944–45, for example, de Guingand became deeply involved in the arrangements carried out by his Civil Affairs Section to deliver food to the starving citizens of recently liberated Holland. Furthermore, as the war entered its last weeks, de Guingand oversaw the arrangements for food to be rushed to the starving Dutch citizens in the Nazi-controlled enclave of northwestern Holland. Again in these last days of the war, much of de Guingand's time was also consumed supervising the preparations for the British Military Government of Germany once the war ended, and with planning the tasks of demobilizing the German armed forces and repatriating refugees and displaced persons.[9] Yet at various periods during 1944–45, de Guingand performed three more specialized (and crucial) operational roles as a senior planning officer, an air support liaison officer, and an inter-Allied liaison representative.

One of de Guingand's most significant roles as chief of staff of the 21st Army Group was to act as a principal staff planning officer. When he took up his appointment on 10 January 1944, he retained his old rank of (acting) major-general. His predecessor had been a lieutenant-general, but Montgomery had already asked de Guingand to retain his existing rank on the grounds that if he were promoted, all of the army group's brigadiers would demand promotion to major-general. This request came to haunt de Guingand during 1946 when he was considering retiring.[10] In early January 1944, Montgomery drew up the initial outline plan for Operation Overlord, the D-Day landings, based on his modification to the existing scheme developed by the office of the Chief of Staff to the Supreme Allied Commander (COSSAC). He then set de Guingand to direct his staff officers in their efforts to flesh out the plan and implement it.

During the ensuing twenty-two weeks of planning, Montgomery spent most of his time motivating his subordinate field commanders and the troops, and left the day-to-day running of the planning almost entirely to de Guingand. He commenced every day during this period with a full-scale conference of the army group staff to coordinate their daily business. He also attended the regular triservice planning conferences run by the three service chiefs of staffs involved in Overlord, and participated in supreme allied commander Dwight Eisenhower's weekly briefings. In addition, de Guingand also became heavily involved in coordinating the Fortitude deception plan, designed to fool the Germans as to where the Allied forces would land. During these hectic days, de Guingand said, he "did not see" Montgomery "very often."[11] On several occasions, when Montgomery met with de Guingand to discuss his progress, the commander also asked his chief of staff to check and comment on drafts of his operational plans or speeches. Just prior to Montgomery's 15 May 1944 presentation of plans at St Paul's School, for example, he asked de Guingand to comment on his notes for this key briefing.[12]

The twenty-two weeks of planning Overlord represented a continuation of the zenith of de Guingand's relationship with his superior, reached in 1943, despite the fact of their physical separation as Montgomery frequently went away to address the troops. At times in these months the general displayed an almost avuncular feeling toward his younger staff officer. On 18 February 1944, for example, Montgomery held a tea party in his offices to celebrate the christening of de Guingand's daughter Marylou. The commander had cleared his desk completely for the celebration—except for one pending tray that he thoughtfully kept so that de Guingand could have somewhere to "park the baby when it gets tired."[13]

It was during the last few weeks prior to Overlord that Montgomery increasingly became concerned with the state of air support for the forthcoming invasion. The lack of experience among Lt.-Gen. Miles Dempsey's British Second Army staff worried him, as did the pockets of skepticism apparent within the Royal Air Force's tactical and strategic commands. Consequently, some forty-eight hours after D-day, Montgomery sent de Guingand, with his rich experience of air support matters, to the air headquarters at Stanmore to act as a brigadier, general staff (air) (BGS [Air]).[14] De Guingand was to use his moral authority and diplomacy to ensure that the strategic air arrangements to support Allied ground operations ran smoothly.

During these first weeks of the invasion, Montgomery also faced another problem in that there remained insufficient space within the Allied beachhead in Normandy for the RAF's Tactical Air Headquarters to move across to the continent as planned. To remedy this situation, Montgomery entrusted de Guingand, then still commuting between the army group's main headquarters near Portsmouth and the Stanmore Air Centre, to coordinate the army's daily requests for tactical air support and to monitor the air-support staff work undertaken by Dempsey's headquarters. On 11 June, for example, the watchful de Guingand reported back to his superior his concerns about the manner in which the Second Army had planned its air arrangements. Montgomery had proposed a plan to drop an airborne division behind the German lines, with which Dempsey's forces were to link up during their next offensive. De Guingand reported to his Chief that even though Air Marshal Trafford Leigh-Mallory, the air commander in chief, had not yet approved this deployment, the Second Army staff had commenced their planning of the operation anyway. A few days later, events proved de Guingand correct, as Leigh-Mallory vetoed the plan as potentially too costly in terms of casualties, and all of the Second Army's staff work proved wasted.[15] By July, with more room in the Allied bridgehead, the RAF Tactical Headquarters moved to France and de Guingand duly handed over these arrangements to the G(Air) Section of the Second Army staff.

Despite Montgomery's continuing reliance on his chief of staff in the early phases of the Normandy campaign, de Guingand observed with some trepidation the formation of Montgomery's Tac HQ at Cruelly in Normandy. While de Guingand understood the necessity for such arrangements in the Eighth Army, he remained concerned that now as an army group commander in charge of four armies, Montgomery would isolate himself from his chief of staff at the main headquarters and attempt to run the campaign by himself from his Tac HQ. To alleviate these concerns de Guingand persuaded his superior to accept Col. Leo Russell, an experienced operations staff officer from main headquarters, to run Tac HQ. Unfortunately, Russell and Montgomery's personalities clashed and the colonel was sacked. De Guingand entertained the suspicion that his Chief saw Russell as his observer and hence removed him.[16]

Yet despite this growing physical separation, Montgomery continued to rely heavily on de Guingand's advice during the first month of Overlord, as the following incident makes clear. Prior to the D-Day landings, Secretary of State for War James Grigg had warned de Guingand that British armor might use the fact of German tank superiority as an excuse for "stickiness." In Normandy, once postcombat reports emerged that confirmed this superiority, Montgomery grew concerned that this information would undermine Allied morale. The general, having asked his chief of staff what he should do, was told categorically that the reports had to be stopped. Within days Montgomery had closed down the entire postcombat reporting system in order to prevent the troops from developing "Tiger phobia."[17]

Although both of the specialized roles undertaken by de Guingand made key contributions to the success the Allies achieved during the 1944 Normandy campaign, his most important role as Montgomery's chief of staff throughout the entire 1944–45 Northwest Europe campaign was that of a senior inter-Allied liaison officer. Here de Guingand's cosmopolitan colonial experiences, charm, and diplomacy proved their value, particularly as Montgomery's arrogance and forthright manner, not to say his pursuit of a British agenda in the campaign, infuriated many of the senior American commanders.[18] During the early phases of the Overlord planning process, Montgomery relied on de Guingand to liaise with Col. Charles H. "Tic" Bonesteel, head of the American section at 21st Army Group headquarters.[19] Yet de Guingand's most important inter-Allied liaison role was his relationships with supreme allied commander Dwight Eisenhower, and with the latter's chief of staff Maj. Gen. Walter Bedell Smith. In the weeks prior to Overlord, Montgomery tasked de Guingand to discuss with Eisenhower the impact the proposed Anvil landings in southern France would exert on the D-Day invasion. Subsequently, during the first weeks of the Normandy campaign, Montgomery—now located at his Tac HQ in Normandy—relied on de Guingand at Southwick near Portsmouth to brief Eisenhower personally on the daily progress of the Allied forces.

De Guingand's role as an inter-Allied liaison officer became increasingly important during the autumn of 1944 as serious tensions undermined Anglo-American cooperation. From late August 1944, Montgomery began his insubordinate campaign against Eisenhower in what became known as the "Broad-Front versus Narrow Thrust" controversy. Eisenhower's proposed strategy for the ongoing campaign was for all three Allied army groups to attack on a wide front into Germany, a plan that eased inter-Allied tensions by ensuring that no national commander received logistical priority over his peers, and also avoided overloading any one section of the Allied logistic network. Montgomery, however, wanted to concentrate Allied striking power to the north of the Ardennes and accord it logistical priority for the conduct of a single narrow thrust north of the Ardennes and onto Berlin.

Montgomery's strategy was based on both operational and partisan national considerations. Operationally, Montgomery realized that in late August and early September 1944 the Allies possessed a unique opportunity to deal the decisive blow against a German army that had lost its cohesion after its debacle in Normandy. Usually cautious, Montgomery now wanted to seize this opportunity to finish off the disorganized Germans before they recovered. Second, the narrow-thrust strategy fitted the partisan national agenda Montgomery had pursued in the theater. He remained acutely aware, as did Churchill, of the British army's dwindling numerical participation in the campaign, as American military might increasingly exerted itself. Montgomery wanted to nurture Britain's prestige in the campaign by seeking at this point to spearhead the triumphant Allied advance onto Berlin. For most of the campaign, however, British manpower shortages had prevented Montgomery from spearheading the Allied advance. But with logistical priority accorded to his northern thrust, Montgomery hoped to win the glory of advancing onto Berlin while the enemy remained in disarray.

This impassioned debate about strategy, however, was also entwined with an associated one concerning command. Montgomery had never accepted the fact that Eisenhower had replaced him by personally assuming command of all the land forces on 1 September 1944. In part Montgomery was rightly concerned about Eisenhower's lack of field experience, but he also recognized that this appointment was crucial to his ability to steer the campaign's strategy to suit both British and his own personal interests. By assuming command of American formations north of the Ardennes in a narrow thrust, Montgomery hoped effectively to become land forces commander of the north, the first step to being reinstated as the overall theater ground commander, and hence regain control over theater strategy.[20]

An increasingly unwell de Guingand was caught awkwardly in the middle of this protracted and increasingly bitter debate. During autumn 1944 his physical isolation from Montgomery increased as the distance between their respective headquarters grew, and as his Chief increasingly came to rely solely on his own judgment. The cooperative distance that now existed between Montgomery and his chief of staff was made clear during the discussions over the launching of Market-Garden, the field marshal's atypically bold offensive in which Lt.-Gen. Sir Brian Horrock's XXX Corps sought to link up with airborne forces dropped at key locations ahead of the ground forces. During the first week of September as this plan emerged in embryo, Montgomery became alarmed about de Guingand's ill health and on 9 September sent him on sick leave. De Guingand telephoned Montgomery from his sickbed to explain his reservations that it was now too late to launch a delayed Market-Garden because German cohesion was recovering fast. Yet Montgomery simply brushed away these objections on the grounds that de Guingand was out of touch with events at the front.[21] Events would prove de Guingand's caution to be correct.

As de Guingand's isolation from Montgomery grew that autumn, his contact with Eisenhower and Bedell Smith also intensified. Ironically, Montgomery had encouraged this development by sending de Guingand in his place to attend conferences with Eisenhower as this strategic debate became increasingly embittered. Though Montgomery wanted to avoid discussion with officers like Eisenhower, whom he could not bully into compliance, he also recognized that de Guingand's diplomatic skills were crucial to soothing American anger. As de Guingand's working relationship with Bedell Smith became increasingly strong, he found himself in the unenviable position of defending Montgomery's northern thrust strategy to the Americans, even though he personally (though privately) believed it wrong. Given that it was politically impossible to halt the American advance, de Guingand calculated that Montgomery's northern thrust could not be supported logistically unless Antwerp was captured first, but his Chief did not want the delay of clearing the approaches to this key port along the Scheldt estuary. After the war, de Guingand blamed himself for not persuading his superior to open Antwerp first before entertaining thoughts of an advance onto Berlin, but at that time he was both too physically isolated from his chief and too unwell to fight a tough battle on this issue.[22] The failure to clear the Scheldt, as Montgomery later admitted in a rare moment of honest self-appraisal, constituted a "bad mistake," although it would be fairer to describe it as his biggest mistake of the war.[23] It was only later, in 1947, that Montgomery learned of de Guingand's reservations about the narrow-thrust strategy in his chief of staff's otherwise innocuous memoir *Operation Victory*. In it de Guingand stated that this matter constituted "the only major issue" of the entire war "over which I did not agree with my Chief."[24]

Montgomery's relations with Eisenhower reached their nadir in late December 1944, amid the recriminations involved in the Allied response to the German surprise counterattack in the Ardennes. On 30 December Eisenhower finally lost patience with the insubordinate British field marshal and drafted a letter informing Montgomery that if his activities continued he would be forced to refer the whole issue to the Combined Chiefs of Staff. De Guingand saw the draft and persuaded Eisenhower not to send it until he had discussed the matter with his Chief. The next day de Guingand told Montgomery about the letter. At first the field marshal refused to accept the seriousness of the situation as there was. He believed no British officer could replace him. When a horrified Montgomery heard from de Guingand that the diplomatic but scarcely operationally brilliant field marshal Sir Harold Alexander had been suggested as a replacement, he asked his chief of staff to draft an abject apology to Eisenhower to defuse the crisis. Montgomery ended the sickly message "your very devoted subordinate."[25] De Guingand had certainly saved his Chief from a serious situation. But gradually over the ensuing years, de Guingand's memories of these events became increasingly distorted and eventually he came to believe that he had actually saved Montgomery from the sack that New Year's Eve.[26] These retrospective exaggerations, however, should not detract from recognition that de Guingand, the chief of staff, played a crucial role in the success the Allies achieved in Northwest Europe by holding together a fractious Allied coalition.

Despite both the increasing distance between Montgomery and de Guingand, and the latter's worsening health, the field marshal continued to value his chief of staff's services right through to the 8 May 1945 victory over Nazi Germany. By early in 1945, however, the strain of de Guingand's duties combined with his difficult intermediary role in the Montgomery-Eisenhower dispute again drove him to ill health. Despite de Guingand's wish to remain, army doctors recommended that he be relieved of his appointment on health grounds so that he could have several months of rest and treatment. Montgomery, however, still valued sufficiently de Guingand's contribution to attempt to fend off the doctors' demands until after VE-Day. In the meantime he persuaded the medics to accept a compromise where de Guingand continued his duties but attended hospital once a fortnight. During this period, the field marshal also introduced Maj. William F. Bovill to de Guingand's office to keep track of the chief of staff's decisions while he remained in poor health.

But in these last weeks of the war, such acts of assistance by Montgomery were interspersed with instances of cruel and insensitive behavior. On Luneberg Heath on VE-Day, for example, when Montgomery took the German surrender, de Guingand was noticeably absent. The field marshal had told de Guingand not to attend—he was not going to share the tiniest sliver of glory that day with anyone else, however deserving.[27] This complex, paradoxical, and inconsistent attitude of Montgomery toward his faithful chief of staff—sometimes appreciative, other times cruel—continued during the years after the war. The ongoing relationship between the two men continued despite heartbreaking rejections by Montgomery, like the Vice-CIGS incident and his refusal to allow de Guingand to return to Alamein with him, disagreements that were occasionally interspersed with his half-hearted attempts at reconciliation. The connection between the two, whether bitter or amiable, was only separated by Montgomery's death in 1976.[28]

Notes

1. This career profile is based on Maj.-Gen. Sir Francis de Guingand, *Operation Victory*, rev. ed. (London: Hodder, 1960); de Guingand, *Generals at War* (London: Hodder and Stoughton, 1964); de Guingand, *From Brass Hat to Bowler Hat* (London: Hamish Hamilton, 1979); Maj.-Gen. Charles Richardson, *Send for Freddie: The Story of Montgomery's Chief of Staff Major-General Sir Francis de Guingaud* (London: William Kimber, 1987), all passim. For the Vice-CIGS incident, see also Arthur Gwynne Jones Chalfont, *Montgomery of Alamein* (London: Athenaeum, 1976), 279–81.
2. Gen. Sir Charles Richardson, *Flashback: A Soldier's Story* (London: William Kimber, 1985), 06.
3. Richardson, *Send for Freddie*, 143, 150–51.
4. De Guingand, *Generals at War*, 69, 80; Richardson, *Send for Freddie*, 151–52, 166, 169.
5. Richardson, *Send for Freddie*, 158–59.
6. Maj.-Gen. David Belchem, *All in the Day's March* (London: Collins, 1978), 14. During his 11 January 1944 address to the 21st Army Group Staff, Montgomery stated that de Guingand "gives all decisions on all staff matters once I have made my plan. Everyone is under him," Imperial War Museum, Montgomery Papers, quoted in Nigel Hamilton, *Monty*, vol. 2 (London: Hamish Hamilton, 1983), 492.
7. Richardson, *Send for Freddie*, 89.
8. De Guingand, *From Brass Hat*, 12; Richardson, *Send for Freddie*, 86.
9. De Guingand, *Operation Victory*, 350–70 passim.
10. Richardson, *Send for Freddie*, 145.
11. De Guingand, *Operation Victory*, 290.
12. Hamilton, *Monty*, 2:582.
13. Richardson, *Send for Freddie*, 148.
14. Richardson, *Flashback*, 177.
15. Stephen Hart, *Montgomery and "Colossal Cracks": The 21st Army Group in Northwest Europe 1944–45* (Westport, CT: Praeger, 2000), 147.
16. Hamilton, *Monty*, 2:565–66; Richardson, *Send for Freddie*, 149.
17. De Guingand, letter to Montgomery, 24 June 1944, Public Records Office, Kew, WO205/5B; Hart, *Montgomery*, 40.
18. For a sustained analysis of this agenda, see Hart, *Montgomery*, 62–67.
19. Richardson, *Send for Freddie*, 151.
20. Hart, *Montgomery*, 64–67.
21. De Guingand, *From Brass Hat*, 15–16.
22. Richardson, *Send for Freddie*, 160–63.
23. Bernard Montgomery of Alamein, *Memoirs* (London: Collins, 1958), 297.
24. De Guingand, *Operation Victory*, 328–29.
25. IWM, Montgomery-Simpson correspondence, cited in Richardson, *Send for Freddie*, 171.
26. De Guingand, *Generals at War*, 109; Nigel Hamilton, *Monty*, vol. 3 (London: Hamish Hamilton, 1989), 274–76. For an analysis of participants' accounts of the Northwest

Europe campaign, see G. E. Patrick Murray, *Eisenhower and Montgomery: The Continuing Debate* (Westport, Conn.: Praeger, 1996), passim.

27. Richardson, *Flashback*, 192.
28. For the continuing influence that Montgomery exerted on his wartime colleagues long after 1945, see Hart, *Montgomery*, 134, 137.

CHRONOLOGY OF FREDERICK MORGAN

5 Feb 1894	Born, Paddock Wood, Kent, England.
1907–12	Attended Clifton College.
1912–13	Attended the Royal Military Academy, Woolwich.
18 Jul 1913	Commissioned into the Royal Artillery and posted to India.
1914–18	Served in World War I, France. Wounded and twice Mentioned in Dispatches.
18 Aug 1919	Assigned as adjutant, 26th Field Brigade, India.
4 Sep 1922	Assigned as staff officer, Northern Command, India.
1927–28	Student, Staff College at Quetta.
1929–30	Assigned to 70th Field Battery, India.
1 Feb 1931	Assigned as a staff officer to MGRA, India.
1934–36	Commanded 4th AA Battery and then served nine months in antiaircraft assignments at Portsmouth and then Malta.
15 Mar 1936	Assigned to the War Office, London, Staff Duties Branch.
28 May 1938	Assigned as GSO1, 3rd Infantry Division.
8 Aug 1939	Promoted to brigadier and assigned as commander, Support Group, 1st Armoured Division.
4 Nov 1940	Assigned as brigadier, general staff, II Corps.
28 Feb 1941	Assigned as general officer commanding, Devon and Cornwall Division.
30 Oct 1941	Assigned as general officer commanding, 55th Infantry Division.
14 May 1942	Assigned as general officer commanding, I Corps District.
14 May 1942	Promoted to acting lieutenant-general.
23 Apr 1943	Appointed COSSAC.
24 Aug 1944	Knighted.
1944–45	Assigned as deputy chief of staff to supreme commander, Allied Expeditionary Force.

Sep 1945	Appointed director, UN Relief and Rehabilitation Agency in Germany.
29 Dec 1946	Retired from the army.
26 Aug 1951	Appointed controller, United Kingdom Atomic Energy Commission.
19 Mar 1967	Died, Northwood, Middlesex, England.

Frederick Morgan

Phillip Green

The British and their imperial allies were the only countries that fought the Germans from the first to the last day in both world wars, and Sir Frederick Morgan, KCB, belongs to a generation of British soldiers, including among many others Sir Harold Alexander, Sir Claude Auchinleck, Sir Bernard L. Montgomery, and Sir William Slim, which played a full part in both conflicts, as junior officers at the front in the first and in senior positions in the second. Morgan must not be confused with another British General Morgan, a virtual contemporary and also an artilleryman. W. D. Morgan (1892–1977), usually known by his nickname of "Monkey," ended the war as Alexander's chief of staff in the Mediterranean.

Frederick Morgan's claim to military fame, and the peak of his career, came in 1943–44 when he was tasked by the Combined Chiefs of Staff with planning the Normandy invasion, the largest amphibious assault ever launched. For this he was given the title Chief of Staff to the Supreme Allied Commander (COSSAC). This acronym was used to designate both Morgan and his headquarters. He played no part in the assault he had planned and spent the last year of the war as deputy chief of staff at Eisenhower's Allied Supreme headquarters. In Morgan we therefore see the chief of staff in one role only, that of the planner.

Educated at Clifton and the Royal Military Academy at Woolwich, Morgan was commissioned into the Royal Artillery in 1913 and went straight to India. On the outbreak of World War I, he returned to Europe with the Indian Corps, that country's contribution to the British Expeditionary Force (BEF), and spent the whole war in France. (It was to be a remarkable feature of his career that all his war service in both conflicts was in France, almost all his peacetime service in India.) He was twice Mentioned in Dispatches and suffered shellshock from a near miss that almost killed him. After recuperating he returned to duty as a staff officer at Canadian Corps headquarters.

Between the wars Morgan spent sixteen years in India, splitting his time between regimental and staff appointments. He attended the Quetta Staff College and then served three years on the staff of the major general, Royal Artillery (MGRA), the commander of all artillery units and establishments in India. The magnificent Indian army, for historical reasons almost a century old, had no artillery of its own, except for a few pack (i.e., mountain) batteries designed for use on the North-West Frontier and other remote areas. While on the MGRA's staff, Morgan played a significant part in forming the new and modern Indian Artillery, which was to perform so well in World War II. He returned home in 1936 to serve at the War Office before becoming GSO1 of the 3rd Infantry Division.

At the beginning of World War II, Morgan was appointed commander (with the rank of brigadier) of the support group of the 1st Armoured Division—the first such division in the British army. It was sent to France in May 1940, but Morgan had no chance to command his group (of two artillery regiments, two infantry battalions, and a squadron of engineers). With the Germans advancing relentlessly on Dunkirk, his units were constantly sent to plug gaps elsewhere. He eventually returned safely to Britain via Brest. From then until early 1943 he remained in Britain, first as a divisional, then as a corps commander.

By then, of course, the United States was in the war, and the first major Allied operation, the invasion of French North Africa, was about to take place. The Allies were worried that the Germans might respond with an attack on Gibraltar through Spain. If Gibraltar fell, the entrance to the Mediterranean would be closed. To guard against this possibility Morgan was told to plan an amphibious assault on Spanish Morocco with his own corps, so that if need be the Allies could control the entrance from the southern shore. It is interesting to recall that Britain's first overseas military base, from 1662 to 1683, was in Tangier on the African side of the straits. Had this operation gone ahead it would have put the clock back almost three centuries. In the event, however, it was not needed and Morgan's divisions were taken from his command and fed into the main battle in Tunisia. A corps commander without a corps, his next task was to plan a possible invasion of Sardinia—another operation that never took place.

Following their North African success, the Allies had to decide what to do next. Even American and British power combined would not be enough to carry out decisive assaults on occupied Europe from the north and south simultaneously. One or the other had to be given priority. The British, with centuries of experience in European wars, favored the southern option: the Americans, who would provide the most troops, the northern one. At Casablanca in January 1943, the Allied leaders agreed to go for a direct assault on the north coast of France in 1944, with a smaller invasion of southern France as a supporting attack. The man to command this enterprise, the supreme allied commander, was not nominated, but it was decided to appoint his chief of staff, COSSAC, straightaway to get on with the detailed planning. The choice fell on Morgan, still a corps commander without a corps, and to ensure that it would be a truly Allied effort he was given an American deputy, Brig. Gen. Raymond Barker.

A chief of staff without a commander is almost a contradiction in terms, but that was Morgan's position. He later described himself as a John the Baptist who "would prepare the way and straighten out as much of the path as possible, reporting his progress from time to time to the Combined British and American Chiefs of Staff." When this august body issued their directive to Morgan in April 1943 they were far from precise:

Our object is to defeat the German fighting forces in North-West Europe. To this end the Combined Chiefs of Staff will endeavor to assemble the strongest possible forces (subject to prior commitments in other theatres) in constant readiness to re-enter the Continent if German resistance is weakened to the required extent in 1943. In the meantime the Combined Chiefs of Staff must be prepared to order such limited operations as may be practicable with the forces and material available.

General Sir Alan Brooke, the chief of the imperial general staff (CIGS), when briefing Morgan for the job was no more helpful, but was at least blunt and to the point. "Well, there it is. It won't work, but you must bloody well make it." Morgan described the Combined Chiefs' directive politely as a "somewhat hazy background," and against it he had to make three plans simultaneously. The first was a deception plan designed to make the enemy think the assault was coming in 1943 and that it would be in the Pas de Calais. A directive issued by Hitler that year indicates that the deception worked, though he may have reached this conclusion anyway. "Those are the very points at which the enemy must and will attack; there [the Pas de

Calais]—unless all indications are misleading—will be fought the decisive invasion battle." The second was for a rapid return to Europe with whatever forces were available at the time should Germany suddenly collapse. The third was for the real assault, Operation Overlord, to take place as early as possible in 1944.

To his great task Morgan brought the experience gained in thirty years of service: frontline duty in some of the bloodiest battles ever fought and staff experience in war and peace at division, corps, and army levels. His command background was not so impressive. Effectively, though he had risen to corps commander, he had never commanded in battle, and his highest peacetime command had been an antiaircraft battery. He was, though, used to working in an international environment, having fought and cooperated with Australian, Canadian, French, and Indian units at various times in his career. His recent experience of planning invasions of Morocco and Sardinia in an amphibious and international setting was obviously an enormous asset; moreover, during this period he had met and got on well with Gen. Dwight D. Eisenhower. A man of great charm and moral courage, Morgan had a strong personality and the reputation of having one of the sharpest minds of his army generation.

The invasion of France across the English Channel was not going to be easy and history offered little encouragement. The Romans in AD 43 and the Normans in 1066 had crossed successfully from France to Britain, but since then British victories—by the Royal Navy over the Spanish Armada and over the French at Trafalgar and by the Royal Air Force in the Battle of Britain—had thwarted the ambitions of Philip of Spain, Napoleon, and Hitler. There were no instances of large-scale invasions the other way, from Britain to France. With their mastery of the sea and air the Allies could undoubtedly land an invasion force relatively unscathed. But could they project a force sufficiently strong to fight its way through Hitler's Atlantic Wall, establish a beachhead, and fight off the inevitable counterattacks?

It was a daunting prospect, but it was not until Eisenhower became supreme allied commander at the beginning of 1944 and had time to study the plan in detail that the Allies, in particular the Americans, fully appreciated the magnitude of the task they had set themselves. The near-disaster at Anzio was to show what could go wrong with an amphibious assault. There the initial landing force was too weak to push inland before the German counterattacks started and found itself trapped near the beaches, in Churchill's words, "like a stranded whale," and almost thrown back into the sea.

Morgan was not, though, starting from square one. Ever since Dunkirk the British had been thinking about how to return to Europe, and their Combined Operations headquarters had given some thought to the problem—in outline if not in detail. Much of practical value had been learned from the failure at Dieppe and from a series of successful commando raids, from the Lofoten Islands in the north to St. Nazaire in the south, about the tactics and specialized equipment that would be needed. Early on Morgan was given a resumé of all British deliberations and lessons learned to date. He was lucky, too, in that Barker, his American deputy, had already been working on a general project for Anglo-American cross-Channel operations.

Morgan's first task was to set up his planning team, which had to encompass three nationalities and three services. After almost sixty years of NATO it is easy to forget that the degree of inter-Allied cooperation and integration envisaged was something never before attempted. Moreover, though the two main Allies shared a common language and political culture, apart from a short time in 1918 they had never fought together. They had no common military traditions, and had different organizations, staff systems, and to some extent tactical concepts. When Morgan read the first directive Eisenhower sent him (concerning Spanish Morocco) he commented that it was written in good English and doubtless in accordance with the teaching of the U.S. Army Staff College, but it was very difficult for a British officer to understand its military meaning. The new allies had a lot to learn about each other and had to do so quickly.

In forming his team, Morgan worked on the principle that the most suitable available officer should fill a post, regardless of his nationality; he avoided the temptation of earmarking specific jobs for a specific nationality, and this went a long way to building up a genuine supranational staff. Morgan was full of praise for the part played by his deputy Barker. The two got on extremely well, a matter of crucial importance, and their staff took their cue from this example. Barker, a New Englander, was an Anglophile to such an extent that some of his compatriots accused him of being in the pocket of the British. Equally, Morgan became such a confirmed and loyal servant of the Combined Chiefs that he was accused of being unduly under American influence. With the value of hindsight we can say that these accusations indicate that Morgan and Barker both got their difficult tasks right, to the immense benefit of the Allied cause.

Morgan was a hardworking man, a completely professional soldier and staff officer, and when the need arose, which was often, he lived in the headquarters for days on end. He also was a good delegator who encouraged his team to make decisions at as low a level as possible; when they were unable to do so, they were to bring the problem to Barker and himself for decision. In his autobiography, Morgan recounts that in his headquarters the relevant government department set up a mess that was unusually luxurious by the standards of wartime London. In the friendly and doubtless convivial atmosphere that prevailed Morgan states that "pre-prandial, prandial and post-prandial discussion seemed at least as productive as more formal sessions around the committee table." He ran a tight ship, but with a human touch.

The directive he had received in April was refined on 25 May, and his first deadline was to present an outline plan to Churchill, Roosevelt, and the Combined Chiefs of Staff at Quebec in July, a plan that had to convince them the invasion was feasible. One of Morgan's British officers, Brig. Kenneth McLean, was given the responsibility of making the presentation. First he had to convince Churchill, who probably in his heart of hearts still favored the traditional British approach via the Mediterranean. This was done in the best Churchillian fashion with the great man lying in bed in his stateroom on board the *Queen Mary* in the mid-Atlantic, maps and charts scattered all around him and the inevitable cigar in hand. The outline plan that Churchill accepted was then put to the Quebec Conference and approved. Churchill further proposed that an American should command the operation in view of the eventual preponderance of American troops in the invasion. This was agreed, but still the supreme allied commander, to whom Morgan should have been reporting, was not nominated.

The plan put forward on Morgan's behalf at Quebec had to provide satisfactory answers to three fundamental questions: where? when? how? It also had to differ in one fundamental respect from the preliminary work carried out by Lord Louis Mountbatten and others. All earlier work had been concerned solely with the practicalities of the actual landing. Morgan had to go beyond that; his planning process had to start at the end, where the ultimate aim of Overlord was the invasion of Germany, and then work back from there to ensure that the landings and subsequent development made that possible.

"Where" was simply a choice between the Pas de Calais and Normandy. The former is closer to southern England and thus offered a shorter sea approach and better Allied air cover. It had, though, stronger defenses and was close to the enemy's main reserves. The ports of southeast England were smaller than those farther west, being designed for cross-Channel rather than oceangoing traffic, and would not have sufficed on their own. Normandy is farther from England, but promised compensating advantages. The German defenses were less strong and there were suitable beaches. The Cotentin

Peninsula would provide some protection from the prevailing westerly weather, and an extended beachhead covering most of northwest France could be envisaged. Secure behind the rivers Seine and Loire, this would include the ports of Brest and Cherbourg, where American reinforcements could disembark without having to stage through Britain. Normandy, which had been advocated by Mountbatten when he was head of Combined Operations, was Morgan's choice.

The answer to "when" had, of course, already been indicated at Casablanca: as early as possible in 1944. Winter weather in the Channel meant that only the months May to September were worth considering. A combination of high tide on the beaches and full moon for the parachute landings was a requirement. The first such opportunity came in May and that was the date Morgan originally selected.

The key point in working out the "how," and also the "where," was the Mulberry artificial harbor. No matter how successful the initial operations were, it would not be possible to maintain a large modern army of between one and two million men ashore unless it had an adequate port. In the case of Overlord this meant the capability of handling 12,000 tons a day. This was undoubtedly a factor in making the Germans decide that the Pas de Calais was going to be the Allies' objective. They would have found it much harder to defend Calais and Boulogne there than Cherbourg in Normandy, lying as it does at the tip of a peninsula. This factor, they thought, would attract the Allies to the Pas de Calais. To quote Churchill:

> Their High Command had no doubt said to themselves, "this [Normandy] is a good sector for raids up to ten or twenty thousand men, but unless Cherbourg is taken in working order no army in any way equal to the task of an invasion can be landed or supplied. It is a coast for a raid, but not for wider operations."

From the German viewpoint this would have been a logical deduction—but they knew nothing about Mulberry.

Mountbatten's headquarters had already given some thought to building an artificial harbor, but it was Morgan's senior naval officer, Commodore John Hughes-Hallet, RN, who refined the idea and made it into a practical proposition. Two Mulberries were to be built and towed across the Channel a short time after D-Day. Each comprised a number of piers, fixed at the landward end but with their seaward ends floating to cope with the twenty-foot tides. A line of sunken block-ships would provide breakwaters. In this sheltered water large vessels could lie at anchor and discharge their cargoes onto small landing craft; smaller vessels could come alongside the piers. Without Mulberry harbors the invasion of Europe could not have taken place in the way it did, and Morgan and his team would have been forced to make a different plan dependent upon the early capture of a major port. Produced in secret, they enabled him to introduce an invaluable element of surprise into the plan for Overlord.

There were many problems to be overcome, not all strictly military. The plan obviously had to be based not on what was ideal, but upon the assets that were available to COSSAC in the real world. Two constant shortfalls were to be the number of landing craft (especially LSTs [Landing Ships, Tank]) and aircraft for the airborne assaults.

Another problem was Morgan's unusual status as a chief of staff with no commander to report to. He was constantly dealing with officers senior to himself, making demands on them not on behalf of a supreme commander but in his own right. Not all cooperated as well as he would have liked, but in fairness to them it must be remembered that unlike Morgan, who was planning a future operation and had no real-time task, they were commanders responsible for actual operations of war every day of the week. This improved when Eisenhower was finally nominated as supreme allied commander and Montgomery appointed to lead the initial assault. Eisenhower traveled via Washington, sending Montgomery ahead to London with full authority to act as his representative in planning matters. Montgomery's first act on arrival in early January 1944 was to call for a detailed presentation of the plan. He was critical of a number of points and ordered changes to be made. Some on Morgan's staff were upset at what they saw as criticism of their hard work—doubtless Montgomery had spoken with his customary bluntness!—but not so Morgan himself. He realized his lack of experience as an operational commander and the problems resulting from his unusual status, and was happy to have the experienced and victorious Monty to refer to.

The major change that had to be made concerned the number of divisions in the initial assault and the width of the beachhead they were to establish. Churchill had already shown Montgomery the Overlord blueprint at Marrakesh (where the prime minister was convalescing from pneumonia) and his immediate assessment was that the COSSAC plan for only three divisions assaulting on a narrow front on D-day was not realistic. The plan called for another thirteen divisions to land across the same beaches by D+12, a further ten by D+24. The potential for chaos in the congested initial landing area was very great, as was its vulnerability to counterattack. When acquainted with the matter Eisenhower and Bradley both agreed with Montgomery.

Morgan was, of course, constrained by the number of landing craft available. Based on the figures he had been given it was impossible to land more than three divisions on D-Day. More landing craft had to be found. The solution, to which Eisenhower and the British Chiefs of Staff agreed in March, was to increase the D-Day divisions to five, three British and two American. Once this important decision had been made at the senior level, Morgan and his team could get to work and recast the Overlord plan accordingly. Landing craft for one of the additional divisions came from postponing Overlord from May to June and using that month's production for the invasion. Craft for the second division were found by postponing indefinitely Operation Anvil, the two-division secondary invasion of southern France timed to coincide with Overlord. This was probably a blessing in disguise, with the divisions thus saved better employed keeping up the pressure in Italy, the only place in which the Anglo-American armies were actually fighting the Germans until D-Day.

Civil affairs was the thorniest problem of all. Until they crossed the Rhine the Allies would be liberating friendly countries, not invading enemy ones. But how were liberated territories to be governed until their own legitimate governments could take over? What were the soldiers to do if faced by a resistance movement, possibly under Communist influence, claiming the right to act as a government before the London-based government-in-exile could be returned? Most difficult of all, which was the legitimate government of France, the one in Paris that had governed the country under German occupation, or Charles de Gaulle's Committee of National Liberation in London? And was the prickly de Gaulle merely another military subordinate under Eisenhower's command, and a fairly lowly one at that, or a head of state in waiting?

Morgan called civil affairs his "headache of headaches" and it diverted too much attention from military matters. The solution was to add the right expert to his staff. On a visit to Washington in autumn 1943 to brief the Combined Chiefs he asked Roosevelt for Ambassador Anthony J. Drexell, and almost immediately Drexell joined Morgan in London as a colonel.

The way the two armies were deployed in southern England, the Americans to the west and the British and Canadians to the east, meant that they would land in Normandy in that formation. In turn, when they broke out of Normandy and wheeled east toward the Rhine the Americans would be on the southern flank and the British on the northern one. The inevitable result would be that the American army would liberate Paris and most of France, the British the smaller countries—Belgium, Holland, and Denmark. France with its two potential governments was going to be the most difficult civil affairs problem, and Roosevelt thought that the British, as France's longtime neighbors, could cope with this better. (Had he, one wonders, studied the history of Anglo-French relations over the centuries?) Quite apart from the political ramifications, this drastic change would have great military consequences. Either two enormous armies would have to swap places across southern England or their invasion axes would have to cross in mid-Channel. Neither was militarily possible and the idea was quickly dropped, but while it lasted it absorbed valuable staff time and effort.

A similar red herring was the proposal made at a fairly late stage to invade Norway instead of France, the underlying reason probably being the fear of unacceptably high casualties in Normandy. Strategically this made little sense, and tactically the crossing of the North Sea would not be possible for landing craft. Oceangoing vessels, of which there were not enough, would be needed and they would have to steam into fjords to disembark their troops at harbors. The idea never stood a chance, but refuting it took up more valuable time.

Another diversion, this a military one that deserved serious consideration, was the threat of German V-1 and V-2 rockets. In late 1943 intelligence estimated that attack by these weapons was imminent and that the Allied air forces lacked the capability to destroy their launch sites. The question whether this would hinder the invasion and if so what alterations to the plan needed to be made then arose. Morgan took the view that to make drastic changes to Allied preparations on the basis of a mere threat would be to dance unnecessarily to the enemy's tune; if the bombardment materialized, then the troops would simply be under enemy fire on this side of the Channel and earlier than expected. His commonsense advice was accepted.

At last, toward the end of January 1944 the supreme allied commander, Eisenhower, arrived in London to take up his responsibilities. Morgan was able to hand over to him two things: a well-thought-out plan that was fundamentally correct and only needed refinement; and in the shape of his COSSAC planning staff the embryo of the international headquarters that would be needed to execute the plan. To quote Eisenhower: "he had in the months preceding my arrival accomplished a mass of detailed planning, accumulation of data, and gathering of supply that made D-Day possible."

Having been COSSAC for almost a year he might have expected to continue as Eisenhower's chief of staff, especially as Gen. George C. Marshall had led Morgan to believe that if he were released from Washington to lead the invasion, he would want to retain Morgan as chief of staff. But Marshall was not appointed, and Eisenhower had already forged a strong and successful relationship with Maj. Gen. Walter Bedell Smith in the Mediterranean. It would have been folly to break this up and, professional soldier that he was, Morgan accepted the situation loyally. He was offered a corps in Italy, but he was very conscious of his lack of command experience. He thought he had spent so much time on the staff answering the bell for someone else that he doubted his ability to ring the bell himself.

Instead, wishing to see his plan come to fruition, he took the post of deputy chief of staff at Eisenhower's headquarters. There his advice often conflicted with the ideas of Montgomery, now commanding the 21st Army Group, something the latter did not take to kindly. In his memoirs he wrote that Morgan "considered Eisenhower was a god; since I had discarded many of his plans, he placed me at the other end of the celestial ladder." Montgomery carried this animosity into the postwar era, and in his memoirs he gave scant praise to Morgan's COSSAC achievements.

Morgan's final assignment was a relatively unimportant job compared to his time as COSSAC, but at the end of it he had the satisfaction of being present when Ike accepted the German unconditional surrender at Rheims— something he was entitled to feel he had played a major part in bringing about. Morgan was honored by the king with a knighthood for his war services and also received American and French decorations.

Morgan held two important posts after the war. In 1945 and 1946, still a serving officer, he was seconded to be director of the United Nations Relief and Recovery Administration in Germany. With his international experience and organizing ability he was ideal for this post, but it was not a happy time. He believed that international Zionists, aided and abetted by the Soviets who were keen to undermine Britain's position in the Middle East, were using the organization for their own purposes to the detriment of more needy, non-Jewish refugees. As a soldier this was anathema to Morgan and he spoke out against it. After surviving an attempt to dismiss him he resigned. He left the army shortly afterwards.

Morgan's five years as controller of the Britain's Atomic Energy Commission (1951–56) were much happier. In this civilian capacity Morgan, who had gone to war in a horsedrawn army in 1914, witnessed the first British H-bomb tests—a startling reminder of how far and fast military technology had advanced in a mere forty years.

Morgan died in 1967. His name and reputation will always depend on his COSSAC time, less than one year in a career spanning thirty-four. To have been responsible for planning the largest amphibious assault in history, a plan that was successfully put into practice with only one major amendment, is no mean achievement. For this he had to form and then lead the first ever truly international headquarters and to blend together officers of two different military traditions whose countries had virtually no previous common war experience.

An essentially modest man, he brought to this difficult task a well-trained military brain, the ability to see the wood from the trees, and a determination to overcome all difficulties. He had indeed risen to Brooke's challenge and "bloody well made it work." Above all, it was his tact and humanity, plus the realization that he was no longer simply a British officer, but answerable instead in this novel supranational situation to Allied superiors, that inspired his team and got it working in the right way. With no commander from whom to seek advice, he was left very much to his own devices, despite his lack of senior command experience in battle. It is interesting that in his autobiography he queried the British custom of alternating trained staff officers between staff and regimental or command appointments. Based on his own experience he believed there was a case for recognizing the staff as a separate and specialized breed early on in their careers.

His success was a major contribution to the Allied victory. The Allies were to reap the benefit of his work in the Cold War as well, as the principles and methods for running an international headquarters he established at COSSAC were to be the foundation stone of NATO.

Selected Bibliography

Churchill, Winston S. *The Second World War*. 6 vols. London: Cassell, 1959.
Gelb, Norman. *Ike and Monty: Generals at War*. New York: William Morrow, 1994.
Montgomery, Bernard L. *Memoirs*. London: Collins, 1958.
Morgan, Frederick. *COSSAC's Memoirs: Overture to OVERLORD*. London: Hodder and Stoughton, 1951.
———. *Peace and War, a Soldier's Life*. London: Hodder and Stoughton, 1961.

CHRONOLOGY OF WALTER BEDELL SMITH

5 Oct 1895	Born Indianapolis, Indiana.
5 Oct 1911	Enlisted, Indiana National Guard.
1913	Enrolled in Butler University, but soon withdrew.
Nov 1917	Commissioned second lieutenant, National Guard.
Apr–Sept 1918	Served in France, seeing action at the Marne and Aisne.
1918–25	Remained on active duty with a regular commission.
Apr 1925	Served as assistant to the chief coordinator, Bureau of the Budget, Washington, D.C.
1929–31	Assigned to the 45th Infantry Regiment, Fort William McKinley, Philippines.
Sept 1929	Promoted to captain.
1930–31	Attended the Infantry School at Fort Benning, Georgia.
1932–33	Remained at Fort Benning as secretary of the Infantry School.
1933–35	Attended Command and General Staff College, Fort Leavenworth.
23 Jun 1937	Graduated from U.S. Army War College, Washington, D.C.
1 Jan 1939	Promoted to major.
Oct 1939	Appointed assistant secretary of the General Staff, War Department.
Sept 1941	Elevated to secretary of the General Staff, with promotion to lieutenant colonel.
Feb 1942	Assigned as U.S. secretary of the Combined Chiefs of Staff (Anglo-American).
Sept 1942	Assigned with the rank of brigadier general as Eisenhower's chief of staff of the European Theater of Operations.
Nov 1942	Promoted to major general and assumed duties as chief of staff of Allied Forces, North Africa and the Mediterranean.
Sept 1943	Secretly signed the Italian surrender document in Lisbon.
Mar 1944	Assigned as a lieutenant general as chief of staff, Supreme Headquarters Allied Expeditionary Forces.
May 1945	Headed Allied delegation to accept the surrender of Germany.

June 1945	Assigned as chief of staff of U.S. forces in divided Germany.
Jan 1946	Assigned as chief of Operations and Plans Division, Joint Chiefs of Staff.
Feb 1946	Succeeded W. Averill Harriman as U.S. ambassador to the Soviet Union.
Mar 1949	Assumed command of First Army, Governors Island, N.Y.
Sept 1950	Appointed director of the Central Intelligence Agency.
July 1951	Promoted to general.
Feb 1953	Appointed undersecretary of state. Headed the U.S. delegation at the Geneva Conference on Indochina.
1 Oct 1954	Retired from the U.S. Army.
Oct 1954	Became vice president of American Manufacturing and Foundry.
9 Aug 1961	Died of heart failure at Walter Reed Hospital.

Walter Bedell Smith

Carl O. Schuster

B orn in 1895 to a middle-class Catholic family in Indianapolis, Indiana, Walter Bedell Smith entered a world in which the United States was neither a world power nor seemingly interested as a nation in becoming one. Despite growing up in a family with no tradition of career military service, young Smith developed a deep and passionate interest in all things military during his earliest childhood and retained it to the end of his days. He reveled in his maternal grandfather's experiences with the German army in the Franco-Prussian War and the activities of another ancestor in America's war for independence. A sickly child who demonstrated little interest in studies or sports, he outwardly evinced few other qualities that marked him as a soldier or combat leader.

The young Smith maintained a large collection of toy soldiers and took them everywhere and even recruited his boyhood friends into an informal association that drilled and practiced military-style marching. Knowing his mother objected to all forms of military service, Smith overcame her opposition to his joining the Indiana National Guard by telling her it was a social club that offered him employment as well as social opportunities. He initiated his military career by entering Company D, 2nd Indiana Infantry on 5 October 1911, his sixteenth birthday. Although it wasn't a full-time military position, Smith saw it as a stepping-stone to a commission in the Regular Army. Most would have told him his was an impossible dream. He didn't even have a high school diploma or the academic record required to enter West Point, at that time the only peacetime path to a Regular Army commission. Nonetheless, his determination and the course of world events combined to move him along his chosen path.[1]

Smith's dedication and hard work rewarded him in the Indiana National Guard. It was an indifferently led, poorly trained, and only lightly motivated force in those days. In that environment, Private Smith's dedication and self-discipline stood out. Although he briefly flirted with college, attending a few courses at nearby Butler University, Smith's father's declining health forced him to drop out and take work as a mechanic in a nearby factory. His dull factory job made his National Guard activities a pleasant escape. His leadership and dedication to duty led to rapid promotions, first to corporal, then sergeant.

Continental and world events then provided the opportunities that Sergeant Smith required. Although he did not participate in the fighting that followed America's 1916 intervention in Mexico's civil war, his staff work in the Indiana National Guard headquarters during mobilization was noted by most of the National Guard's senior leadership. Sergeant Smith may not have enjoyed his duties on the staff, but his obvious talents were apparent to his superiors and provided the launch pad for his professional advancement. All he needed was another opportunity. It came in April 1917 when the United States declared war on Germany.[2]

Faced with the need to mobilize for a major overseas war, the U.S. Army had to expand its officer corps from 5,959 to more than 200,000 in less than a year. To accomplish that, the Army drew platoon and company officers from the National Guard and the population at large. Sixteen officer-training schools were established to build the officer corps, and National Guard units were directed to nominate "talented men of officer potential" to be trained at these schools. In recognition of his leadership during a 1913 flood and his outstanding staff work in 1916, Smith's company commander recommended him. In late August 1917 Smith departed for officer training at Fort Benjamin Harrison, where he excelled at the training and received his commission as an infantry second lieutenant in the National Guard on 27 November 1917. He was then immediately posted to the 4th Infantry Division, a Regular Army unit.[3]

The 4th Infantry Division was a division in name only. Its regiments had been broken up to provide cadres for the training of the vast drafts of newly mobilized men. The officers received training from veteran French and British officers brought back to the United States to teach the Americans about modern warfare. Lieutenant Smith was assigned to Company A, 39th Infantry Regiment. The division left for Europe on 9 May 1918 with its training incomplete.[4] Smith's regiment, for example, had not participated in field training above the company level.

The German 1918 offensives were in full swing as the 4th Infantry Division marched to its assembly areas in France. The British 16th Division took over the American unit's training. Unfortunately, Germany's battlefield successes forced the 4th Infantry Division's training to be cut from the planned four weeks to only eight days. The division marched out to marshalling areas near the Marne, where the French discovered that their enthusiastic American allies were still practicing the infantry tactics of 1914–15. Shocked, they recommended that the Americans be absorbed into regular French formations. The American Expeditionary Force (AEF) commander, Gen. John J. Pershing, resisted.[5] The American 4th and 28th Infantry Divisions were held back in defense of the French capital while the Second Battle of the Marne was conducted without them. As the last German offensive petered out in mid-July, the Americans were moved up to support the Allied counterattack. The 4th Infantry Division still had not conducted field training as a complete division.

Attached to the French 33rd Division, Lieutenant Smith's 39th Infantry Regiment was supposed to attack behind French units in order to minimize American casualties, but aggressive German counterbattery fire forced the Americans to advance independently and under heavy artillery fire. Advancing in dense solid lines in accordance with American doctrine of the time, the unit suffered heavily whenever it encountered resistance. Fortunately, they were fighting a surprised German unit on the edge of collapse. The Germans withdrew, giving the 39th Infantry Regiment its first military victory. It was Smith's first and last combat action as a platoon leader. In the confusion of misunderstood orders between the American infantry units and their French artillery supporting units, the Americans were shelled accidentally. Unable to withdraw through the barrage, the American battalion attacked the German unit in front of them. More than half of the unit was killed or wounded—Lieutenant Smith was among the latter.[6]

His wounds were not serious and his convalescence was short, but the attack highlighted the problems facing an American army using obsolete tactics and having few properly trained staffs to organize and plan operations. Thus, when he tried to return to his unit, Smith instead found himself directed to the U.S. Army's ad hoc General Staff School at Langres. He wound up there because the Regular Army establishment was wary of European-style general staffs and therefore had directed that the bulk of the appointments to the course consist of Reserve and National Guard officers. Smith did well in the course and subsequently was seconded to the War Department General Staff in Washington, D.C., as a newly promoted first lieutenant.

In September 1918 Smith was assigned to the newly established Military Intelligence Division (MID). From a prewar strength as a branch in the Plans Division consisting of three officers and clerk, the MID grew to more than 1,200 personnel by war's end. Smith's work in developing the MID's systems and procedures was quickly recognized and appreciated. He then was transferred and assigned as the staff adjutant and intelligence officer of the 379th Infantry Brigade at Camp Sherman, Ohio. With experienced staff officers in very short supply, an officer of Lieutenant Smith's background was priceless, and he was soon drawn up to the divisional headquarters.

Working in the 95th Infantry Division adjutant's office, Smith processed recruit and divisional unit records far more often than he examined intelligence reports. The 1918 flu epidemic severely curtailed the division's training schedule and the war ended before the unit was ready. Camp Sherman was then converted to a demobilization center, where once again Lieutenant Smith's administrative skills came to the fore. With the war over, Reserve and National Guard officers of talent were offered the opportunity to request a commission in the Regular Army. Smith applied and studied hard for the competitive exam. His staff record, combat service, and high examination score resulted in his selection as one of the 14,000 accepted out of 40,000 applicants. He finally had achieved his dream of a military career in the Regular Army.[7]

The interwar U.S. Army was embroiled in a series of philosophical and doctrinal struggles between those opposed to reorganization and the development of a General Staff, and those who advocated reforms. With the army unpopular as a result of its involvement in putting down the Red Strikes of 1919, most military leaders preferred to pursue small reforms that did not threaten the established order. Doctrine stagnated and command positions were dominated by those who had served as field-grade officers in France.

In that environment Lieutenant Smith found himself isolated in an Army officered by West Point graduates intent on defending the traditional Army. He served in a successive number of staff assignments, and he attended the Infantry School and the Command and General Staff College at Fort Leavenworth. His contemporaries found him tough and uncompromising, while his superiors recognized him for his intellect, hard work, and loyalty. His abrupt demeanor as an instructor at the Infantry School deterred students from asking questions. He demanded strict adherence to the school solution to tactical problems. He and his wife largely kept to themselves, socializing only as required by duty. Nonetheless, he progressed in step with his contemporaries, finishing the Army War College in 1937. Two years later he was assigned to the secretariat of the War Department General Staff, where he met and worked for Gen. George C. Marshall. It was a fortuitous posting.

As World War II approached, Major Smith differed little from his peer group, except that he had no formal college education and was a Catholic. What separated him professionally from his counterparts was the 1930–33 period he spent as a student and then as an instructor at the Infantry School and his contact with General Marshall in the General Staff Secretariat. At the former he met then–Maj. Omar Bradley, who later recommended to Marshall that "Beetle" Smith be appointed to the War Department General Staff. Smith became the assistant to the chief of the secretariat, Col. Orlando Ward. In that capacity, Smith was charged with a number of complex responsibilities, including liaison with the White House. Under the reforms Marshall started in 1939, the secretariat was responsible for ensuring that information, orders, and the vast details of a rapidly expanding army reached the right people, units, and offices at the right time. Smith's hard work and efficiency quickly drew him into Marshall's inner circle, and he soon proved very adept at running a headquarters. More important, he was one of only a small handful of officers with the credibility and confidence to approach General Marshall directly.[8]

Colonel Ward's promotion and departure in late September 1941 resulted in Smith's promotion to lieutenant colonel and assignment as chief of the secretariat. He quickly became the U.S. Army chief of staff's de facto chief of staff. Smith brought order to the encroaching chaos of an army preparing for war. By the time of the Pearl Harbor attack, Smith had established an effective staff structure that could handle the massively expanding requirements.

With the war's outbreak, Smith was selected to head the secretariat of the Anglo-American Combined Chiefs of Staff (CCS), formed in January 1942 to coordinate, plan and direct the bilateral coalition's grand strategy. He also was appointed chief of the joint secretariat of the American Joint Chiefs of Staff (JCS), established in February 1942. In those combined jobs, the newly promoted Colonel Smith had to ensure the fair and equitable treatment of potentially contentious issues affecting the competing interests of the American armed services on the Joint Staff, and the equally difficult challenges of the differing perspectives between the two allies on the CCS. He executed his latter duties more diplomatically. The strong, taciturn Smith became one of the better-known and liked members of the CCS organization. His Washington tours had taught him tact, diplomacy, and the art of evasive conversation.

Smith was promoted to brigadier general in September 1942 and assigned as Maj. Gen. Dwight Eisenhower's chief of staff for the European Theater of Operations (ETO).[9] Two months later Smith became a major general and chief of staff to now full-General Eisenhower, as Ike became the commander of Allied Forces in North Africa and the Mediterranean. Smith would remain Eisenhower's chief of staff for the remainder of the war. As in all his previous assignments, Smith proved a loyal, hard-working, and efficient subordinate.

Smith was the first to handle the increasingly acrimonious relations among the primary Allied commanders whose strategic and operational visions differed drastically. The Patton-Montgomery rivalry is the best known, but Allied air commanders such as Carl A. Spaatz and Sir Arthur Tedder had equally differing perspectives on air operations. When things got truly out of hand, it was Smith who had to play the hard-nosed enforcer, keeping Eisenhower free to play the reasonable fatherly figure who smoothed the waters in the end. Smith, for example, was the arbiter who carried the competing Patton-Montgomery plans for the Sicily invasion to Eisenhower for resolution. He served a similar role as chief referee between the competing visions for invading mainland Italy once Sicily was secured. In doing so, Smith earned Eisenhower's undying trust—so much so that Eisenhower detailed Smith to handle the negotiations and signing of Italy's secret surrender in September 1943.[10]

As Allied planning for the invasion of France advanced, Smith followed Eisenhower to Britain to direct the staff planning for what became Operation Overlord. With that posting came promotion to lieutenant general and the title of Chief of Staff, Supreme Headquarters Allied Expeditionary Force (SHAEF). Few, including many professional military officers, appreciated the complexity and challenges that faced SHAEF as it prepared to invade the Continent. Germany had more than one-half million troops stationed in France, many in heavily fortified positions. More important, France's coastal waters and key port facilities were heavily mined and defended. Just transporting the Allied armies to France under such conditions was a major logistical and transportation problem requiring the planning and coordination of near-simultaneous naval and air movements from more than twenty ports and 200 airfields. Adding air and naval gunfire support requirements to the equation, plus the need to land and deploy ground forces while being fired upon by a determined and well-armed opponent, resulted in a planning and execution nightmare of indescribable intricacy. The plan not only had to be complex and integrated, but it had to be flexible enough to accommodate changes dictated by enemy action. The responsibility for ensuring that all the necessary requirements and alternatives were examined and resolved fell to SHAEF's chief of staff, Lt. Gen. Walter Bedell Smith.

Eisenhower was clearly the commander and it was his strategic vision that shaped the staff's planning and the command's execution. But it was Smith's strong guiding hand that directed the plan's development and ensured that all preparations were completed in an integrated conclusion. He also fought the political battles to prevent the SHAEF staff from being torn apart by directions and requirements coming in from outside the staff. Smith warned Eisenhower of both American and British tendencies to undercut SHAEF's authority by seeking minor organizational adjustments to the command's subordinate command relationships, the cumulative effects of which would undermine Eisenhower's command authority. Unity of command had to be preserved and Smith fought all the early battles, saving Eisenhower for the major ones. The result was that Eisenhower retained control over all the command elements for Operation Overlord, as well as the staff planning elements. That unity of purpose and authority was essential to D-Day's success.

To understand the immensity of Smith's task, one need only to look at the fact that without capturing a single operational port, SHAEF landed more than one million Allied troops on the Normandy beachhead in the first week following 6 June. The logistical support and direction of operations ashore fell to Smith and the SHAEF staff. As in the planning of the landing itself, Smith drove the staff in the execution of Eisenhower's intent.

By June 1944 the Eisenhower-Smith relationship had become so strong that Smith was able to anticipate Eisenhower's requirements and decisions as the campaign for France unfolded. Smith, for example, had to coordinate the preparation and presentation of the contending plans for driving across France, because logistical constraints limited the Allies' freedom of maneuver ashore. The Allies at that point had only the supply, transport, and debarkation capacities to support either one sustained drive or a steady broad advance across France.[11]

Both Montgomery and Patton called for a narrow, rapid drive across France to roll up the German armies and enter Germany before Hitler could transfer or rebuild the forces required to defend the German border. Militarily, the British army was not capable of sustaining such a drive without American troops and resources in support. Politically, that was not acceptable to the United States, the country providing the bulk of the troops and supplies to the campaign. Patton's idea was equally unacceptable politically. For very good domestic political reasons and postwar Anglo-American relations, British troops could not be relegated to a secondary role. They had fought too long and too hard to be left out at the end. Both Eisenhower and Smith understood that, if many other American and British leaders did not.

Smith proved so adroit at handling the political problems that Eisenhower delegated to Smith the responsibility for handling the Soviets, Free French, and other potentially volatile political factions. Doing this had two advantages for Eisenhower—it gave him plausible deniability in case anything went wrong, and it enabled him to study the situation carefully before he became involved. It also helped that Smith generally resolved the political problems effectively.

Conservative and risk-averse in his thinking, Smith used logistics to control Eisenhower's most difficult American subordinate, Lt. Gen. George S. Patton, commander of the U.S. Third Army. Wary of what he believed to be Patton's reckless approach to operations, Smith deliberately limited the Third Army's supplies. He also used the lure of supplies in his unsuccessful effort to convince Montgomery to delete Arnhem as an objective of Operation Market-Garden, the massive airborne assault into the Netherlands. SHAEF, however, did not have total control over logistics arrangements in France. Unlike the command arrangements in the Mediterranean Theater, in France logistics was a national responsibility, leaving Smith with direct authority only over the American supply system. This arrangement became increasingly difficult as ammunition, fuel, and personnel shortages grew. By October 1944 units were being cannibalized to sustain the now-stalled Allied advance.[12]

Although daring and embarrassing to the Allies, the German winter offensive that resulted in the Battle of the Bulge highlighted SHAEF's ability to command the Allied armies. In contrast to the hesitations and debates that characterized decisionmaking for the drive across France, Eisenhower and SHAEF responded quickly and decisively to the German offensive. Command lines were redrawn and forces allocated and redirected to first contain and then destroy the German thrust. Patton and Montgomery clearly fought the battles, but they did so under the guiding hand of and with resources provided by SHAEF. The details of that direction and the planning were conducted under Smith's stern hand and thorough leadership.

The battle for France and the invasion of Germany were the highlight of Smith's military career. Although he would go on to serve in key government positions of authority and responsibility, he would never again enjoy the broad powers and access to power he had enjoyed as Eisenhower's chief of staff. He was Eisenhower's strong right hand and intimate professional associate. It was

Smith who headed the delegation that accepted Germany's formal surrender in May 1945.

Immediately after the war Smith served as the chief of staff of U.S. Forces in the Western Zone of occupied Germany. In January 1946 he was scheduled to return to the United States as chief of the Operations and Plans Division of the Joint Chiefs of Staff, but he was then redirected to replace Averill Harriman as the U.S. ambassador to the Soviet Union, while retaining his military rank as a lieutenant general. Smith represented the United States at the Paris Peace Conference. Unfortunately, he approached his ambassadorial duties the same way he did military duties—with cold tenacity and little if any flexibility. It did little to reassure the Soviets of American intentions, but he served as an indicator of potential American resolve. Smith was still at that post when the Soviet Union initiated the Berlin Crisis by trying to starve the city in an effort to drive out the Allied forces. Smith negotiated directly with the Soviet premier Josef Stalin and Foreign Minister Vyacheslav Molotov.[13]

In March 1949 Smith returned to the United States as commander of the First Army, headquartered on Governor's Island, New York. It was not the post Smith wanted and it appeared that his hopes for a fourth star and a meaningful Army command were becoming less and less likely. Disappointed, he used his free time to write a book about his service as American ambassador, *My Three Years in Moscow*. It was a revealing if not highly acclaimed book that accurately portrayed Soviet goals in Europe and around the world and the need for sustained American commitment to the defense of freedom.

Unfortunately, Smith's health began to decline, and he became plagued by a stomach ulcer. Nonetheless, President Truman appointed him in September 1950 to head the newly established Central Intelligence Agency. That position finally led to his fourth star in July 1951. Two years later he left the CIA when President Eisenhower appointed him as undersecretary of state to John Foster Dulles. Smith, however, never established the close professional relationship with Dulles that he had enjoyed with his superiors in the military.[14]

Faced with a growing stomach ulcer problem and constant pain, Smith weathered on in hopes of gaining a fifth star and perhaps appointment as Army chief of staff. As that dream evaporated, Smith retired from the Army in 1954. Bitter at not being accorded the recognition that he felt he deserved, he turned to commercial activities. He became a director of the United Fruit Company and cooperated fully in the overthrow of Guatemala's Arbenz government. Some have criticized Smith's ethics because he negotiated with the dictatorship while involved in the U.S. government's planning for the coup.

Smith proved as adept at earning money as he had been at running a military headquarters. Unfortunately, his lack of sincere human warmth deprived him of any long-lasting personal friendships. Even those who respected and trusted him felt no personal feelings toward him. Most of those who worked around him during World War II considered him insincere and mean-spirited. His wartime machinations to shift blame for SHAEF's logistical problems to Gen. J. C. H. Lee earned him the enmity of many. As Smith's health declined, he became increasingly bitter. At the end he even felt that Eisenhower had used and betrayed him. Smith died alone on 9 August 1961, leaving an estate in excess of $2.5 million, earned in the six years since his retirement. He was buried near General Marshall in Arlington Cemetery.[15]

Notes

1. D. K. R. Crosswell, *The Chief of Staff: The Military Career of General Walter Bedell Smith* (New York: Greenwood Press, 1991), 3–6.
2. Ibid., 7–8.
3. Edward M. Coffman, *The War to End All Wars* (New York: Oxford University Press, 1968), 8–9.
4. Ibid., 10–13.
5. Edward Cray, *General of the Army: George C. Marshall, Soldier and Statesman* (New York: Cooper Square Press, 2000), 54–55.
6. Crosswell, *Chief of Staff*, 15–17.
7. Ibid., 20–29.
8. Ibid., 62–84.
9. Ibid., 90, 105.
10. Ibid., 182.
11. Russell F. Weigley, *Eisenhower's Lieutenants* (Bloomington: Indiana University Press, 1981), 269.
12. Crosswell, *Chief of Staff*, 269–70.
13. Ibid., 326–31.
14. Ibid., 332–34.
15. Ibid., 338–40.

CHRONOLOGY OF HOBART RAYMOND GAY

16 May 1894	Born in Rockport, Illinois.
Jun 1917	Commissioned second lieutenant, Cavalry.
Oct 1917	Promoted to first lieutenant.
Jul 1920	Promoted to captain.
1923–24	Attended Cavalry School.
1924–25	Attended Special Advanced Equitation Course, Cavalry School.
1925–29	Assigned as instructor, Special Advanced Equitation Course.
Jun 1934	Transferred to Quartermaster Corps.
Aug 1935	Promoted to major.
1938–39	Attended Quartermaster School.
1939–41	Assigned as post quartermaster, Fort Myer, Virginia.
Aug 1940	Promoted to lieutenant colonel.
Aug–Dec 1940	Attended Army Industrial College.
Jan 1941	Assigned as division quartermaster, 2nd Armored Division.
Dec 1941	Promoted to colonel.
Jul 1942– Apr 1944	Assigned as chief of staff, I Armored Corps, Western Task Force, U.S. Seventh Army, and U.S. Third Army.
Jun 1943	Promoted to brigadier general.
Apr 1944	Assigned as assistant chief of staff (Administration), U.S. Third Army.
3 Dec 1944– Oct 1945	Assigned succcessively as chief of staff, U.S. Third Army.
Mar 1945	Promoted to major general.
Oct 1945	Assigned as chief of staff, Fifteenth Army.
Jan 1946	Assumed acting command of the Fifteenth Army following the accidental death of Gen. George Patton.
Feb 1946	Assigned as commanding general, 1st Armored Division.
April 1946	Assigned as commander, 2nd Constabulary Brigade, Germany.
Aug 1947	Assigned as commanding general, Military District of Washington.

Sep 1949– Feb 1951	Assigned as commanding general, 1st Cavalry Division, Korea.
Feb 1951	Assigned as deputy commanding general, Fourth Army, Fort Sam Houston, Texas.
Jul 1952	Assigned as commanding general, VI Corps, Camp Atterbury, Indiana.
Apr 1953	Assigned as commanding general, III Corps, Fort MacArthur, California.
Sep 1954	Promoted to lieutenant general and assigned as commanding general, Fifth Army, Fort Sheridan, Illinois.
31 Aug 1955	Retired.
1955–1963	Superintendent, New Mexico Military Institute.
19 Aug 1983	Died, El Paso, Texas.

CHRONOLOGY OF HUGH JOSEPH GAFFEY

18 Nov 1895	Born in Hartford, Connecticut.
Oct 1917	Commissioned second lieutenant, Field Artillery.
Oct 1918	Promoted to first lieutenant.
Jul 1920	Promoted to captain.
1922–23	Attended Field Artillery School.
Dec 1935	Promoted to major.
1935–36	Attended Command and General Staff College.
Aug 1940	Promoted to lieutenant colonel.
Feb 1942	Promoted to colonel.
Oct 1942	Assigned as commander, Combat Command B, 2nd Armored Division in Operation Torch.
Aug 1942	Promoted to brigadier general.
Mar 1942	Assigned as chief of staff, II Corps.
Apr 1943	Promoted to major general.
May 1943	Assigned as commanding general, 2nd Armored Division.
Apr 1944	Assigned as chief of staff, U.S. Third Army.
Dec 1944	Assigned as commanding general, 4th Armored Division.
Mar 1945	Assigned as commanding general, XII Corps.
Sept 1945	Assigned as commanding general, Armor School, Fort Knox, Kentucky.
17 Jun 1946	Killed in plane crash, Fort Knox, Kentucky.

Hobart R. Gay and Hugh J. Gaffey

Robert Larson

In July 1926 George S. Patton Jr. wrote his good friend Dwight Eisenhower to congratulate him on graduating first in his class from the U.S. Army Command and General Staff College. He mixed his praise for his friend's achievement, however, with reservations over the value of the course as a preparation for leaders in future wars. The key problems in modern war, he wrote, were "what it is that makes the Poor S.O.B. who constitutes the casualty lists fight and in what formation he is going to fight." Admitting he did not know the answer to the second problem, he had no hesitation in asserting that the key to the first was leadership. He recommended Eisenhower read Ardant du Picq's *Battle Studies*, a work renowned for its argument that an unquenchable determination to conquer was the essential ingredient for success in war. The commander's task was to provide the impetus for that determination and Patton concluded his comments with the assertion that "The victor in the next war will depend on Execution not Plans and the execution will depend on some means of making infantry move under fire."[1]

Such comments do much to reinforce Patton's image as a hard-driving commander who relied on flamboyant leadership to achieve success. But this obscures the reality that he was also a deeply thoughtful and highly professional commander who had thoroughly mastered the skills necessary to lead large formations in war. It also obscures the fact that Patton fully understood the importance of staff work and of having the right man as his chief of staff to complement himself. In Hobart R. Gay and Hugh J. Gaffey he found two men who filled this need.

Maj. Gen. Hugh J. Gaffey with Gen. George Patton. (Hobart Gay is not pictured.)

130

There is a general assumption that the typical commander–chief of staff relationship is one where the former is mostly in the field conducting operations while the latter remains at the headquarters supervising and coordinating the activities of the staff, or, to put it succinctly, the commander is "Mr. Outside" and the chief of staff is "Mr. Inside." In the U.S. Army in World War II, however, such a neat compartmentalization was difficult to maintain at the field army–level headquarters because it was not authorized a deputy or assistant commander.[2] Consequently, while the chief of staff was not the designated successor to the commander should the latter be permanently removed, he often acted in the capacity of an assistant commander otherwise.

This dual responsibility was spelled out in FM 101-5, *Staff Officers Field Manual* of 1940. It defined the chief of staff as "the principal assistant and adviser to the commander" and, without explicitly dividing them as such, described two broad areas for which he was responsible. The first was supervising the staff in performing its functions. He was to establish policies for and coordinate the work of the General and Special Staff sections, direct the staff in preparing the detailed instructions to implement the commander's decisions, keep the commander continually abreast of the situation of both friendly and enemy forces and prepare for future contingencies, and assemble routine staff reports and, with the commander's approval, send copies to higher headquarters. The second area of responsibility was to assist the commander in the performance in his duties, by which he was to "[r]epresent the commander during his temporary absence or when authorized to do so" and "[b]y personal observation . . . [see] that the orders and instructions of the commander are executed."[3]

Patton certainly expected his chief of staff to be active in both roles. His deputy chief of staff throughout the war, then-colonel (later general) Paul Harkins, later recalled that "Patton wanted to get things done and when he wanted something done the staff were the do'ers,"[4] and in this context the chief of staff can be termed the "chief doer." A Third Army after-action report from May 1945 specifically stated that the duties of the chief of staff were not only to integrate the work of the staff sections but also to insure "the correct interpretation and execution by all subordinate units of orders received."[5] In practice this meant that Patton's chief of staff often found himself in the position of having to make decisions in Patton's name without being able to consult him beforehand. The fact that this could involve division or corps commanders who were senior in rank to him made the position particularly sensitive.

Two men fulfilled these functions for Patton in the course of World War II: Hobart R. Gay from July 1942 to March 1944 and again from December 1944 to the end of the war, and Hugh J. Gaffey from March to December 1944. They brought very different personal qualities and professional experience with them. Gay had spent seventeen years in the cavalry, four of them as an instructor in the advanced equitation course of the Cavalry School, and was widely known in the army as an excellent horseman. Described by one historian as a "splendid companion" who liked to ride and hunt, he had a jesting, jovial manner that earned him the nickname "Hap" for happy. During an interview many years later, he described himself as "just a country boy" and merely one of the team at Patton's headquarters. Some thought he lacked depth and intellectual capacity and that his horizons never went beyond troop movements; a few less-charitable individuals described him as "dumb loyal."[6]

Gay was also an experienced logistician, however, and it was in this context that he first met Patton. He had transferred to the Quartermaster Corps in 1934 and in July 1939 was assigned as post quartermaster at Fort Myer, Virginia, which was then commanded by Patton. In January 1941 he became Patton's chief quartermaster officer in the 2nd Armored Division and when Patton took command of the I Armored Corps in January 1942, Gay followed him again in the same capacity. That July Patton selected him as his chief of staff. Gay's administrative abilities and logistical experience undoubtedly played a major role in Patton's decision. According to Gay, Patton normally communicated directly with his intelligence and operations officers but gave his logistics officer only broad guidance and had Gay give specific orders. "It was the supply thing," he commented.[7]

Both were also avid horsemen and this was certainly important in cementing their relationship. Three days after Gay arrived at Fort Myer in 1939, Patton asked him to ride a difficult horse he had just bought. The horse promptly broke a leg on the first jump and Gay was naturally horrified until Patton put his arm around him and said, "Thank God I'll never have to ride that S.O.B."[8] They became so close that in May 1943, when recommending Gay for promotion to brigadier general, Eisenhower noted that both men had expressed a strong desire that Gay continue in his position for the duration of the war.[9]

This undoubtedly would have occurred had Eisenhower not intervened. In late February 1944 he told Patton that while he would not give him a direct order to replace Gay, he wanted him to do so. According to Patton, Eisenhower admitted that Gay was an "extra efficient chief of staff" but claimed that he lacked the "presence" to represent Patton at other headquarters or to take Patton's place should he be killed. In short, Gay had fallen victim to the fact that there was no assistant commander for the Third Army and he had to fill both roles. Patton disagreed with this reasoning but, still under a cloud because of the infamous slapping incidents in Sicily, felt he owed Eisenhower his position and should follow his wishes in this matter. On 6 March he called Gay into his office and told him that Eisenhower said he would have to go. Patton recorded that Gay took the news well, but Patton expressed his own view when he wrote, "It was most distasteful."[10] In any event, Gay did not go far. The deputy chief of staff, Paul Harkins, was made deputy for operations and Gay was appointed to the newly created position of deputy chief of staff (administration).

In sharp contrast to Gay, Hugh Gaffey was an experienced and highly regarded combat commander. He was commissioned in the field artillery in 1917, graduated from the Field Artillery School in 1923 and the Command and General Staff College in 1936 and considered one of the army's early armor experts.[11] He had served briefly as Patton's chief of staff at II Corps in North Africa and later successfully commanded the 2nd Armored Division in Sicily. He had a reputation as a tough tanker and much preferred command to staff work, but agreed to serve as Third Army chief of staff out of a sense of loyalty to Patton. Gaffey retained the position until December when he took command of the 4th Armored Division, at which time Gay replaced him without any apparent objections from Eisenhower.

The obvious differences between these two men raise the inevitable question as to whether or not they functioned differently as the Third Army chief of staff. An examination of the Third Army War Diary indicates that for the most part they did not; rather, the dual role of an army chief of staff and the different circumstances under which the Third Army operated were far more important in determining their role and actions.

The Third U.S. Army became officially active at noon on 1 August 1944 as the Allies were breaking out of the Normandy bridgehead.[12] Placed on the right of the Allied line, it moved rapidly south and west into the Brittany Peninsula and then swung east. By the evening of 19 August, its forward elements had crossed the Seine and by 10 September were pushing on the Mosel in eastern France. These spectacular advances placed enormous strains on all aspects of Allied operations, not the least of which were faced by senior staff officers.

Official activities at Third Army headquarters normally began with a 0900 hours daily staff conference with the entire command group and staff present.

They discussed the situation and objectives for the day as well as any problems that might arise and make the decisions necessary. After this, Patton, Gaffey, and the two deputy chiefs of staff settled on their tasks for the day. Normally, either Patton or Gaffey and one member of each staff section would spend the day at the front. A second staff conference with just those staff members involved in operations normally took place at about 2000 hours.

The most striking aspect of Gaffey's activities in this period is the extent to which he was away from Third Army headquarters. According to the war diary and Gaffey's personal daily log, he was out visiting units for thirteen of the thirty-one days in August and for nineteen of the thirty days in September. On some of these days, he left shortly after the morning conference and did not return until 1700 or 1800 hours. The diary also indicates that both he and Patton were away at the same time on some days. It is clear that at this time of highly mobile operations when conditions were extremely fluid, Patton used Gaffey primarily as another set of eyes and ears to help direct units of the Third Army and see that his orders were being followed.

The Third Army War Diary does not normally describe what Gaffey saw or did on these trips, but there are some exceptions. On 7 August, for example, two American airmen who had been shot down behind German lines returned and reported that the city of Angers on the Loire River was almost deserted of German troops. Patton ordered Gaffey to go to the XX Corps, in whose sector the city lay, and direct them to send forces from the 5th Infantry Division to take the city. At 1600 hours Gaffey telephoned back that the mission was under way and at 1745 called again to say that Angers would be taken by the end of the day. He returned to Third Army headquarters that evening.

A week later Gaffey received an even more unusual assignment for a chief of staff. The Allies were then trying to close the Falaise pocket and, on 16 August Bradley ordered Maj. Gen. Leonard Gerow to take command of the 80th (less one regiment) and 90th Infantry Divisions and the French 2nd Armored Division to close the pocket from the south. No one thought Gerow could arrive for at least two days, so Patton organized the divisions into a provisional corps of the Third Army and made Gaffey its commander. He also ordered Gaffey not to wait for Gerow but to plan and launch an attack as quickly as possible to prevent the Germans from escaping. Gerow arrived at the headquarters early on the morning of the seventeenth—much earlier than expected—and a German counterattack stalled the American plans. Gaffey's command was unexpectedly short and barren of results. The incident loses none of its significance, however, for it demonstrates that Gaffey was as much a deputy commander as he was a chief of staff.

The end of September marked the end of the period of rapid advances and the beginning of the slogging match for Lorraine. Gaffey's activities changed at this time as well. In October— excluding a few days for an official visit to England—he was only away from Third Army headquarters for nine days and five of them were for trips to 12th Army Group headquarters. For several days, Gaffey simply noted in the war diary "performed routine administration," a comment totally absent from entries of the heady days of the rapid advance through France.

On 3 December Patton appointed Gaffey to command the 4th Armored Division and Gay resumed his old position. By the middle of the month, the Third Army had closed in on the West Wall, and Patton was preparing for a major assault on this line scheduled to begin on 22 December. At this time, the Third Army consisted of two corps on line: Maj. Gen. Walton Walker's XX Corps on the left with the 10th Armored and 5th, 90th, and 95th Infantry Divisions; and Maj. Gen. Manton Eddy's XII Corps on the right with the 4th and 10th Armored and 35th, 80th, and 87th Infantry Divisions. In addition the as-yet-untried III Corps under Maj. Gen. John Milliken was in reserve with the 26th Infantry Division, which had just received a large number of replacements and was scheduled to undergo a thirty-day training period. The 4th Armored and 80th Infantry Divisions were in XII Corps Reserve to prepare to lead the attack on the West Wall.[13]

These plans, of course, were disrupted by the German Ardennes offensive, which began on 16 December. According to Harkins, Patton had recognized the possibility of a German offensive in this area as early as December 12, and directed his staff make a study of possible Third Army responses.[14] He did not learn of the attack until the evening of 16 December, however, and, admitting later that he did not recognize the seriousness of the situation, told Eddy the next day to have the 4th Armored Division committed to action as quickly as possible to prevent it from being diverted to the north.[15] He also had a conference with Eddy planning the attack on the West Wall. The only action taken that day in response to the new situation was to postpone the decision to move the army headquarters forward from Nancy to St. Avold where it would have been better situated for the attack on the West Wall.

Patton did not learn the full extent of the German threat until 1030 hours on 18 December. At that time, he attended a meeting at Bradley's headquarters, following which he called Gay and told him to hold the 4th Armored and 80th Infantry Divisions in place, inform the commanders of those units that they were going to the III Corps, and arrange for transportation for the latter division. Patton also told Gay that he was going to visit the XX Corps and would probably not return to Nancy until late.

Gay informed Eddy of this change of plans and later received a call from Col. Halley G. Maddox, Third Army G-3, who passed on an order from Patton that the III Corps staff report to Nancy that evening for a meeting. When Bradley called later that day, Gay reported that Third Army could have one combat command of the 4th Armored Division on the road that night and the rest of the division and the 80th Infantry Division on the road by the next morning. At the conference that evening, routes were drawn up for the movement of the two divisions.

Early on the morning of 19 December Patton met with the commanders and key staff officers of the III and XII Corps. They drew up alternative plans for a shift in the boundary between XII Corps and the Sixth Army to its south and an attack by that corps in the Luxembourg area once it had taken up its new positions. Patton and Harkins then left for a SHAEF conference with Eisenhower at Verdun. Here Patton shocked many of the assembled officers by declaring that he could attack the German southern flank in three days. Shortly thereafter, Patton called Gay to tell him of the results of the conference and say that Harkins would return to Nancy that evening with the details; he would visit the XX Corps and did not expect to return that night.

The story of the Third Army's shift of front from east to north and attack on the German left flank beginning on 22 December has often been told. Many consider it Patton's finest hour, but he himself admitted "the remarkable movement of the Third Army from the Saar to the Bulge was wholly due to the superior efficiency of the Third Army staff, particularly General Gay, General Muller, Colonel Nixon, and Colonel E. Busch, quartermaster of the Third Army."[16] He spoke no more than the truth.

The essence of the plan was that the XX Corps on Patton's left (minus one division) would remain in place facing east and now form his right; the XII Corps, which had been Patton's right, would be withdrawn from the line (its place taken by the Seventh Army, to which it would transfer some of its units) and move north behind the XX Corps to the vicinity of the city of Luxembourg; the III Corps, consisting of the three Third Army divisions not on line, would move north and take up positions to the left of XII Corps and form the initial striking force of the attack; and the VIII Corps, which had been part of the First Army and had been badly mauled in the initial German drive, was now transferred to the Third Army and would form its left. To coordinate the placement of units in their new positions and prepare the attack, Patton established a forward tactical echelon at Luxembourg with himself and a small part of the Third Army staff on 20 December, while Gay remained at the main headquarters in Nancy to direct the movement of the units to the north.

The complexities of Gay's mission were formidable. He had essentially three tasks to perform: first, to relieve those units on the line that were being redirected to attack the southern shoulder of the bulge; second, to insure the smoothest possible movement of those units to the new front over the road net; and third, to coordinate the transfer of divisions and supporting units from one higher headquarters to another as the entire Third Army line was readjusted. All of these tasks had to be done simultaneously and as quickly as possible over difficult terrain, under extremely poor weather conditions, and with the limited daylight available in northern Europe in December. And, of course, Gay had to know exactly where everyone was every minute of the day should Patton call and ask.

The Third Army War Diary reflects the hectic pace of events. On 20 December Gay and other members of Third Army staff met with Seventh Army staff members to coordinate the latter's takeover of the XII Corps sector and to work out a schedule for the relief of specific units and transfer of others to the Seventh Army. Gay had several further telephone conversations with Seventh Army during the day to follow this up. He also ordered one regimental combat team of the 5th Infantry Division to move to a position east of Luxembourg; transferred the 6th Armored Division from the XII to the XX Corps; transferred Task Force Pickett from the III to the XX Corps; directed headquarters XII Corps to move to Luxembourg the following day; and directed Manton Eddy to move the 602nd Tank Destroyer Battalion less one company to VIII Corps headquarters that night on a route to be provided by the Third Army G-3.

On 21 December Gay directed the tank destroyer battalion and the tank battalion attached to the 35th Infantry Division to move to Luxembourg no later than the following day, and he ordered the 35th Infantry Division out of the line to billets vacated by the 26th Infantry Division near Metz where it would receive much-needed replacements and prepare to join the XII Corps in the north as quickly as possible. Later, Patton called to order all units moving north to carry gas masks and Gay met with Third Army G-4, Col. Walter G. Muller, to issue the order and have the latter follow it up.

Finally, Gay received a call from the SHAEF chief of staff regarding reporters' complaints about the Third Army's public relations officer and agreed to have SHAEF's public relations officer investigate the situation and follow his recommendations.

Once the orders to move had been given, Gay had to monitor all movements and intervene to resolve any problems that arose. This he continued to do from 23 to 27 December, when he reported to Third Army headquarters at Luxembourg. For eight days he had operated from Nancy while Patton was in Luxembourg. The war diary reports occasional conversations but no meetings between them during this period. Points of confusion were bound to arise with so many units being transferred from one higher headquarters to another and Gay had to deal with them on his own. On 23 December, for example, Seventh Army called regarding a SHAEF order transferring the 87th Infantry Division to Third Army. Gay knew nothing about this and was only able to resolve the matter the next day when he learned that the order intended the division to go to SHAEF reserve, not the Third Army.

Another problem arose on 24 December when Harkins called to relay a message from Patton ordering one regimental combat team of the 35th Infantry Division to begin moving north immediately to join the III Corps. The division had only completed its assembly around Metz on the previous day and was still receiving replacements. Knowing this, Gay replied that he was sure that no element of the division was ready to move. He also objected to the placement of the division, saying that it should go to the XII Corps farther east so as to be able to strike the bulge closer to its base. Harkins relayed Gay's objections to Patton and called back later with an order that the division alert one regimental combat team for movement as of the following day. The division eventually moved on the twenty-sixth and went to the III Corps, but to replace another division that was shifted to the right. And as a final note, after daily conversations with the SHAEF representative, the Third Army public relations officer was relieved on 26 December, when a suitable replacement was found and a directive issued regarding relations with the press corps.

During the last four months of the war, Gay spent by far the greatest part of his time at Third Army headquarters. In March, for example, the war diary records only three visits to subordinate units as they were preparing to cross the Rhine, and none during the first two weeks of April as the army moved rapidly through Germany. He was, however, very involved in Third Army operations and had considerable leeway in making operational decisions on his own. On 9 March, for example, Eddy reported that his XII Corps had secured a bridge over the Moselle near Trier and Gay told him to exploit it fully. He then called Patton who approved the order. On 26 March, before leaving for a conference at SHAEF Headquarters, Patton told Gay to use his own judgment in approving a plan of attack over the Rhine by the XX Corps. In both instances these actions appear to be quite normal for the Third Army.

In conclusion, Patton used Gaffey and Gay not only as his chiefs of staff as that role is normally perceived, but also as assistant commanders capable of acting in his place and making the decisions he would have had he been there to make them. Despite their different backgrounds, both men performed these duties in an outstanding manner—and, in the end, that is all that really matters.

Notes

1. Martin Blumenson, *The Patton Papers*, vol. 1, *1885–1940* (Boston: Houghton Mifflin, 1972), 801–2. Capitalization in original.
2. U.S. War Department, *Table of Organization and Equipment*, No. 200-1 (Washington, D.C.: Superintendent of Documents, 26 October 1944), 2.
3. U.S. War Department, *FM 101-5: Staff Officers Field Manual; The Staff and Combat Officers* (Washington, D.C.: Superintendent of Documents, 1940) 7–8.
4. Paul D. Harkins, oral interview by Maj. Jacob B. Couch Jr. in Dallas, Texas, April 28, 1974, Senior Officers Debriefing Program, Paul D. Harkins Papers, Archives, U.S. Army Military History Institute, Carlisle Barracks, Pa.
5. Third U.S. Army "G-3 Operational Report" dated 18 May 1945, Halley G. Maddox Papers, Archives U.S. Army Military History Institute, Carlisle Barracks, Pa.
6. Martin Blumenson, *The Patton Papers*, vol. 2, *1940–1945* (Boston: Houghton Mifflin, 1984), 757; Gay interview, 17 (A brief biography of Gay can be found in Hobart R. Gay, oral interview by Col. Willard L. Wallace, 4–5 October and 15–16 November 1980, Senior Officer Oral History Program, Project 81 G, Appendix A, Archives, U.S. Army Military History Institute, Carlisle Barracks, Pa.); Blumenson, *Patton Papers*, 2:757.
7. Gay interview, 17.
8. Ibid., 9.
9. Eisenhower to George C. Marshall, 8 May 1943 in Alfred D. Chandler, ed., *The Papers of Dwight David Eisenhower: The War Years* (Baltimore: Johns Hopkins University Press, 1970), 2:1118.
10. Blumenson, *Patton Papers*, 2:419–21.
11. Obituary, *New York Times*, 18 June 1946, 11. On Gaffey as an early pioneer in the U.S. Army's tank development see Albert N. Garland and Howard M. Smyth with Martin Blumenson, *Sicily and the Surrender of Italy* in *U.S. Army in World War II: The Mediterranean Theater of Operations*, Stetson Conn, gen. ed. (Washington, D.C.: Office of the Chief of Military History, 1965), 95–96.

12. Unless otherwise noted, all further references are to the Third U.S. Army War Diary, 1 August 1944–8 May 1945, Hobart Gay papers.

13. Headquarters Twelfth Army Group, "Order of Battle as of 15 December 1944," Chester B. Hansen Papers, Box 28, Archives, U.S. Army Military History Institute, Carlisle Barracks, Pa.

14. George S. Patton, *War As I Knew It* (Boston: Houghton Mifflin, 1995), 128 n. 13.

15. Ibid., 130.

16. Ibid., 135.

CHRONOLOGY OF ALEKSEY INNOKENTEVICH ANTONOV

15 Sep 1896	Born in Grodno, son of Tsarist Russian artillery officer.
1915	Student at Petrograd University and a factory worker.
1916	Attended Pavlovsk Military College.
Dec 1916	Appointed Praporshchik (ensign), Life Guards Jager Regiment.
1917	Combat service with South West Front. Wounded and decorated for bravery in June. Evacuated to Petrograd. Elected assistant adjutant of the Life Guards Jager Reserve Regiment. Fought in defense of Petrograd against the Kornilov Coup in August.
1918	Demobilized and enrolled in the Petrograd Forestry Institute. Recalled to the colors as deputy chief of staff of the 3rd Brigade of the 1st Moscow Workers' Division.
1919–21	Served in Russian Civil War as brigade staff officer with 1st Moscow Workers Division and the 15th Inzensk Rifle Division.
1922–28	Served as head of Operations Section, 15th Inzensk Rifle Division, in the Ukraine.
1928–31	Student at Frunze Military Academy.
1931–34	Served as chief of staff, 46th Rifle Division, in the Ukraine.
1932–33	Student at the operations faculty of the Frunze Military Academy.
Oct 1934	Appointed chief of staff of the Mogilev-Yampolsk Fortified Region.
Aug 1935	Appointed head of the Operations Department, Kharkov Military District.
Sep 1935	Commended for work in the organization of the Kiev Maneuvers.
Nov 1936	Student at the General Staff Academy.
1936	Appointed chief of staff, Moscow Military District.
Dec 1938	Appointed senior lecturer, General Tactics Department, Frunze Military Academy.
4 Jun 1940	Promoted to major general.

Jan 1941	Appointed deputy head, General Tactics Department, Frunze Military Academy.
Mar 1941	Appointed deputy chief of staff, Kiev Special Military District.
30 Aug 1941	Appointed chief of staff, Southern Front.
27 Dec 1941	Promoted to lieutenant general.
28 Jul 1942	Appointed chief of staff, North Caucasus Front.
4 Sep 1942	Appointed chief of staff, Black Sea Group of Forces.
20 Nov 1942	Appointed chief of staff, Transcaucasus Front.
11 Dec 1942	Appointed first deputy chief of General Staff and head of the Operations Directorate.
4 Apr 1943	Promoted to colonel general.
20 May 1943	Appointed first deputy chief of General Staff.
27 Aug 1943	Promoted to army general.
18 Feb 1945	Appointed chief of the General Staff.
25 Mar 1946	Appointed first deputy chief of the General Staff.
Nov 1948	Appointed first deputy commander in chief, Transcaucasus Military District.
1950	Appointed commander in chief, Transcaucasus Military District.
Apr 1954	Appointed 1st Deputy Chief of the General Staff.
May 1955	Appointed chief of staff of Warsaw Pact Armed Forces and first deputy chief of General Staff of the Soviet Union.
18 June 1962	Died in Moscow; buried at the Kremlin Wall.

Aleksey Innokentevich Antonov

Michael Orr

In the eyes of his contemporaries, Aleksey Antonov was "a born staff officer."[1] Both his father and grandfather were officers in the Imperial Russian Army and he grew up in garrison towns. He went on exercises with his father while still a boy but his father's death in 1908, when Antonov was twelve, must have disrupted his plans for a military career. When World War I broke out in 1914 the Antonovs had to move to Petrograd and the impoverished Aleksey combined studies at university with factory work. His military service began as a praporshchik (ensign) in the Life Guards Jager Regiment and he was wounded in the summer battles of 1917. Convalescence at home in Petrograd put him close to the center of events between the February Revolution, which led to the tsar's abdication and the October Revolution, which brought Lenin and the Bolsheviks to power. When Antonov returned to the reserve unit of his regiment he was elected assistant adjutant, not an unusual event as the Russian army dissolved in chaos.[2]

This was the ideal background for someone who was to rise to high rank in the Red Army during World War II. Antonov's family circumstances prepared him for a military career but he was not disposed to serve with the counterrevolutionary White Russians. His mother's father had actually been deported to Siberia for his opposition to the Tsarist regime. Men like Antonov were the foundation of the new Red Army, gaining practical experience during the Russian Civil War, studying the theoretical side in the first courses at the new staff colleges. (Antonov was a star pupil in the Frunze Military Academy's first course on operations and the first course at the General Staff Academy, both of which were created to provide staffs for higher formations

143

and the General Staff.) Luck was on Antonov's side because he was not senior enough to be one of the formation commanders who suffered so heavily during Josef Stalin's purges in 1937–38. Instead, Antonov was one of those promoted to fill their places. In 1937 Antonov was one of the thirty or so General Staff Academy students who graduated early on appointment to key posts. (Others included Aleksandr Vasilevskiy, Ivan Bagramyan, Nikolai Vatutin, Andrei Grechko, Matvei Zakharov, and Leonid Govorov, who all played distinguished roles during the war.)

Antonov was one of the organizers of the Kiev Maneuvers of 1935, from which were developed the armored formations that spearheaded the Red Army's victorious offensives from 1943 to 1945. As a senior member of the Tactics Department at the Frunze Military Academy from 1938 to 1941, he was one of the authors of the tactical manuals with which the Red Army began the war.[3] He left the Frunze in March 1941 to become deputy chief of staff to the Kiev Special Military District, which was expected to face the main attack in any future German offensive. Luckily perhaps for Antonov, the main German blows came farther north, on the Moscow and Leningrad axes. During the catastrophic first months of the war Antonov maintained his reputation for unshaken competence, which was strengthened when the Russians began to launch their first, limited counterattacks.

In November 1941, as chief of staff of the Southern Front (army group), Antonov planned the counterstroke, which forced Paul Ewald von Kleist to abandon Rostov and withdraw behind the Mius River. In January 1942 the Southern Front played a successful role in the limited Barvenko-Lozovaya operation. In both these operations Antonov meticulously supervised the regrouping of limited assets to create a strike grouping, disguised by strict camouflage and deception measures. As a result, the Germans were surprised by both attacks and in the Barvenko-Lozovaya operation Antonov produced an artillery plan that exploited German expectations of standard Soviet tactics to cause heavy casualties just before the offensive actually began.[4]

As the Wehrmacht began its summer offensive into southern Russia, the Southern Front was forced back into the Caucasus. The front headquarters was dissolved and between July and December 1942 Antonov acted as chief of staff in three different headquarters. As chief of staff of the Black Sea Group he played a vital role in the Tuapse defensive operation. He worked tirelessly, catching a couple of hours sleep a day, wrapped in his greatcoat, next to the telephone. When the group headquarters was criticized by Moscow for reducing the forces defending the Tuapse sector in order to create a counterattack force, Antonov was ready to accept responsibility. By the skillful regrouping of forces, he ensured that the defenses held firm. Despite the pressure under which he was working, Antonov found time to organize the production of a manual describing the lessons learned during the Black Sea Group's operations.[5]

As chief of staff Antonov telephoned a situation report to Moscow every day, usually speaking directly to the chief of the General Staff, Gen. Aleksandr Vasilevskiy, a classmate at the General Staff Academy in 1936. On 10 December Vasilevskiy proposed that Antonov should become his deputy and head of the Operations Directorate of the General Staff. Next day Antonov was told that Stalin had approved the appointment. However, this did not mean that Stalin had confidence in him, as Antonov soon found when he arrived in Moscow. Stalin suggested that Antonov might be more useful coordinating operations at the front, and he spent most of the first three months of 1943 as Stavka representative to the Bryansk, Voronezh, and Central Fronts. Having passed this examination, Antonov returned to Moscow and was trusted with the daily briefings and given more and more responsibility.[6]

The war on the eastern front was approaching its turning point. The balance of success was tilting toward the Soviets, as at Stalingrad, but the failure of Georgi Zhukov's Operation Mars offensive in November 1942 and Erich von Manstein's successes in the spring of 1943 demonstrated that the Germans were far from defeated. The Red Army was beginning to deploy vast forces, but these resources had to be organized more effectively. Antonov played a vital role in that process. To understand that role we need to examine the peculiarities of the Soviet command structure.

Stalin was not merely head of the Soviet government, but also supreme commander in chief, the head of the military chain of command. He was advised and assisted by the *Stavka*, a word that is hard to translate into English. "Headquarters" is found in dictionaries, but Stavka lacked most of the attributes of a headquarters, especially its staff. Its closest equivalent in the West was the small group of military and political advisers whom Churchill kept from their beds on most nights while he discussed the conduct of the war. Stavka was also a mix of senior military and political figures, but it directed day-to-day military operations in a way that Churchill was never allowed to do. Stavka directives were the basis of all plans and Stavka representatives coordinated operations in the field and monitored their progress. Like the State Defense Committee (GKO), to which it was subordinated, Stavka's real power came from Stalin's presence. It suited Stalin to issue his orders in Stavka's name, but their force derived from his brutal reputation.

The General Staff was at Stavka's beck and call and thanks to Stalin's working methods, its personnel were often distracted from their real work. When Antonov arrived at the General Staff he found staff officers spent much of their time hanging about in what they called the "dressing room," the chief of the General Staff's waiting room, in case they were needed to answer questions telephoned from Stavka, that is, from Stalin himself. There were many talented officers in the Operations Directorate, such as Antonov's future deputy, Sergei Shtemenko, but they were overstressed by their irregular working hours and uncoordinated work schedules. Antonov's first major contribution was to bring order to the General Staff's daily routine and its relationship with the supreme commander in chief, Stalin. His masterstroke was to produce a work schedule for the General Staff that laid down not only the times of the regular briefings to Stavka during the day and who was to give each briefing, but also specified rest hours for the staff. Thus Antonov himself was to sleep from 5 or 6 AM to noon and Shtemenko from 2 PM to 6 or 7 PM. Antonov took this three-page memorandum to Stalin for his approval and then it became the unshakeable routine by which the Soviet war effort was managed, tying down Stalin himself as well as the staff.[7]

As head of the Operations Directorate Antonov was responsible for the day-to-day coordination of Soviet operations. The strategic direction of the Soviet war effort was very different from that of the Western Allies or Nazi Germany. The Allies in particular were fighting a war in several theaters and were fighting a triservice war. Moscow was fighting along a continuous front stretching from the Arctic to the Black Sea, but did not declare war on Japan until after the German surrender. The Red Navy was a coastal force, operating to secure the army's flanks and the air force was not a strategic striking force. From 1944 there were other national forces incorporated in the Soviet order of battle, but they were firmly subordinated to the Soviet chain of command, not autonomous allies as in the West.

Stavka and the General Staff were effectively fighting a one-theater war and controlled operations directly. No Soviet commander had the independence of Dwight Eisenhower, Harold Alexander, Douglas MacArthur, or Chester Nimitz in planning or directing operations. Although the day-to-day battles on the eastern front were waged by front commanders, they were linked to Moscow by secure telephone and teletype communications so that they could discuss the progress of operations several times a day. The great strategic operations were planned in considerable detail in Moscow and executed by the front headquarters under the supervision of Stavka representatives. In Germany strategic command was bedeviled by competition between Hitler's OKW and the service headquarters, such as OKH. Stavka and the General Staff were not rivals; rather, the General Staff was Stavka's means of command.

Antonov became the key link between Stalin and the General Staff, and to understand his role it is necessary to appreciate how the General Staff worked. The Operations Directorate was subdivided into a number of "directions" consisting of a chief and five to ten staff officers.[8] There was a direction for each Front and its officers were responsible for keeping up to date with the situation in that sector. The directions in turn reported to the head of the Operations Directorate so that his maps were updated before the three daily briefings to Stavka.

Antonov had no time for wordy reports; once the Operations Directorate machinery was running smoothly, the heads of directions usually just compared their maps with his and briefly discussed any variations. (Antonov was responsible for standardizing map-marking procedures so that any officer could immediately read another's map.) Antonov was also in regular contact by telephone with the chiefs of staff of the various fronts, so he could check that the information he was receiving tallied with the directions' data. Lesser men would have been swamped by this mass of reports, but Antonov worked calmly and even pedantically, absorbing and analyzing the data. He was never known to lose his temper, a remarkable trait in an army known for its short-fused generals. His orders were given equally quietly and as requests not commands. Although he was soft-spoken, he was not softhearted. Antonov would not accept the slightest error, nor would he tolerate careless presentation.[9]

The Operations Directorate maps were the basic briefing documents when Antonov or Shtemenko reported to Stalin. A 1:200,000-scale map was maintained for each Front and a 1:1,000,000 summary map showing the whole eastern front, with regularly updated duplicates in Stalin's study. Stalin would ring the Operations Directorate every morning between 10 and 11 AM and Shtemenko would brief him on events overnight, standing in front of the map boards. At about 4 PM. Antonov would telephone a situation report, but the main business of the day was his personal report to Stalin. Most of the evening would be spent preparing the maps and documents until the summons came, usually after 11 PM. General Shtemenko described the daily routine in his memoirs:

After the telephone summons we would get into a car and drive through deserted Moscow to the Kremlin or the "Near House"—Stalin's dacha at Kuntsevo. . . . A long rectangular table stood in the left hand part of the room. . . . On this we would spread out the maps, from which we would then report on each front separately, beginning with the sector where the main events were happening at the moment. We used no notes. We knew the situation by heart and it was also shown on the map.

Other members of the Politburo and Stavka usually attended the briefings but they were aimed at Stalin, who would stalk around the room as he listened, usually smoking a pipe filled with tobacco from Hercegovina Flor cigarettes. Afterwards Antonov and Shtemenko would produce their red folder of draft directives and other high-priority documents. Stalin would approve them or dictate amendments. From 1943 such directives were most often dispatched under the signatures of Stalin and Antonov and often Antonov alone. If time permitted Antonov would produce his blue folder of requests from fronts and other routine matters. When Stalin was in a good mood, Antonov might ask Shtemenko for the green folder, which contained recommendations for decorations and promotions and other matters that were not urgent. Finally, they would be released at 3 or 4 AM, returning to their offices to put into action the decisions taken at the conference.[10]

The chief of the General Staff, General Vasilevskiy, was used by Stalin as a Stavka representative at the front. He was away from Moscow for at least twenty-two of the thirty-four months that he held the post of chief of the General Staff.[11] When he was away Antonov took over and it became clear that the double workload was too much. Shtemenko was therefore appointed head of the Operations Directorate on 19 May 1943, and Antonov became first deputy chief of the General Staff and thus effective chief for much of the war. The separation of roles released Antonov from some of the day-to-day routine and made it possible for him to give more of his attention to planning future operations.

It is this side of his work which is most neglected, especially in western sources. If Antonov had only been the "office manager" of Stavka and the General Staff, his contribution, though important, would not have deserved inclusion in this book. But his greatest achievement was that, despite the burden of supervising current operations, he found time to prepare for the future, particularly as the initiative on the eastern front passed from the Germans to the Red Army. This first became apparent in the preparations for the defensive battle at Kursk in the summer of 1943.

When the Russian spring imposed its usual halt on operations the Soviet High Command was forced to consider how it should meet the expected German summer offensive against the Kursk salient. General Vatutin of the Voronezh Front was urging a preemptive attack. Stalin was inclined to support the idea, distrusting the Red Army's ability to fight a defensive battle against the Wehrmacht after the disasters of the previous two summers. Zhukov was summoned back to Moscow to discuss the summer campaign on 11 April and told that he, Vasilevskiy, and Antonov were to prepare a map and proposals for a conference with Stalin the following evening. The three generals agreed on the need for the Red Army to stand on the defensive in the strongest possible position and defeat the German armor before beginning an offensive.

> [S]ince there was full agreement between us, everything was ready by the evening. Besides all his other merits, Antonov had a brilliant skill for presenting material and while Vasilevskiy and I drafted the report for Stalin, he quickly drew up a situation map and a map showing the planned operations by the fronts in the Kursk bulge.[12]

At the conference Stalin accepted the generals' concept of operations and Vasilevskiy and Antonov were ordered to begin detailed planning. Antonov was naturally fully involved in the conduct of the defensive battle and the offensives that followed. In August he noticed opportunities to break into the German rear at Kharkov, which had been missed by the commanders at the front, and he twice flew down to meet Zhukov and the front commanders to coordinate future operations. Antonov's working notebook shows that during the autumn he was studying options for the winter campaign, which he was able to present to Vasilevskiy and Zhukov when they returned to Moscow.[13]

The Byelorussian offensive of June 1944 (Operation Bagration) shows Antonov's staff work at its best. At the end of the winter campaign the Red Army was making its greatest advances in the Ukraine. During the spring thaw the Soviet High Command had to decide whether to continue to make their main effort in the south when operations resumed in the summer. The alternatives were to concentrate on the Baltic coast or in Byelorussia. Antonov quickly ruled out the Baltic option and decided that an offensive in the Ukraine would involve an unacceptable risk from German Army Group Center in Byelorussia. However, the latter force was exposed to converging attacks by Soviet forces attacking into the "Byelorussian balcony." Once Stalin had accepted that the main Soviet effort should be made in Byelorussia,

Antonov began the meticulous calculations and map studies that produced outline plans that could be discussed with front commanders when they were brought back to Moscow. He said himself that he "loved to think things through over a map" and in this way he planned the redeployments that would be necessary to create strong enough strike groupings or ensure that enemy forces on the flanks could be pinned down. In preparing the final draft directive Antonov spent a week personally rechecking all the operational calculations on which the plan was based.

A central part of Antonov's concept was the *maskirovka* camouflage and deception plan. He had shown his skill in deception in the early days of the war, but the Operation Bagration plan was probably his masterpiece. The aim was to convince the Germans that the Red Army would make its main effort in the Ukraine and along the Baltic coast. False troop concentrations were organized on both sectors. All six Soviet tank armies remained in the south until the eve of the offensive and over two-thirds of German armored formations remained in the Ukraine to meet them. At the last moment, four tank armies moved north, under strict concealment. Regrouping was only carried out at night and assembly areas were well camouflaged. The communications blackout was total; radios were even sealed to prevent their use and written documents strictly limited.[14]

The plan was typical of Antonov's operational thinking in that the main aim was to destroy a major enemy grouping, not merely to occupy territory. In June Army Group Center was effectively destroyed by the encircling Soviet Fronts, which drove on into Poland. Sequenced operations in the Ukraine, the Baltic states, and Norway kept up the pressure on the Germans. By the late summer maps of the Berlin area lay on Antonov's desk and his notebook was being filled with calculations about the resources required for the capture of the German capital. As always, Antonov had the knack of not allowing himself to be so involved in the current battle that he lost sight of the next steps in the war. He also found time to expand the General Staff section that studied war experience and to ensure that its studies were widely circulated. In February 1945 Vasilevskiy took over command of the 3rd Byelorussian Front after General Chernyakovsky was killed. Antonov became chief of the General Staff and a member of Stavka, a formal recognition of his importance in the Soviet command structure.[15]

However, like the better-known field commanders such as Zhukov, Antonov suffered from Stalin's jealousy after of the war. (He had also earned Beria's enmity.) He was never promoted to the rank of marshal of the Soviet

Union, though he was awarded the Order of Victory, the only recipient who was not a marshal. Vasilevskiy returned as chief of the General Staff and then in 1948 Antonov was shunted off to the Transcaucasus Military District, at first as deputy commander and from 1950 as commander. After Stalin's death, Antonov was recalled to Moscow and given his old job as first deputy chief of the General Staff. When the Warsaw Pact was founded in May 1955, he was also given the post of chief of staff to its armed forces. After the revolts in Poland and Hungary in 1956, Antonov played a crucial part in building the Warsaw Pact into a functioning military alliance, with a common doctrine and training. His personal charm disguised the reality of Soviet domination. Although his health was not perfect after the war he worked to the last, dying in his office on the morning of 18 June 1962.[16]

The concept of operational art was basically developed within the Soviet General Staff during the interwar period. Aleksey Antonov was one of the first students to be trained in operational art and became one of its most competent practitioners. For over two years he was effectively Stalin's chief of staff and played a crucial role in planning and executing the strategic operations, which determined the outcome of the land war in Europe. With his encyclopedic memory, organizing abilities, skill in presenting information, and calmness in a crisis, he was a model of the qualities required by a staff officer at any level. It is often the fate of a chief of staff to be forgotten while more flamboyant commanders remain in the limelight but in a work devoted to chiefs of staff we must recognize Antonov's place among the elite of his profession.

Notes

1. Aleksey Khorev, *Knight of the Order of Victory* (Moscow: Red Star, 20 March 1993), 5.
2. I. I. Gaglov, *Army General A. I. Antonov* (Moscow: Sovetskii Pisatel, 1987), 4–11 (the only biography of Antonov and the source of most biographical details in this chapter).
3. *The Military Academy Named After M. V. Frunze* (Moscow: Voyenizdat, 1980) 114.
4. David Glantz, *Soviet Military Deception in the Second World War* (London: Routledge, 1989), 43–46, 75–77.
5. Gaglov, *Army General A. I. Antonov*, 68–73.
6. Ibid., 77–82; A. M. Vasilevskiy, *A Life-Long Occupation* (Moscow: Politizdat, 1974), 282; S. M. Shtemenko, *The Soviet General Staff at War 1941–1945, Book 1* (Moscow: Progress Publishers, 1985), 191.
7. Shtemenko, *Soviet General Staff at War*, 180–93; John Erickson, *The Road to Berlin*, vol. 2 of *Stalin's War with Germany* (London: Weidenfeld and Nicolson, 1983), 42.

8. N. Lomov and V. Golubovich, *On the Organization and Methods of Work of the General Staff* (Moscow: Military Historical Journal, February 1981), 15. The Russian terms are *Operativnoye Upravleniye* (Operational Directorate) and *Napravleniye* (Direction).

9. Gaglov, *Army General A. I. Antonov*, 86–87; Shtemenko, *Soviet General Staff at War*, 191–93.

10. Shtemenko, *Soviet General Staff at War*, 182–86.

11. Anatoliy Kvashnin and Makhmut Gareyev, *Thought Fights First* (Moscow: Red Star, 4 May 2000), 2.

12. G. K. Zhukov, *Reminiscences and Reflections* (London: Novosty, 1974), 147.

13. Gaglov, *Army General A. I. Antonov*, 92–105.

14. For Antonov's work for the Belorussian operations see Gaglov, *Army General A. I. Antonov*, 113–24; Shtemenko, 307–8, 334; Zhukov, *Reminiscences and Reflections*, 239–42; Erickson, *Road to Berlin*, 198–99; David Glantz and Jonathan House, *When Titans Clashed* (Lawrence: University Press of Kansas, 1995), 195–99.

15. Gaglov, *Army General A. I. Antonov*, 106, 131–32, 136–37.

16. Ibid., 147–59; Dmitri Volkogonov, *Stalin, Triumph and Tragedy* (London: Weidenfeld and Nicolson, 1991), 472; Richard Woff, "Antonov," in *Stalin's Generals*, ed. Harold Shukman (London: Weidenfeld and Nicolson, 1993), 19; Malcolm Mackintosh, *The Evolution of the Warsaw Pact* (London: Institute for Strategic Studies, 1969).

CHRONOLOGY OF VASILY DANILOVICH SOKOLOVSKY

21 July1897	Born in the village of Kozliki near Grodno in western Belarussia.
1918	Volunteered for the Red Army.
1918–21	Served in the Russian Civil War as a company, battalion, regimental, and brigade commander.
1921	Attended the Red Army General Staff Academy in Moscow.
1922	Involved in the suppression of the Basmachi rebel movement in Soviet Central Asia.
1922–29	Served as a divisional chief of staff and commander of Soviet forces in Turkestan, Soviet Central Asia.
1937–38	Survived Stalin's Great Purge of 1936–38, in which 30,000 Red Army officers were executed or tortured and imprisoned.
Fall 1939	Appointed chief of staff of the Moscow Military District.
Jan 1941	Appointed deputy chief of the Soviet General Staff.
Oct 1941	Appointed chief of staff, Western Front.
Feb 1943	Appointed commander of the Western Front.
Apr 1943	Promoted to full army general.
Jul 1943	Commanded the Western Front in Operation Kutozov.
Aug–Oct 1943	Commanded Operation Suvorov and liberated Smolensk.
Apr 1944	Removed from command of the Western Front.
May 1944	Appointed chief of staff to Marshal Konev's 1st Ukrainian Front.
Apr–May 1945	Served as deputy commander of Zhukov's 1st Belarussian Front during the Battle of Berlin; awarded the Order of the British Empire, conferred on him by Field Marshal Sir Bernard L. Montgomery.
1945–49	Served as deputy commander in chief, then commander in chief of Soviet forces, Germany.
10 Apr 1946	Appointed military governor of the Soviet Zone of Occupation in Germany.
Jul 1946	Promoted to marshal of the Soviet Union.
1948–49	Directed the unsuccessful Soviet blockade of Berlin.
30 Mar 1949	Appointed first deputy minister of defense.

1952–60	Served as chief of the Soviet General Staff.
1960	Appointed inspector general, Ministry of Defense.
1962	Editor of *Military Strategy*, an official and authoritative work on the principles of Soviet military strategy.
10 May 1968	Died at the age of seventy-one.

Vasily Danilovich Sokolovsky

Stephen Walsh

Marshal Vasily Danilovich Sokolovsky was one of the greatest staff officers in the Red Army's history. He served as chief of staff of the Western Front from October 1941 to February 1943 and was chief of staff of the 1st Ukrainian Front between May 1944 and April 1945. He ended the war as deputy commander of the 1st Belarussian Front. As commander of Soviet forces in Germany from 1946 to 1950, he was instrumental in establishing Soviet authority in Eastern Germany. Sokolovsky's career reached its zenith in 1952 with his appointment as chief of the General Staff, a position he held until his retirement in 1960. He died on 10 May 1968.

Sokolovsky was not just a staff officer. In 1943 and 1944 he commanded the Western Front. However, in comparison with his achievements as a staff officer Sokolovsky was a mediocre field general. This essay will analyze Sokolovsky's wartime career, which was synonymous with the crisis, recovery, and eventual triumph of the Red Army. It will conclude that Sokolovsky was an outstanding chief of staff, but as a field commander he lacked the instinctive flair of Marshal Konstantin K. Rokossovsky or Marshal Georgy K. Zhukov.

Born in 1897 in the village of Kozliki near Grodno in western Russia, Sokolovsky joined the Red Army in 1918, seeing extensive action in the Civil War of 1918–21, rising to the rank of brigade commander. After graduating from the Red Army General Staff Academy in 1921, Sokolovsky spent the 1920s enforcing Bolshevik rule in Soviet Central Asia. He survived the purges of 1936–38 and in January 1941, following Zhukov's appointment as chief of the General Staff, Sokolovsky became his deputy.

Marshal Vasily Danilovich Sokolovsky with Gen. of the Army Dwight D. Eisenhower.

On 2 October 1941 the Germans launched Operation Typhoon, their assault on Moscow. In ten days at Vyazma and Bryansk the Germans engulfed the Soviet Western, Bryansk, and Reserve Fronts, leaving Moscow with no organized defense; a shaken panic infected the streets. However, heavy rainfall slowed the German advance and provided the respite needed to reconstitute Soviet defenses. On 10 October Lt. Gen. Ivan S. Konev was sacked as commander of the Western Front and replaced by Zhukov with Sokolovsky as his chief of staff.[1]

Sokolovsky's task was to reorganize the Western Front. He used a fallback position, the Mozhaisk Line, as a rallying point. By 15 October, through scraping up remnants of broken formations and integrating reserves, new armies had been established. In a classical display of the role of the chief of staff, Sokolovsky managed to impose order on the chaotic aftermath of a crushing operational defeat. This achievement is borne out by the failure of the German spearheads to break the line. The importance of this improvised reorganization of Soviet defenses can hardly be overestimated. It gave Zhukov some control and time to consider his options, and it enabled the movement of reserves and equipment.

However, improvisation would not halt a full-scale German attack on Moscow. It was essential to put flesh on the bones of the Mozhaisk Line if the Soviet Union was not to become another German carcass. At Vyazma the Soviets proved unable to combine linear defense with depth. At Moscow, Zhukov's strategy sought to utilize depth to defend key points while holding a coherent line. It was Sokolovsky's job to implement these ideas at the operational and tactical levels. He was aided by the terrain, as forests, marshland, and numerous rivers canalized the German assaults along predictable axes, preventing them from conducting fluid armored operations and making anything more than fleeting tactical surprise difficult to achieve. It was also easier to acquire intelligence. By 13 November 1941 Sokolovsky claimed that only two German divisions remained undetected. Sokolovsky's prediction that the main German attack would fall on the Soviet right wing ensured that Rokossovsky's Sixteenth Army was suitably reinforced. It was 80,000 strong in positions twenty kilometers deep.[2] These timely deployments forced the Germans into frontal assaults, enabling the Red Army to fight on approximately equal terms for the first time in the war by combining depth and attrition.

In strategic terms the Soviet Union's manpower resources enabled it to survive 1941. In October 1941, however, the Red Army was a wasting asset with Sokolovsky's staff reduced to combing the hospitals. As historian John Erickson pointed out, "practically everything depended on the proper concentration of what was available going to the right place at exactly the right time."[3] The organization and control that Sokolovsky maintained under extreme pressure were the foundation of Soviet survival, as he juggled the Western Front's assets to translate Zhukov's ideas into reality. The infrastructural assets of Moscow help to explain this achievement, but do not reduce it.

By November 1941 Soviet eastern reserves were being moved to the Moscow region as intelligence indicated that Japanese eyes were on the Pacific. Sokolovsky integrated tough Siberians into the frontline, but husbanded experienced formations to train inexperienced troops. He constantly refashioned and redeployed shattered units into existing divisions in the line. This ability to regenerate divisions was influenced by Moscow's pivotal position in the Russian railway system. Field Marshal Fedor von Bock, commanding German Army Group Center, believed that "this gives the Russians time to fill up their beaten divisions and reinforce their defenses, especially since they are in control of most of the railways and roads around Moscow."[4] This was a major advantage in terms of tactical and operational mobility. As Sokolovsky orchestrated Soviet troop movement with flexibility and economy of effort, the Germans thrashed around, unable to overcome difficult terrain and unpaved roads breaking up in shocking weather. If command is to be effective, appropriate communications must exist to facilitate control, the actual expression of command. Moscow's proximity permitted Sokolovsky a knowledge of events and control of resources that enabled Zhukov to fight the Battle of Moscow.

Soviet logistics were underpinned by Moscow. Sokolovsky could rely on effective rear services, while the Germans' failure to provide for the speedy conversion of the Russian railway gauge to offset their crippling dependency on the roads came to haunt them. This contrast, the result of German overconfidence, was decisive in the struggle for Moscow. Western Front's staff proved superior to their German counterparts. Soviet soldiers were more accustomed to freezing temperatures but "if the Red Army soldier was not fed, he died, and if he was not clothed he succumbed to frostbite. His rifle and cannon needed ammunition and his horse had to have fodder."[5] Moscow was beneficial, but superior resources, the product of greater foresight, had to be used intelligently. Sokolovsky, whatever his "advantages," planned and fought the battle of Moscow more efficiently than the Germans.

In late November 1941 the Germans reached what Clausewitz termed the culminating point of the offensive. In a fearsome encounter at Istra, the SS *Das Reich* Division described its clash with the Siberians of Rokossovsky's

Sixteenth Army as "the heaviest of the Eastern campaign and with the highest number of casualties."[6] At Tula to the southwest of Moscow, the Germans also proved unable to break the Soviets. On 1 December 1941 the Germans began their final assault in nightmarish conditions of minus 35 degrees Celsius, but were halted on 4 December. The following day the Soviets attacked.

On 29 November 1941 Sokolovsky and his staff, demonstrating extraordinary mental and physical resilience in defense, simultaneously planned a counteroffensive. The aim was simply to force the Germans away from Moscow, as Sokolovsky advised that the shattered state of the troops ensured that anything more ambitious would be unwise. It was Stalin, on 20 December 1941, who ordered the encirclement and annihilation of Army Group Center. Sokolovsky's husbandry of the Western Front's reserves and resources enabled an overnight transition from defense to attack. Zhukov's timing was exemplary against the demoralized Germans, who knew the attack on Moscow had failed but who had no defensive positions. Sokolovsky relied on *maskirovka*, a systematic process of camouflage, disinformation, and deception to achieve surprise, which proved total. However, this was due more to German preoccupation with their own plight and underestimation of Soviet resilience than to Sokolovsky's brilliance.

The Moscow counteroffensive succeeded despite many Soviet commanders' lack of experience or incompetence in offensive warfare. It was a shocking blow to German morale, which teetered on the edge of collapse. On 10 December 1941 the commander of the German Second Army, Gen. Rudolf Schmidt, ordered "individuals who make defeatist remarks to be singled out and shot as an example."[7] As the Germans retreated, Stalin's overconfidence led him on 5 January 1942, against the recommendations of the Western Front, to order a general offensive. There had been little sustained preparation for such an operation, and the Germans fought with a tenacity and skill born of desperation, as catastrophe seemed imminent. As Sokolovsky had warned, the Red Army did not possess the power or skill to crush the Germans. In February 1942 the Soviet offensive, its strength dissipated by Stalin's interventions, began to wane. By March 1942 the Germans had recovered their equilibrium.[8]

During the spring of 1942, Sokolovsky remained with the Western Front. A highly effective German deception plan, Operation Kremlin, initially duped the Soviets into believing that the German strategic objective was Moscow and not the southern oilfields.[9] The Moscow region became quieter as the Germans moved south to a date with destiny at Stalingrad. Sokolovsky's front adopted a watching brief over the German forces to the west of Moscow.

In August 1942, following Zhukov's promotion to deputy supreme commander in chief, Konev returned to the Western Front with Sokolovsky as his chief of staff. As such, Sokolovsky was involved in the planning of Operation Mars, conceived and supervised by Zhukov and launched on 25 November 1942. The objective was to destroy the German Ninth Army in the Rzhev salient, removing the threat to Moscow. It was a disaster. It was later claimed, even when rarely acknowledged, that Mars was merely a diversionary operation designed to lure German attention and reserves away from Operation Uranus, the encirclement of the German Sixth Army at Stalingrad. The genuine historical record does not support this. It was intended that Mars would be followed in December 1942 by Operation Jupiter (in the same way that Uranus was exploited by Operation Saturn). Conducted by the Western Front, the aim was to reach Vyazma and destroy Army Group Center.[10] This "cosmic" strategic design was frustrated by the poor performance of the Western Front, and the skillful employment of German reserves. By mid-December, awash with blood, Mars was terminated. Sokolovsky's role in this debacle is obscure. The operational plan was reasonable enough even if the strategic conception was inordinately ambitious. However, at the tactical level, as at Moscow, many Soviet commanders struggled to handle their forces in the agile fashion necessary to bring success in maneuver warfare.

The Western Front took time to recover, but kept up its constant harassment of the German forces. In March 1943 the Germans withdrew from the Rzhev salient in Operation Buffalo. In recognition of his performance as chief of staff, Sokolovsky was given command of the Western Front in April 1943. The front was to play an important, if subsidiary, role in the battles of the forthcoming year, as the Red Army first wrested the initiative from and then drove the Wehrmacht out of the Soviet Union. The spring of 1943 represented a turning point for both Sokolovsky and the Red Army, which set about creating the force structure that would enable it consistently to transform isolated tactical and operational triumphs into strategic victories.

In the period June 1941 to November 1942, the Red Army abandoned its sophisticated interwar theories of deep battle for survival. In spring 1943 the Soviets began to transform the fighting power and sustainability of the Red Army under talented and battle-scarred commanders, who had the ability to handle large formations with imagination. Soviet rifle (infantry) brigades, divisions, and corps were expanded and given additional armored, engineer, signal, antitank, and aviation units to make them combined arms armies capable of conducting breakthrough operations. The Soviet air force began to develop the quality and quantity of man and machine that enabled it first to negate German air superiority, and later to wrest control of the air, as the Luftwaffe was diverted west to defend the skies of the Reich.[11] The Soviet High Command emphasized artillery to ensure that German tactical defenses could be reached quickly. The "artillery offensive" was developed with the Soviet High Command allocating artillery divisions and later corps to particular commands in accordance with tactical, operational, and strategic requirements. However, successful penetration only *created* the opportunity for deep operations; it did not *conduct* them.

The central theme of the interwar years had been the requirement to conduct operations in depth to deny the enemy the ability to react in a coordinated manner following a Soviet breakthrough. At Moscow the Red Army proved unable to translate tactical into operational success because it lacked the ability to sustain the offensive. The Red Army's most significant structural development in the spring of 1943 was the creation of five elite all-arms formations known as tank armies, designed to make deep operations a reality by exploiting breakthroughs to depths of up to 500 kilometers.[12] These tank armies, consisting of two tank and one mechanized corps plus additional supporting units, were to prove devastatingly effective in denying the Germans the ability to fight effectively. Such was the speed of their exploitation and disruption of cohesion between operational and tactical commands. As Sokolovsky took command of the Western Front, a new Red Army was born in the spring of 1943. It would mature and triumph, but Sokolovsky's performance did not match his earlier achievements.

Hitler sought to reclaim the initiative on the eastern front through a victorious battle of annihilation in the Kursk salient. Soviet strategy envisaged the destruction of German armored mobility on the deep defenses at Kursk, before launching a massive counteroffensive. The counteroffensive, named Operation Kutozov, foresaw the annihilation of German forces in the Orel salient, to the north of Kursk, through the coordinated use of the forces of the Western, Bryansk, and Central Fronts. Western Front's left-wing was to advance southwest toward Khotynets, while the Bryansk and Central Fronts marched west and northwest respectively to meet them, thus trapping German forces in the pocket.

Sokolovsky was a reticent and very correct professional officer. This professionalism was tested when a dispute arose about how to breach the German defenses in the Orel salient. In April 1943 Sokolovsky outlined Western Front's plan without dissent, but when Stalin asked for comments,

Lt. Gen. Ivan K. Bagramyan, commander of the Eleventh Guards Army, the Western Front's main striking force, intervened and proposed an alternative. The German defenses were among the strongest on the eastern front, fortified in depth and manned by tough experienced troops. Bagramyan thought Sokolovsky's proposed solution, a broad front attack, appropriate to the problem of ensuring a tactical breakthrough, but inimical to the operational objective of a deep exploitation to Khotynets, as it would expose the Eleventh Guards' flank. Bagramyan proposed a more limited operation identifying Bolkhov as the initial objective, the successful attainment of which would create the right conditions for operational exploitation.[13] This plan was accepted, much to Sokolovsky's irritation. The question of how to make speed of breakthrough, tempo, and depth compatible with security was at the heart of the operational dilemmas confronted by the Soviet generals.

Soviet commanders sought to "dilute" German defenses by deploying on a broad front, forcing defense of the entire frontage while disguising the main point of effort to facilitate concentration of force on the chosen axes of breakthrough. Tactical assaults across the line would fix enemy units in position, denying them flexibility, while massive concentrations of Soviet artillery and infantry would annihilate the enemy in selected areas. The timely committal of exploitation forces, the crucial decision faced by front commanders, sought to transform tactical annihilation into operational maneuver in depth, shattering the cohesion of the enemy. This was Sokolovsky's intention, but the limited breadth of the Western Front's sector, and the strength of the German defenses and reserves suggest that Bagramyan was correct.

The Western Front began Operation Kutozov on 12 July 1943. The attack, led by Bagramyan's Eleventh Guards Army with a massive concentration averaging 420 guns and 50 tanks per kilometer, was dramatically successful. By 13 July the Eleventh Guards Army had penetrated sixteen miles and Model's German Ninth Army was forced to abandon its assault on the northern face of the Kursk salient. By 20 July the Eleventh Guards Army was forty-five miles into the German defenses, and in conjunction with the Bryansk and Central Fronts, Sokolovsky's Western Front appeared on the verge of a major operational victory. The Soviet High Command, however, had failed to anticipate the Western Front's success, deploying the Third Tank Army in the Bryansk Front's sector. By the time Lt. Gen. Vasily M. Badanov's Fourth Tank Army arrived on 20 July, the opportunity was gone and German reserves arriving in strength had restored the line.

On the Soviet High Command's orders, the Fourth Tank Army was to take Bolkhov, which Bagramyan argued would involve a brand-new and inexperienced formation designed for deep operations, in a specialist breakthrough attack. A furious row ensued between Bagramyan and Badanov, in which Sokolovsky sided with Badanov. On 26 July the Fourth Tank Army was mauled, making no progress, while the following day they advanced less than a mile. Orel was taken on 5 August, but the German crisis had passed and they withdrew in good order.[14] Sokolovsky does not emerge with credit from this episode: either he took revenge on Bagramyan or his professional judgment was seriously flawed. The incident cost Badanov his command while Bagramyan received command of the 1st Baltic Front in October 1943, retaining his command while Sokolovsky eventually lost his in April 1944. Operation Kutozov flattered to deceive, but ultimate responsibility for its relative failure lay with the Soviet High Command, not Sokolovsky.

Sokolovsky meanwhile retained his position and in August 1943 the Western Front undertook Operation Suvorov, the aim of which was to liberate Smolensk. The operation was a subsidiary part of the Soviet drive to the Dnieper River. A secondary objective involved fixing German troops, preventing their transfer to the Ukraine, where the main Soviet blows would fall.[15] Since July 1941 Smolensk had been German Army Group Center's main supply and communications hub. The region was heavily fortified with high-quality troops commanded by Gen. Gotthard Heinrici, a master of defense. The terrain was problematic and Sokolovsky had no significant numerical or material advantage.

After a broad front deployment of the Western Front's nine armies, Sokolovsky planned to attack with four armies—the Tenth Guards, Thirty-third, Sixty-eighth, and Twenty-first—on a sixteen-kilometer front using maskirovka to disguise their concentrations, while the Tenth Army attacked Kirov to distract the Germans. The VI Guards Cavalry Corps and the V Mechanized Corps would exploit. After a visit from Stalin on 3 August, the only time he ever visited the frontline, the Western Front began regrouping as part of its maskirovka plan. However, "Western Front measures to achieve surprise were not noted for their special effectiveness"[16] German intelligence identified where and when the attack would occur and by whom, moving in six reserve divisions.

The attack began on 7 August 1943. Progress was painfully slow in the face of fierce resistance. Sokolovsky ordered extensive regroupings, but these rather chaotic movements confused his own troops as much as the Germans. By means of unsophisticated attrition the Western Front advanced thirty-five kilometers in fourteen days. Although the Germans conceded Spas-Demensk on 20 August, Sokolovsky terminated the attack. Sokolovsky altered the axis of attack from Roslavl to Yelnya and reshuffled the Western Front pack. This was skillfully done, as the Germans failed to decipher his intentions. On 28 August 1943 Sokolovsky renewed the assault with tactical surprise, and in an exemplary attack pierced the German defenses. By 6 September the Western Front had advanced fifty kilometers and taken Yelnya. Sokolovsky regrouped in preparation for the assault on Smolensk, scheduled for 14 September. The Western Front's diversionary operations along the Desna proved highly effective and the German defenses were breached. By 25 September the Germans withdrew, their occupation of Smolensk rendered untenable by the advances of the Western and Kalinin Fronts. The Western Front continued its advance toward Orsha and Mogilev, but encountered strong defenses that brought Operation Suvorov to an end on 2 October.[17]

By October 1943 the Western Front had advanced 150 miles through the strongest defenses on the eastern front, removing the threat to Moscow, while liberating millions of Russians. Sokolovsky pinned down extensive German formations, thus lubricating the Red Army's successful progress toward the Dnieper in the Ukraine. Sokolovsky's Western Front spent the remainder of 1943 and the early months of 1944 trying to destroy the formidable German positions in the "iron triangle" of Orsha-Mogilev-Vitebsk on the Dvina-Dnieper "land-bridge," the gateway to and exit from the Russian heartland. The German defenses were aided by numerous lakes, marshes, and rivers, which in conjunction with unseasonably mild but wet weather frustrated the Western Front.[18]

In April 1944 Sokolovsky paid the price, as the Soviet High Command concluded that the Western Front's troubles were as much the result of "organizational failures" as German defenses.[19] The Western Front was broken up into the 2nd and 3rd Belarussian Fronts under Lt. Gen. Ivan E. Petrov and Lt. Gen. Ivan D. Chernyakovsky respectively. Sokolovsky's command was criticized as being physically and emotionally too distant from the troops. It is ironic, therefore, that his successor, the dashing thirty-eight-year-old Chernyakovsky, was killed in the frontline in East Prussia during February 1945. The Western Front was officially dissolved on 25 April 1944 and with it Sokolovsky's field career came to rather an ignominious end. Nevertheless, as chief of staff of the 1st Ukrainian Front he would preside over the creation and implementation of a masterly deception plan in the Lvov-Sandomierz operation of July 1944. By general consent his organization of the secret deployment of tens of thousands of 1st Ukrainian Front troops in the Sandomierz bridgehead no larger than a small town during December 1944 prior to the Red Army offensive across Poland in January 1945 was one of the great feats of staff work in World War II. Sokolovsky's "organizational failures" did not prevent no less an individual than Zhukov "poaching" him from Konev's 1st Ukrainian Front in April 1945 to be his deputy commander at Berlin. Indeed, it was Sokolovsky who negotiated with Gen. Hans Krebs the final surrender of German troops at Berlin in May 1945. It was the first act in a postwar career that would become intimately associated with the German capital.

Sokolovsky's achievements as a chief of staff rank among the greatest of the century. In the most trying of circumstances with the talented but demanding Zhukov, to say nothing of the menacing presence of Stalin and his malevolent cronies, Sokolovsky played a critical role in the Battle of Moscow, which saved the Soviet Union from disaster and fundamentally altered the course of World War II. He was an austere, professional soldier who famously rebuked an army commander in the middle of the battle of Berlin for crude language used while reprimanding an artillery officer.[20] It seems extraordinary that Sokolovsky was removed from command of the Western Front for among other things "organizational failures." Yet, clearly he did not excel as a field commander. The essential questions faced by a Soviet commander revolved around timing, especially in the commitment of elite exploitation forces designed to conduct operations in depth. To his contemporary, Gen. Sergei M. Shtemenko, who Sokolovsky succeeded as chief of the General Staff, he was "a very careful general, who always looked twice, or even three times before he leapt."[21] In his defense he encountered some of the best troops and strongest defenses that the Germans possessed. But Sokolovsky, an intelligent and studious man, lacked the instinctive boldness for coup d'oeil that Clausewitz thought the foundation of great generalship. In contrast to his contemporaries, Rokossovsky and Zhukov, Sokolovsky did not have a natural feel for the creative arts of high command. He was an excellent officer, a truly outstanding chief of staff, but never more than a competent field general.

Notes

1. David M. Glantz and Jonathan M. House, *When Titans Clashed: How the Red Army Stopped Hitler* (Lawrence: University Press of Kansas, 1995), 79–81.

2. Klaus Reinhardt, *Moscow: The Turning Point? The Failure of Hitler's Strategy in the Winter of 1941–42*, Studies in Military History (Oxford: Oxford University Press 1992), 207.

3. John Erickson, *The Road to Stalingrad*, vol. 1 of *Stalin's War with Germany* (New York: Harper and Row, 1975), 237.

4. Reinhardt, *Moscow*, 94.

5. Albert Seaton, *The Russo-German War* (New York: Praeger, 1971), 241.

6. Reinhardt, *Moscow*, 232.

7. Ibid., 298.

8. Erickson, *Road to Stalingrad*, 297–326.

9. Glantz and House, *When Titans Clashed*, 105–6.

10. David M. Glantz, *Zhukov's Greatest Defeat: The Red Army's Epic Disaster in Operation Mars, 1942*, Modern War Studies (Lawrence: University Press of Kansas, 1999), 19–20.

11. David M. Glantz, *From the Don to the Dnepr: Soviet Offensive Operations, December 1942–August 1943* (London: Routledge, 1991), 370.

12. Glantz and House, *When Titans Clashed*, 155.

13. John Erickson, *The Road to Berlin*, vol. 2 of *Stalin's War with Germany* (London: Weidenfeld and Nicolson, 1983), 75–76.

14. Ibid., 115.

15. Ibid., 129.

16. David M. Glantz, *Soviet Military Deception in the Second World War*, Cass Series on Soviet Military Theory and Practice (London: Routledge, 1989), 188.

17. Erickson, *The Road to Berlin*, 130–31.

18. Ibid., 145.

19. Ibid., 198.

20. Ibid., 561.

21. S. M. Shtemenko, *The Soviet General Staff at War 1941–1945* (Moscow: Progress Publishers, 1985), 251.

Part Two
Korea and Vietnam

CHRONOLOGY OF EUGENE M. LANDRUM

6 Feb 1891	Born in Pensacola, Florida.
20 Aug 1910	Enlisted in the Regular Army; private, 9th Coast Artillery.
1914	Re-enlisted as private (later, sergeant), 17th Infantry.
26 Nov 1916	Commissioned second lieutenant, 20th Infantry; immediately promoted to first lieutenant, 43rd Infantry.
4 June 1917	Promoted to captain, 32nd Infantry.
Dec 1917	Assigned to 27th Infantry, Manila, Philippine Islands. Aide-de-camp to Brig. Gen. Robert Kennon Evans.
Aug 1918	Served with the American Expeditionary Forces in Siberia.
30 Oct 1919	Aide-de-camp to Brig. Gen. Richmond P. Davis, Manila.
Dec 1919	Assigned to 49th Infantry (later, commander, Company M, 17th Infantry), Fort Leavenworth, Kansas.
16 Apr 1923	Assistant adjutant general, War Department General Staff.
7 Mar 1924	Transferred from infantry to the Adjutant General's Corps.
Jul 1927	Assistant adjutant general, Headquarters, Ninth Corps Area, Presidio of San Francisco, California.
16 Nov 1927	Promoted to major.
Jul 1931	Student, Command and General Staff School, Fort Leavenworth, Kansas.
27 Feb 1933	Transferred from Adjutant General's Corps to Infantry.
May 1933	Battalion commander, 6th Infantry.
9 Feb 1934	Assistant chief of staff for supply, Headquarters, Sixth Corps Area, Chicago, Illinois.
13 Aug 1935	Student, Army War College, Washington, D.C.
Jun 1936	Instructor, Infantry School, Fort Benning, Georgia.
1 Apr 1938	Promoted to lieutenant colonel.
1 Dec 1940	Executive officer, Infantry School.
15 Mar 1941	Staff duties, Headquarters, 3rd Infantry Division, Fort Lewis, Washington.
26 Jun 1941	Promoted to colonel (temporary); chief of staff, 3rd Infantry Division.
12 Mar 1942	Promoted to brigadier general (temporary); assistant division commander, 3rd Infantry Division.

Jun 1942	Staff duties, Alaskan Defense Command.
13 Mar 1943	Promoted to major general (temporary).
Aug 1942	Commander, Adak Landing Force; commander, Adak Post.
Mar 1943	Awarded Army Distinguished Service Medal for occupation of Adak.
16 May 1943	Commander, Attu Landing Force.
Jul 1943	Awarded Navy Distinguished Service Medal for the occupation of Attu.
Oct 1943	Commanding general, 87th Infantry Division.
Apr 1944	Chief of staff, VII Corps.
13 June 1944	Commanding general, 90th Infantry Division, Normandy.
28 Jul 1944	Relieved of command, 90th Infantry Division.
Aug 1944	Commanding general, 71st Infantry Division, Fort Benning, Georgia.
Oct 1944	Commanding general, Infantry Advanced Replacement Training Center, Camp Maxey, Texas.
31 Jan 1946	Reverted to permanent grade of colonel.
Mar 1946	G-1 (later, chief of staff), Fifth U.S. Army, Chicago, Illinois.
1948	Chief of staff, Eighth U.S. Army, Japan.
12 Jul 1950	Chief of staff, Eighth U.S. Army in Korea.
4 Sep 1950	Deputy chief of staff, Eighth U.S. Army in Korea.
16 Jan 1951	Awarded first Oak Leaf Cluster to Army Distinguished Service Medal.
28 Feb 1951	Retired with rank of major general.
24 Jul 1967	Died.

Eugene M. Landrum

Donald W. Boose Jr.

In August 1950, after a month-long series of delaying actions, Lt. Gen. Walton H. Walker's U.S. Eighth Army dug in along the line of the Naktong River in the southeast corner of Korea in what came to be known as the Pusan Perimeter. With his army stretched thin, Walker used the roads and rail lines inside the Perimeter to shift his forces, reinforce threatened positions, and counterattack North Korean penetrations. Always on the move, he ranged the front by jeep and light airplane, badgering, cajoling, and encouraging his commanders, gauging the situation, calculating the next move. Until late in the Pusan Perimeter battle, Walker had no general officer deputy and no U.S. corps commanders. He relied on his chief of staff, Col. Eugene M. Landrum, to run his headquarters, coordinate the flow of men and supplies into the theater, and generate the ad hoc reserves without which Walker's desperate defense would fail. Landrum had commanded three divisions as a major general in World War II, but his record was marred by relief from command in Normandy. Now at the end of a forty-year Army career, Landrum proved to have the experience, skills, and character needed for his crucial supporting role.

Eugene Landrum was born on 6 February 1891 in Pensacola, Florida. His father, Samuel Winburn Landrum, had fought some of the toughest battles of the Civil War as an officer in the 38th Alabama Infantry. Wounded at the Battle of Lookout Mountain, he ended the war as a prisoner and returned home to Baghdad, Florida, scarred and weary. "Captain Sam" died in 1895 when young Gene was four. The family said he had finally succumbed to old war wounds and hardships at the hands of the Yankee army.[1] His son would serve that same Yankee army long and faithfully, signing up at age

171

nineteen and putting in his early years servicing the old guns at Atlantic and Gulf Coast fortresses as a coast artillery private. He reenlisted in 1914 and by 1916 was a sergeant in Company M, 17th Infantry Regiment at Eagle Pass, Texas.[2] Landrum marched with the 17th into Mexico as part of Gen. John J. Pershing's punitive expeditions and was on duty in San Joaquin in the fall of 1916 when he received orders reassigning him to the 2nd Infantry Regiment in Hawaii.[3]

Landrum was commissioned on 26 November 1916 and promoted to first lieutenant the same day. Seven months later he pinned on captain's bars and in July 1917 sailed to the Philippines to become Brig. Gen. Robert Kennon Evans' aide-de-camp at Fort McKinley, near Manila. Landrum served out World War I in the Philippines rather than on the battlefields of France. But in 1918 and 1919 he participated in the U.S. intervention in the Russian Far East, commanding an infantry company guarding rail lines in Siberia.

Shortly before leaving for Siberia, Landrum married Frances Yeater, daughter of the acting governor general of the Philippines. In late 1919 the couple moved to Fort Leavenworth, Kansas, where the two Landrum children were born. After four years commanding Company M, 17th Infantry, his old outfit from Mexico days, he transferred temporarily to the Adjutant General Corps, serving at Army headquarters in Washington and in other staff assignments. In 1933 he completed the two-year Army Command and General Staff School course at the top of his class and then took command of the high-visibility Army demonstration battalion at the Chicago World's Fair. After graduating from the Army War College in 1936, Landrum spent the final years of peace at the Infantry School in Fort Benning, Georgia. In 1941 Landrum was assigned to the 3rd Infantry Division, then testing amphibious doctrine on the California coast. When the Japanese attacked Pearl Harbor, Landrum was the division chief of staff. Promoted to brigadier general in March 1942, he served briefly as assistant division commander before being reassigned to Alaska.[4]

Just as Landrum arrived in Alaska in June 1942, Japanese forces attacked and occupied the western Aleutian Islands of Kiska and Attu, beginning a strange and deadly campaign among the craggy islands, icy waters, fogs, and williwaw winds of the thousand-mile-long Aleutian chain.[5] In August 1942, as the first step toward recapturing the lost islands, Landrum was charged with the occupation and construction of an airbase at Adak, halfway along the Aleutian chain and about 250 miles from Kiska. In spite of fog, Japanese submarines, and a storm that struck the beach just as the troops landed,

Landrum put his 4,500-man Adak Landing Force ashore within eighteen hours. Two weeks later the airfield was operational.[6]

On 5 January 1943 U.S. forces occupied Amchitka Island, only forty miles from Kiska. The next step was an amphibious assault on Attu by two regiments of Maj. Gen. Albert Brown's 7th Infantry Division.[7] The force landed on 11 May 1943 but soon bogged down, stymied by the Aleutian weather and terrain and the Japanese defense. Four days into what they had hoped would be a three-day operation, the Alaska commanders called for Gene Landrum, now a major general, to come up from Adak and take over.[8] By the time Landrum arrived on 17 May, the situation had already begun to improve, but two weeks of tough fighting still lay ahead, including a final Japanese counterattack that overran the American frontline. Landrum did not change Brown's campaign plan significantly, but nonetheless made an impact on the operation. He understood the Aleutian weather and terrain and the value of high ground. He insisted on rotating frontline units frequently and ordered his men up into the ridgelines to bypass Japanese positions. During the Attu campaign, he earned the respect of "John Infantryman," as he called his soldiers, and of the correspondents accompanying the landing force, who began referring to him as "Landrum of the Aleutians."[9]

In 1943 U.S. Army Ground Forces began assigning divisions to officers who had already held successful combat commands. Landrum took command of the 87th Infantry Division at Camp McCain, Mississippi, in October 1943.[10] In March 1944 he became chief of staff of Maj. Gen. J. Lawton Collins' U.S. VII Corps, part of Lt. Gen. Omar N. Bradley's U.S. First Army, then in England preparing for the Normandy invasion.

On D-Day, VII Corps landed on the southeast coast of the Cotentin peninsula, a marshy patchwork of small fields cut by winding rivers and lined with hedgerows—thick, dense, heavily wooded earthen dikes that blocked movement and gave the Germans superb cover and fields of fire. Paratroopers of Maj. Gen. Matthew B. Ridgway's 82nd Airborne Division soon secured bridgeheads over the Merderet River, a few miles inland, but were unable to advance farther. On 9 June Collins ordered the 90th Infantry Division to pass through the bridgeheads and attack west. When the 90th, too, failed to make progress through the hedgerows, Collins relieved its commander and sent Landrum in to take charge.[11]

Once again, Gene Landrum found himself taking command in the middle of a battle with subordinates he didn't know. Even as the attack continued, he started an intense training program to build confidence and improve individual and team tactics. But in spite of what Bradley would later characterize as "heroic efforts on Landrum's part," the 90th's progress through the hedgerows was slower than that of the divisions on its flanks.[12]

On 19 June Bradley transferred Landrum's division to Maj. Gen. Troy Middleton's VIII Corps in preparation for the Normandy breakout. Landrum had less than two weeks to improve the division's combat capability before the 90th attacked south against strong German positions. On 14 July, after twelve days of fighting that left more than 10,000 of its soldiers killed or wounded, the battered and exhausted division reached its objectives along the Sèves River.[13] Eight days later, and before it could absorb the thousands of green troops sent to replace its recent casualties, the 90th was ordered to resume the attack. Crossing the Sèves River, the division, in Bradley's words, "took its second dive."[14] One battalion, pinned down and isolated, surrendered to the Germans. Bradley relieved Landrum of command.[15]

General Dwight D. Eisenhower confided to army chief of staff George C. Marshall that the relief from command was "nothing against Landrum," whom he would be glad to have back in command of a division that he had trained himself.[16] But when Landrum did train up another stateside division, the 71st, Eisenhower changed his mind. Cabling Marshall in September 1944 that he had decided not to ask for Landrum, Eisenhower sent back another general to take command of the 71st.[17]

Landrum finished out the war commanding the Infantry Advanced Replacement Center at Camp Maxey, Texas, and, when the war ended, he agreed to stay on active duty at his permanent rank of colonel. In 1946 he became chief of personnel (G-1) of Lt. Gen. Walton H. Walker's Fifth Army in Chicago.[18] Walker, who had commanded XX Corps under Gen. George S. Patton in World War II, had brought his wartime chief of staff, Col. William A. Collier, with him to Chicago. Collier was a former brigadier general who, like Landrum, had dropped back to the rank of colonel to stay on active duty. The two men had contrasting personalities: Landrum was contemplative, soft-spoken, and kindly; Collier was edgy, sharp-tongued, and demanding. Both got results and together they made a capable, complementary team.[19] When Collier was reassigned to Korea, Walker made Landrum his chief of staff and in 1948 asked Landrum to accompany him to the Eighth Army in Japan.[20]

As Eighth Army chief of staff, Landrum was in an unusual situation. No deputy commander position was authorized for a field army, so the chief of staff served as "principal assistant and advisor to the commander" as well as "principal coordinating agency of the command."[21] The authorized rank for an army chief of staff was major general, but Walker had no doubt that Landrum, whom he invariably called "General Landrum," could handle the job.[22]

Walker and Landrum had joked about going to a cushy assignment in Japan, but they soon became involved in the demanding task of trying to turn the Eighth Army from an occupation force into a combat-ready field army. Walker's command, four understrength infantry divisions and supporting units, was the major Army element of Gen. Douglas MacArthur's Far East Command (FEC). A potentially formidable force, Eighth Army had serious weaknesses when Walker and Landrum arrived. From 1945 until 1949 U.S. forces in Japan were committed almost exclusively to occupation duty and had been whittled down by tight budgets. Eighth Army had no corps headquarters or corps artillery. Few of the divisional artillery units had a full complement of guns, and most of the infantry regiments had been reduced from three to two battalions and had lost their tank companies. Light tanks replaced medium tanks in the divisional tank battalions.[23]

Walker and Landrum could do little about the shortages and equipment deficiencies, but they could improve combat effectiveness through training. In 1949, as the Eighth Army's occupation duties wound down, Landrum developed and supervised a training program intended to turn Eighth Army into an "effective, integrated air-ground-sea fighting team."[24] However, the program was based on what MacArthur and Walker believed was the most likely war scenario, a Soviet invasion of Japan from the north, not war in Korea. Furthermore, personnel turbulence and equipment shortages interfered with training, and Eighth Army was committed to battle long before the program was completed.[25]

On 25 June 1950 the North Korean People's Army (KPA) attacked across the 38th parallel. As the lightly armed Republic of Korea Army (ROKA) fell back, President Harry S. Truman decided to assist, initially with supplies and equipment, later with U.S. combat forces. The first U.S. ground troops—a task force from the 24th Infantry Division—arrived in Korea on 2 July and engaged the North Koreans on 5 July. On 6 July MacArthur alerted Walker that he was to take command of all U.S. ground forces in Korea. Walker asked Collier, then commanding the base at Kobe, to fly to Korea and establish an advance command post while Landrum prepared the army headquarters for the move. Walker visited Korea the next day, conferring with the 24th Infantry Division commander before returning to Japan.[26] On 12 July Walker returned to Korea and opened the headquarters of Eighth U.S. Army in Korea (EUSAK) in the southeastern city of Taegu, about sixty miles northwest of the major port city of Pusan.[27] Collier stayed on in Korea as deputy chief of staff, while Landrum flew back and forth between Taegu and Yokohama, carrying out his chief of staff responsibilities in Korea while keeping an eye on Eighth Army (Rear) activities in Japan.[28]

On 17 July Walker received operational control of the ROK Army. Some ROKA units were attached directly to U.S. units, but Walker or Landrum transmitted instructions to the rest of the ROK Army through the ROKA chief of staff.[29] EUSAK was also designated the ground component of the newly established United Nations Command (UNC). Sixteen UN nations eventually provided combat forces to the UNC, but in July and August the only ground forces were those of South Korea and the United States.[30]

The main avenue of approach through South Korea runs from Seoul in the northwest to the small city of Taejon eighty-five miles to the south. It then runs eighty miles southeast, through a narrow valley in the Sobaek Mountains, to Taegu, then south to Pusan. When Walker took command, the U.S. 24th Infantry Division was trying to slow the North Korean advance along that main avenue of approach, but had been pushed back toward Taejon. The 25th Infantry Division was just arriving in Pusan and the 1st Cavalry Division was preparing to load out to Korea.[31] ROK Army forces, now recovered from the initial shock of the North Korean attack, were fighting tenaciously to hold the mountain passes north of Taegu and to block a North Korean advance down the east coast.

With the North Koreans pushing deep into South Korea, Walker had no choice initially but to conduct a delay, committing U.S. forces into the fight piecemeal to slow the enemy advance until he could organize a coherent defense line. On 14 July Walker met with Landrum to determine where and how he would conduct that defense. In preparation, Landrum phoned all the major units in or en route to Korea to determine their location and status and gathered information on logistics, lines of communication, and terrain. Walker's pilot, Eugene M. (Mike) Lynch, spent the previous two days flying low over the Korean countryside in a light plane with Collier and the army assistant G-3, Col. Allan D. MacLean, reconnoitering the terrain.[32] When Landrum arrived carrying an armload of annotated terrain maps, Walker asked, "When and where can I stop the enemy and attack him?"[33]

He had to hold Pusan, the only deepwater port in South Korea, and enough territory west and north of Pusan to provide depth to the defense. The obvious location for a main line of resistance was the Naktong River, which runs south for about eighty miles from the mountain town of Naktong-ni, forty miles northwest of Taegu, to within ten miles of the south coast before turning east to empty into the Korea Strait near Pusan. Sixty miles of mountainous terrain from Naktong-ni to the east coast town of Yongdok would provide a northern anchor for the defense. After his meeting with Landrum, Walker ordered the U.S. 24th Infantry Division and ROK forces to "execute maximum delay" and to stop the North Koreans west and north of the Naktong River–Yongdok line.[34]

Over the next two weeks, the remnants of the 24th Infantry Division (whose commander, Maj. Gen. William F. Dean was captured by the North Koreans near Taegu), reinforced by the 25th Infantry and 1st Cavalry Divisions, slowly gave ground, then fell back behind the barrier of the Naktong. By 1 August U.S. and ROK forces in Korea finally established a coherent defense line along the 140-mile-long Naktong River–Yongdok line: the Pusan Perimeter.[35]

The ideal pattern of defense, given enough forces to carry it out, would have been an "area" or "positional" defense in which most of the defending forces are deployed forward along a continuous line of fixed positions and backed up with small mobile reserves.[36] In 1950 a division conducting such a defense would normally be assigned a six- to eight-mile front. But the calculus of terrain and forces available to Walker denied him that option. His U.S. divisions and the relatively well-equipped ROK 1st Infantry Division would have to hold fronts of thirty to forty miles along the Naktong River. The remaining four Korean divisions, with less mobility and firepower but aligned in more defensible mountainous terrain and supported by UNC air and naval forces, would defend fronts of about twelve miles.[37]

Eighth Army's superior mobility and interior lines gave Walker the opportunity to conduct a "mobile defense," an operation developed by armor officers in World War II. In a true mobile defense most of the defending force is held in reserve as a counterattack force while the remainder holds a series of strong points.[38] Since Walker did not have enough forces to maintain a large mobile reserve, he used ad hoc forces from units in quiet sectors and from newly arriving units. Taking advantage of the network of roads and railways, he moved these "fire brigades" to reinforce threatened sectors and to destroy or eject KPA forces that penetrated the main line of resistance.

Throughout August and early September, Walker conducted what one military historian has called "the largest, most successful mobile defensive operation in U.S. military history."[39] The North Koreans attacked on four avenues of approach. One thrust was along the south coast toward Pusan. Another was across the Naktong River about thirty miles south of Taegu where twice the KPA broke through Eighth Army's thin frontline. They also attacked repeatedly toward Taegu, where fiery tank rounds crashing down a long straight stretch of road gave rise to the nickname the "Bowling Alley." By mid-August, KPA forces had pushed down the east coast about thirty miles, but while the North Koreans compressed the perimeter, Eighth Army held the line.

It was a virtuoso performance by Walker, but it required a trusted deputy to conjure up the reserves and to keep a steady hand on the headquarters while Walker flew over the battlefield or traveled by jeep around the front. Gene Landrum's entire career and the years he had spent building mutual friendship, respect, and confidence with Walker now culminated in this trusted deputy role. Nicknamed "Old Timer," Landrum also had the admiration and respect of the Eighth Army staff.[40] He spent his days with the intelligence and operations sections and in close contact with the Air Force Joint Operations Center. Every night, he phoned each of the frontline divisions to determine their status and keep the commanders informed. He kept track of every unit in or deploying to Korea so that whenever Walker returned from the battlefront, Landrum could answer the question, "Landrum, how many reserves have you dug up for me today?"[41]

He didn't operate alone. Walker's G-3, Col. John A. Dabney, worked closely with Landrum at the main headquarters, as did Collier, the deputy chief of staff, who backstopped Landrum during his trips back to Japan. Collier and MacLean, another trusted and competent officer, also served as Walker's eyes, ears, and voice in the field, often being referred to as the "tactical gofers."[42] But there were very few other experienced staff officers in Eighth Army and, after Dean was captured, Landrum was the only officer in Korea besides Walker who had previously commanded a division in combat.[43]

Walker's outstanding performance in defending the Pusan Perimeter is widely recognized today but there were some doubts at the time about both Walker and Landrum. Direct dialogue between MacArthur in Tokyo and Walker in Korea was infrequent and generally limited to MacArthur's visits to Korea. Otherwise, their communication was filtered through MacArthur's chief of staff, Maj. Gen. Edward M. Almond, who appears to have had little confidence in either Walker or Landrum.[44] In late July a colonel from Army Field Forces headquarters came to Korea to inspect Eighth Army. On 9 August 1950 he briefed Lieutenant General Ridgway, U.S. Army Deputy Chief of Staff for Administration, who was then visiting Korea with Presidential Special Assistant W. Averell Harriman. On the basis of his brief observations, the colonel delivered a scathing indictment of Walker and his command. He said he was "not impressed" with Landrum and recommended he be replaced by a "younger stronger chief of staff."[45] Walker's senior aide-de-camp, Col. Layton C. Tyner, later noted that Walker and Landrum had been fighting an intense war of movement with an undermanned staff for four weeks with little sleep or rest, and he questioned how "a bunch of visiting VIPs" could arrive at a valid assessment.[46]

However unfairly, the report persuaded Ridgway, who contemplated recommending Walker be relieved from command, to arrange for Maj. Gen. Leven C. Allen, executive secretary to the secretary of defense, to be sent out to Korea to replace Landrum.[47] On 4 September 1950 Landrum stepped gracefully aside and Allen took over as Eighth Army chief of staff. Walker refused to send Landrum back to the States, but kept him on as deputy chief of staff, a job Landrum shared with Collier until the following January. Walker also made an unsuccessful attempt to get Landrum promoted to brigadier general.[48]

The North Koreans made one last furious attempt to breach the Pusan Perimeter in early September, but their offensive had reached culmination. Weakened by fatigue, casualties, and the interdiction of its supply lines, the KPA faltered. Reinforcements had been flowing into Korea, and by 1 September Eighth Army substantially outnumbered the attacking force.[49] By 15 September, the day of the amphibious assault at Inch'on, the last KPA attacks against the perimeter had burned out. The next day Walker's Eighth Army and its ROK allies, bolstered by a British infantry brigade, began the breakout from the Pusan Perimeter. Ten days later, Eighth Army's lead elements, a 1st Cavalry Division task force, linked up with the Inch'on landing force south of Seoul.

On 30 September advanced patrols of the ROK 3rd Division crossed the 38th parallel into North Korea. On 7 October Eighth Army began a general advance into the north. Allen remained with the Eighth Army main command post in Taegu, while Landrum took charge of a newly established advanced command post in Seoul and Collier headed into North Korea with Walker. The advance north was checked by Chinese forces near the end of October, and a month later, just as UN forces began another general advance, the Chinese attacked in strength. By mid-December, the Eighth Army had withdrawn to the 38th parallel and was digging in for the next onslaught.

On Saturday, 23 December 1950, General Walker was killed when his jeep collided with a truck northeast of Seoul.[50] Three days later General Ridgway took command of Eighth Army. Whatever Ridgway may have thought of Landrum as a result of the events in France in July of 1944 or the unflattering assessment of the visiting colonel the previous August, once he actually had the opportunity to see Landrum in action he, too, gained respect for the old colonel's true worth. Ridgway immediately began to rely on both Landrum and Collier, and when the next Chinese attack began, he gave Landrum full responsibility for moving the Eighth Army command post out of Seoul.[51]

Gene Landrum left Korea on 16 January 1951. Ridgway demonstrated his appreciation for his deputy chief of staff by holding a formal farewell ceremony in Taegu even as the Chinese attack continued and Eighth Army prepared for a counteroffensive. At that ceremony, Ridgway presented Landrum with a second Army Distinguished Service Medal (his first was awarded for his successful capture of Adak in 1943). By coincidence, U.S. Army chief of staff Gen. J. Lawton Collins, who had given Landrum command of the 90th Infantry Division in Normandy and had been there when Bradley and Middleton had taken it away, was visiting Korea at the time and attended Landrum's farewell. When he returned to Washington, Collins recognized Landrum's contribution to the defense of Korea by arranging for Landrum to be restored to the rank of major general.[52]

The Pusan Perimeter battles provide many lessons about the defense of an extended front, the use of ad hoc forces and interior lines to conduct a mobile defense, and effective and complementary interaction between a field army commander and a chief of staff. In Korea Gene Landrum's talents, personality, and actions complemented those of his dynamic, aggressive commander. His performance in command of the 90th Infantry Division may be debated, but Landrum's actions as principal assistant and advisor to the Eighth Army commander and principal coordinating agency of the command were exemplary. For forty years Eugene M. Landrum demonstrated professionalism and loyalty to his superiors, to the men who served under him, to the Army, and to the nation. And in the hot, bloody Korean summer of 1950, the Old Timer showed that he had what it took.

Notes

1. Janet B. Hewett, ed., *The Roster of Confederate Soldiers, 1861–1865*, vol. 9 (Wilmington, N.C.: Broadfoot Publishing, 1996), 299; W. Brewer, *Alabama: Her History, Resources, War Record, and Public Men from 1540 to 1872* (Montgomery, Ala.: Barrett and Brown, 1872, reprinted by Alabama State Department of Archives and History, 1966), 647–48;

Eugene M. Landrum Jr., "Major General Eugene M. Landrum, 04-570," unpublished biographical sketch, Box 52, "Alphabetical Files J-M," Clay and Joan Blair Collection, Archives of the U.S. Army Military History Institute, Carlisle Barracks, Pa. (MHI) (hereafter "EML Bio").

2. Unless otherwise noted, the information on General Landrum's life prior to World War II is based on the EML Bio; his official biography, a copy of which is held at MHI; and the relevant annual issues of *The Army Register* and the *Army List and Directory* (Washington, D.C.: War Department, The Adjutant General's Office, various dates).

3. U.S. War Department, "Return from Regular Infantry Regiments, June 1821–December 1916: Return of the 17th Regiment of Infantry," April–October 1916. Microcopy 665, Roll 190 at the U.S. Army Center of Military History, Fort McNair, Washington, D.C.

4. Donald G. Taggart, ed., *History of the Third Infantry Division in World War II* (Nashville, Tenn.: Battery Press, 1987), 4–6.

5. Brian Garfield, *The Thousand-Mile War: World War II in Alaska and the Aleutians* (Garden City, N.Y.: Doubleday, 1969); See also Stetson Conn, Rose C. Engelman, and Byron Fairchild, *United States Army in World War II: Guarding the United States and Its Outposts* (Washington, D.C.: Government Printing Office, 1960); Samuel Eliot Morison, *History of United States Naval Operations in World War II*, vol. 7, *Aleutians, Gilberts and Marshalls, June 1942–April 1944* (Boston: Little, Brown, 1960); chap. 11, "The Aleutians Campaign," in Wesley Frank Craven and James Lea Cate, eds., *The Pacific: Guadalcanal to Saipan, August 1942 to July 1949*, vol. 4 of *The Army Air Forces in World War II* (Chicago: University of Chicago Press, 1950, reprinted, Washington, D.C.: Government Printing Office, 1983), 359–401.

6. Craven and Cate, eds., *The Pacific*, 360, 368–69; Louis Morton, *United States Army in World War II: The War in the Pacific, Strategy and Command* (Washington, D.C.: Government Printing Office, 1962), 420; Conn, Engelman, and Fairchild, *United States Army in World War II*, 270–72; Garfield, *Thousand-Mile War*, 151–61; Morison, *History*, 12–13; EML Bio.

7. For the planning and conduct of the Attu operation, see, in addition to the references for the Aleutians Campaign, above, U.S. War Department, *The Capture of Attu as Told by the Men Who Fought There* (Washington, D.C.: The Infantry Journal, 1944); Edmund G. Love, *The Hourglass: A History of the 7th Division in World War II* (Nashville, Tenn.: Battery Press, 1988), 2–97; and Albert E. Brown "The Attu Operation," unpublished typescript, folder, "Correspondence and Comments Concerning Publication of the Book, *The Capture of Attu*, 1944–1946," Box T-2, Albert Brown Papers, MHI.

8. Morison, *History*, 38–41; Love, *The Hourglass*, 105; Letter, Commander North Pacific Force, U.S. Pacific Fleet, to Maj. Gen. Eugene M. Landrum, A.U.S., 16 May 1943, Subject: Secret Orders, Box T-2, Albert E. Brown Papers, MHI. Landrum was given command of the Attu Landing Force, consisting of two regiments of the 7th Infantry Division plus some other divisional troops and supporting forces. He was not given command of the 7th Infantry Division, which remained without a commander until after the Kiska operation in August 1943.

9. Love, *The Hourglass*, 55; Howard Handleman, *Bridge to Victory: The Story of the Reconquest of the Aleutians* (New York: Random House, 1943), 17, 173–75, 206–33.

"Landrum of the Aleutians," *New York Times*, 21 May, 30 May, and 13 August 1943. Alaska governor Ernest Gruening (whose diary is reprinted in Claus M. Naske, "The Battle of Alaska Has Ended and . . . the Japs Won It," *Military Affairs* 49, no. 3 [July 1985]: 144–51) believed Landrum should have been in command in the first place and credited him with the success of the operation (146, 150).

10. Robert R. Palmer, Bell I. Wiley, and William R. Keast, *United States Army in World War II: The Procurement and Training of Ground Combat Troops* (Washington, D.C.: Government Printing Office, 1948), 440–41; *An Historical and Pictorial Record of the 87th Infantry Division in World War II* (n.p., n.d., available at MHI Library), 17–18.

11. Gordon A. Harrison, *United States Army in World War II: European Theater of Operations: Cross-channel Attack* (Washington, D.C.: Government Printing Office, 1951), 182–86, 280–404; Roland G. Ruppenthal, *Utah Beach to Cherbourg (6 June–27 June 1944)* (Washington, D.C.: GPO, 1948), 14–75, 119–39; John Colby, *War from the Ground Up: The 90th Division in WWII* (Austin, Tex.: Nortex Press, 1991), 36–39; "VII Corps War Diary, 2 June 1944–1 April 1945," entries for 10–12 June 1944, microfilm, MHI.

12. "Heroic efforts": Omar N. Bradley and Clay Blair, *A General's Life: An Autobiography* (New York: Simon and Schuster, 1983), 262. The Germans had shifted their forces, thinning out the units facing the adjacent divisions and reinforcing those opposing the 90th to establish the anchor of their defense. Collins and Bradley, unaware of this at the time, began to be concerned about Landrum's ability to improve the division's performance. Martin Blumenson, "Re-assessing a Reputation," *Military Affairs* 22, no. 2 (Summer 1958): 100; Ruppenthal, *Utah Beach to Cherbourg*, 131–37; Harrison, *United States Army in World War II*, 403–4.

13. Martin Blumenson, *Breakout and Pursuit*. In *United States Army in World War II; European Theater of Operation* (Washington, D.C.: Government Printing Office, 1961), 63–70, 126–27; Colby, *War from the Ground Up*, 89–137; First U.S. Army Situation Reports from 3 July to 14 July 1944, Folders, "FUSA SITREPS #16, 24–71 (June 14–July 11, 1944)" and "FUSA SITREPS #73-108 (July 12, 1944–July 31, 1944), Box 6, Chester B. Hansen Papers, MHI.

14. Omar N. Bradley, *A Soldier's Story* (New York: Holt, 1951), 332.

15. The 90th Division's performance on the Cotentin peninsula and Landrum's relief from command have been the subject of debate. Eisenhower believed that the division "was not well brought up" and blamed its performance on poor training. Eisenhower to Marshall, 5 July 1944, in Alfred D. Chandler, ed., *The Papers of Dwight David Eisenhower: The War Years: IV* (Baltimore: Johns Hopkins University Press, 1970), 1972. A group of 90th Division veterans who collaborated on a history of the division in World War II dispute this and place the blame for the division's bad reputation on poor leadership by Landrum, whom they despise and dismiss as "short, fat, uninspiring" (Colby, *War from the Ground Up*, 149.) They compare Landrum unfavorably with the assistant division commander, Samuel T. Williams, whom they idolized and whom Landrum relieved during the battle. Williams, a courageous and dynamic leader who would rise to the rank of lieutenant general, did not get along with Landrum and undermined his authority. Their ugly confrontation did no credit to either officer, cast a shadow over Landrum's reputation, distracted him from the business of fighting the division, and

deprived him of a competent, if irascible, assistant. For Williams's side of this story as interpreted by his biographer, see Harold J. Meyer, *Hanging Sam: A Military Biography of General Samuel T. Williams, From Pancho Villa to Vietnam* (Denton: University of North Texas Press, 1990), 75–76, 87–97. George Bitman Barth, one of the very few 90th Division officers with prior combat experience, considered Landrum "a very fine man, a man of much experience," but questioned whether Landrum had faith in his officers and in the division (U.S. Army Command and General Staff College Case Study, *Leadership*, M1030-4 [Fort Leavenworth, Kan., n.d.], L4-I-5). General William E. DePuy, who was a staff officer in the 90th, says Landrum wasn't sufficiently visible to the fighting troops and failed to exert active battlefield leadership. See Ronnie L. Brownlee and William J. Mullen III, *Changing an Army: An Oral History of General William E. DePuy* (Carlisle Barracks, Pa.: U.S. Army Military History Institute, n.d.), 31, 32. Martin Blumenson, who wrote the official Army history of the Normandy breakout, argues that Landrum and the 90th were better than they were given credit for. He points out that the 90th was comparable to other divisions overall and in the bloody attack to the Sèves River "the 90th Division under Landrum had actually made a splendid showing that was unappreciated at the time." See *Masters of the Art of Command* (Boston: Houghton Mifflin, 1975), 369. Blumenson argues that the surrender of the battalion at St. Germain-sur-Sèves must be understood in the light of the circumstances, including the arrival of thousands of green replacements for the heavy casualties sustained during the previous attack. See "Reassessing a Reputation," 100–102. Blumenson also points out that Landrum, a former enlisted man, was quiet, thoughtful, and tended to control the division from his command post. These characteristics would stand him in good stead during the Pusan Perimeter battles in Korea but they contrasted with Bradley's image of an ideal commander. See ibid., 370. Some insights into Bradley's thinking can be gleaned from the diary and notes of his aide-de-camp, Chester B. Hansen. See especially the diary entry for 4 July 1944, Folder, "1–10 July 1944," Box 1, Chester B. Hansen Papers, MHI, and an undated memo of conversation between Bradley and Hansen, Folder, "6 June to August 1, 1944 (D-Day to 12 Aug)," Box 8, "War Diaries 1943–1945," Blair Collection, MHI.

16. Eisenhower, letter to Marshall, 2 August 1944, quoted in Blumenson, *Breakout and Pursuit*, 204.
17. Fred Clinger, Arthur Johnson, and Vincent Masel, *The History of the 71st Infantry Division* (Augsburg, Germany: E. Kieser KG, 1946), 23; Eisenhower, messages to Marshall, 24 September 1944 (FWD 15607, EM) and 28 September 1944 (FWD 16127) in *Eisenhower Papers*, ed. Chandler, 4:2196–97.
18. EML Bio, 6; Eugene M. Landrum Jr., letter to Donald W. Boose Jr., 20 January 1999 (hereafter Landrum to Boose, 20 January 1999); R. Manning Ancell with Christine M. Miller, *The Biographical Dictionary of World War II: Generals and Flag Officers* (Westport, Conn.: Greenwood Press, 1996), 181.
19. Official Biography, William Albert Collier (O-7598), at MHI. Collier's friendship with Landrum: Enclosure 1 to letter from William A. Collier to the chief of Military History, 10 March 1958, Folder, "Corr Misc," Box 745 "CMH Appleman," Record Group (RG) 319, National Archives at College Park (NACP), Maryland (hereafter Collier letter).

Contrasting, but compatible personalities of Landrum and Collier: Col. (Ret.) Layton C. Tyner [General Walker's senior aide-de-camp. 1948–50], letter to Brig. Gen. (Ret.) Eugene M. Lynch, 7 December 1998, 3 (provided to the writer by Lynch; hereafter Tyner to Lynch, 7 December 1998).

20. Eugene M. Landrum Jr., letter to Clay Blair, 25 February 1985, Box 52, "Alphabetical Files J-M," Blair Collection, MHI; EML Bio, 6–7; Landrum to Boose, 20 January 1999, 3–4.

21. *Staff Officers' Field Manual: The Staff and Combat Orders, FM 101-5* with changes 1 through 10 (Washington, D.C.: War Department, 1942), 7; *Field Service Regulations: Larger Units, FM 100-15* with change 1 (Washington, D.C.: Government Printing Office, 1942), 51–56; *Table of Organization and Equipment: Headquarters, Army, T/O&E 200-1* with six changes (Washington, D.C.: War Department, 1944), 2, 6.

22. Relationship between Walker and Landrum: Tyner to Lynch, 7 December 1998, 1–3; Landrum to Boose, 20 January 1999, 4. "General Landrum": Cpl. Randle M. Hurst, "The History of the 502nd Reconnaissance Platoon in Japan and Korea 1950," typescript manuscript quoted in Roy E. Appleman, *Disaster in Korea: The Chinese Confront MacArthur* (College Station: Texas A&M University Press, 1989), 336. Hurst was one of the sentries who guarded the Eighth Army commanding general. When, on two occasions, general officers were assigned to the command, Walker temporarily designated them as chief of staff, but kept Landrum on as deputy. When the new arrivals went on to divisional command or other assignments, Walker moved Landrum back to the chief of staff position. Tyner to Lynch, 7 December 1998, 3; Eighth U.S. Army General Orders, 1948 and 1949, "108 Folder #3 Hist/Rpt ACofS G-3 - Eighth Army 1949," Box 1068, RG 407, NACP.

23. "Cushy assignment" EML Bio, 7. The prewar condition of the Eighth Army is described in James F. Schnabel, *United States Army in the Korean War, Policy and Direction: The First Year* (Washington, D.C.: Government Printing Office, 1972), 55–57 (hereafter Schnabel, *Policy and Direction*). More detail and personal insights based on his own experience and interviews with veterans can be found in Brig. Gen. Uzal W. Ent's *Fighting on the Brink: Defense of the Pusan Perimeter* (Paducah, Ky.: Turner Publishing, 1996), 8–15.

24. Transition from occupation duty: General Headquarters, Far East Command, *Annual Historical Report, 1 January 1950–31 October 1950*, Entry 429, Box 346, RG 409, NACP, 6. Training program: Tyner to Lynch, 7 December 1998, 2; Schnabel, *Policy and Direction*, 55–56; Clay Blair, *The Forgotten War: America in Korea, 1950–1953* (New York: Crown, 1987; repr., Doubleday Anchor, 1989), 47–50; Eugene M. Landrum, letter to Roy E. Appleman, received 23 November 1953, Folder, "Letters used in revision," Box 746, "CMH Appleman," RG 319, NACP (hereafter Landrum to Appleman, 23 November 1953). "Effective . . . fighting team": Ent, *Fighting on the Brink*, 10. See also comments by Thomas J. Marnane, who was Eighth Army secretary of the General Staff in 1950, record of interview with Thomas J. Marnane, Box 52, "Alphabetical Files, J-M," Blair Collection, MHI (hereafter Marnane interview).

25. Blair, *The Forgotten War*, 48–50.

26. Colonel (Ret.) Layton C. Tyner, letter to Brig. Gen. Eugene M. Lynch, 11 March 2000 (provided to the writer by Brigadier General Lynch).

27. Ibid.; War Diary, Section I: Prologue, Headquarters Eighth United States Army, APO 301, 25 June–12 July 1950, xvi, Entry 429, Box 1081, RG 407, NACP.

28. Schnabel, *Policy and Direction*, 136–37; Roy E. Appleman, *South to the Naktong, North to the Yalu* in *U.S. Army in the Korean War* (Washington, D.C.: Government Printing Office, 1961), 110–11; enclosure 1 to Collier letter.

29. Appleman, *South to the Naktong*, 112; Layton C. Tyner, letter to Eugene M. Lynch, 11 March 2000 (provided to the writer by Brigadier General Lynch), 4; Eugene M. Lynch, letter to Donald W. Boose Jr., 14 December 1998, 2 (hereafter Lynch to Boose, 14 December 1998); LT. Gen. F. W. Farrell (former chief of KMAG), letter to Roy E. Appleman, 11 June 1958, Folder, "Corr-Misc," Box 745, "Appleman CMH," RG 3119, NACP. Walker sometimes also conferred directly with Republic of Korea President Syngman Rhee. Tyner to Lynch, 11 March 2000.

30. A Royal Australian Air Force fighter squadron and Royal Navy ships and aircraft began combat operations in Korea during the first week of July 1950 and Australian and Dutch warships arrived soon thereafter. But the first non-U.S. UN ground units, two battalions comprising the British 27th Infantry Brigade, did not arrive in Korea until 29 August 1950. Appleman, *South to the Naktong*, 382–83; James A. Field Jr., *History of United States Naval Operations, Korea* (Washington, D.C.: Government Printing Office, 1962), 55–57, 125; Robert O'Neill, *Australia in the Korean War 1950–53*, vol. 1, *Strategy and Diplomacy* (Canberra: Australian Government Publishing Service, 1981), 51–55, 62.

31. The 1st Cavalry Division retained its title and horse cavalry traditions, but since 1942 had been organized and equipped as an infantry division.

32. Appleman, *South to the Naktong* 148–49; Landrum, letter to Appleman, 23 November 1953; Ent, *Fighting on the Brink*, 58.

33. Landrum, letter to Appleman, 23 November 1953.

34. Appleman, *South to the Naktong*, 148–49; Landrum, letter to Appleman, 23 November 1953. The fundamental idea of a defense of the Pusan Perimeter (and an amphibious counterattack at Inch'on) was not original with either MacArthur or Walker. In 1948 the Army Staff G-4 Plans Division developed a series of strategic logistical studies. One of these, SL-17 (completed in June 1950), envisioned such a defense and counterattack following an enemy attack across the 38th parallel. Copies of SL-17 were sent to Far East Command Headquarters immediately after the North Korean attack. See the letter by Col. (Ret.) Donald McB. Curtis in *Army* 35, no. 1 (July 1985): 5.

35. Walker's delay to and defense of the Pusan Perimeter are well described in detail in Ent, *Fighting on the Brink*. See also Appleman, *South to the Naktong*, 109–487, and Blair, *The Forgotten War*, 143–264.

36. Department of the Army, FM 100-5, *Operations* (Washington, D.C.: Department of the Army, 1993), 9-3, 9-4. In 1950, this type of defense had no official name, but was unofficially called a "positional" or "rigid" defense. Department of the Army, FM 100-5, *Field Service Regulations: Operations* (Washington, D.C.: Government Printing Office, 15 June 1944), 120–40; Uzal W. Ent, "With Their Backs to the Wall: Defending the Pusan Perimeter," *Command Magazine*, no. 38 (July 1996): 47.

37. Ent, "With Their Backs to the Wall," 47.

38. While the term "mobile defense" did not appear in Field Manual 100-5 in 1950, there was provision for "Defense on a Wide Front" which envisioned strong points along the main line of resistance backed up with mobile reserves (FM 100-5, August 1949, 140–42). The armored concept of mobile defense was described in Department of the Army, FM 17-100, *Armored Division and Combat Command* (Washington, D.C.: Government Printing Office, 1949), 178, 181–95. The mobile defense was established in Army doctrine when FM 100-5 was revised in 1953. See Department of the Army, Draft FM 100-5, *Field Service Regulations: Operations* (Washington, D.C.: Department of the Army, 1953), 194–96, 198–200. The concept, essentially unchanged, is still Army doctrine. See FM 3-0, August 2001, paras. 8-14 through 8-19. Brigadier General Ent discusses the issue of the mobile defense in Korea in 1950 in "With Their Backs to the Wall," 46–48.

39. Ent, "With Their Backs to the Wall," 47; Tyner to Lynch, 7 December 1998, 2, 4.

40. Tyner to Lynch, 7 December 1998, 1–5; Lynch to Boose, 14 December 1998, letter, 1–3. "Old Timer": Eighth Army War Diary, Section III, PIO Report, 25 July 1950, Entry 429, Box 1085, RG 407, NACP.

41. Appleman, *South to the Naktong*, 335; notes from Maj. Gen. Eugene M. Landrum, rec'd 28 June 54, field in correspondence between Eugene M. Landrum and Roy E. Appleman in Folder, "XVI The First Battle of the Naktong Bulge," Box 744, "CMH Appleman," RG 319, NACP; Landrum letter, 28 June 1954. After August 1950, when Corps U.S. corps headquarters were activated in the Eighth Army, Walker began the practice of calling the corps commanders each night. Tyner to Lynch, 11 March 2000.

42. Appleman, *South to the Naktong*, 392; Marnane interview; Tyner to Lynch, 7 December 1998, 2–4.

43. Brigadier General Eugene M. Lynch, Walker's pilot during the Pusan Perimeter battles, received an indelible impression of Landrum's "knowledge of tactics and combat techniques" and his key role in "developing sound tactical options for Walker, and also in analyzing the alternatives available." General Lynch argues that "much of 8th Army's success in the first months was due to Landrum's thinking and planning. He, more than any other officer I ever met, taught me the true meaning of the principles of war and fundamentals of warfare." Brig. Gen. Eugene M. Lynch, letter to Col. (Ret.) Donald W. Boose Jr., postmarked 18 March 2000 (hereafter Lynch to Boose, 18 March 2000).

44. Ent, *Fighting on the Brink*, 108, 118; Blair, *Forgotten War*, 36.

45. Memorandum for the Record, 9 August 1950, by Lt. Col. Frank W. Moorman, initialed by Lt. Gen. Matthew Ridgway, Folder, "Personal Correspondence Aug to Oct 1950," Box 16, Matthew B. Ridgway Papers, MHI. Ent provides an assessment and rebuttal of the colonel's report in *Fighting on the Brink*, 161–63.

46. Tyner to Lynch, 7 December 1998, 4.

47. Blair, *The Forgotten War*, 185–90; official biography, Maj. Gen. Leven Cooper Allen, USA, MHI; Tyner to Lynch, 7 December 1998, 4,5; EUSAK General Order 52, 4 September 1950, Enclosure 15 to EUSAK War Diary 1–30 September 1950, Sec. I, Summary, Box 1102, Entry 429, RG 407, NACP.

48. Blair, *The Forgotten War*, 645.

49. Ent, "With Their Backs to the Wall," 56. By September 15 EUSAK, including the ROK Army, outnumbered the KPA attacking the Pusan Perimeter approximately two to one: 140,000 vs. 70,000. Appleman, *South to the Naktong*, 547.

50. Appleman, *Disaster in Korea*, 390–93

51. Tyner to Lynch, 7 December 1998, 3; Ridgway notes on typescript, "Some Questions on the Korean War to Gen. Ridgway: Ltr. 11 May 84," Folder, "Correspondence with Gen. Ridgway and Gen. McCaffrey," Box 20, Roy Appleman Collection, MHI.

52. Blair, *The Forgotten War*, 644–45; Official Army Register, I, United States Army Active and Retired Lists (Washington, D.C.: Government Printing Office, 1954), 899.

CHRONOLOGY OF EDWARD M. ALMOND

12 Dec 1892	Born in Luray, Virginia.
15 Jun 1915	Graduated from Virginia Military Institute (VMI).
30 Nov 1916	Commissioned second lieutenant.
25 Jun 1917	Promoted to captain.
June 1918	Commanded 12th Machine Gun Battalion, 4th Division, France.
4 Aug 1918	Received fragmentation wounds to the head near Reims, France.
20 Oct 1918	Promoted to temporary major.
July 1919	Returned to America and awarded the Silver Star.
20 Jan 1920	Reduced to captain as part of postwar reduction in forces.
Oct 1923–Jan 1924	Attended Infantry School, Fort Benning, Georgia. Remained as tactics instructor until 1928.
7 Aug 1928	Promoted to major.
1928–30	Attended Command and General Staff College, Fort Leavenworth, Kansas.
1930	Assigned to the 45th Infantry Regiment.
1933–34	Attended Army War College; upon completion assigned to War Department, Military Intelligence Division, Latin American Section.
1 Sep 1938	Promoted to lieutenant colonel.
1938–39	Attended Air Corps Tactical School, Maxwell Field, Montgomery, Alabama.
1939–40	Attended Naval War College, Newport, Rhode Island.
1941	Assigned assistant chief of staff, G-3, VI Corps.
14 Oct 1941	Promoted to colonel.
Jan 1942	Assigned as chief of staff, VI Corps.
13 Mar 1942	Promoted to brigadier general and assigned as assistant division commander, 93rd Infantry Division, Fort Huachuca, Arizona.
10 Sept 1942	Promoted to major general and assigned as commanding general, 92nd Infantry Division.

1944–45	Combat in Italy.
17 Sep 1945	Assigned as commanding general, 2nd Infantry Division. Training for the invasion of Japan.
Jun 1946	Assigned as assistant chief of staff, personnel, Armed Forces Pacific Command (later Far Eastern Command).
Nov 1946	Elevated to deputy chief of staff, Far Eastern Command.
Feb 1949	Elevated to chief of staff, Far Eastern Command.
24 Jul 1950	Dual-hatted as chief of staff FEC and chief of staff, United Nations Command.
26 Aug 1950	Assigned as commanding general, X Corps, while retaining chief of staff functions.
13 Feb 1951	Promoted to lieutenant general.
April 1951	Relinquished duties of FEC chief of staff. Remained commanding general, X Corps.
July 1951	Assigned as commandant, U.S. Army War College, Carlisle Barracks, Pennsylvania.
1 Jan 1953	Retired from active duty.
1953	Worked for Executive Life Insurance Company of Alabama.
1961–68	Member, Board of Trustees, Virginia Military Institute.
1968–69	President, Board of Trustees, Virginia Military Institute.
11 Jun 1979	Died in San Antonio, Texas.

Edward M. Almond

William Van Husen

T his book examines the principal staff officers whose function was to provide two-way flow of communication between the commander and his subordinate units. The chief of staff also functions as an organizer and planner of combat missions. What a chief of staff is *not* is a combat commander. Ludendorff, Gaffey, Sokolovsky, and others held command positions during their careers, but when they were assigned to a staff position they relinquished their command duties. This was not the case with Edward "Ned" Almond. During the Korean War he developed the plans for a complex amphibious landing and then functioned as a key commander in the execution, while simultaneously retaining the duties of the chief of staff of a joint service unified command.

Edward Almond was born in Luray, Virginia, on 12 December 1892. He attended Virginia Military Institute where he graduated in 1915, third in his class. In November 1916 he was commissioned a second lieutenant. He shipped off to France, where he commanded the 12th Machine Gun Battalion of the 4th Infantry Division. In France Almond participated in the Aisne-Marne and the Meuse-Argonne battles. He finished World War I as a major.

Almond returned to the United States in July 1919 and was assigned as professor of military science and tactics and director of Reserve Officers Training Corps (ROTC) at the Marion Institute in Alabama. Because of the postwar draw-down, he was reduced to captain, returning to the rank of major only in 1928. In 1924 he attended the Infantry School at Fort Benning,

Georgia, and after completion of the course he remained at the school as an automatic weapons instructor.

In 1930 Almond attended the Army Command and General Staff College before being assigned to the Philippines, where he commanded a Filipino battalion under the 45th Infantry Regiment. In 1933 he returned stateside to attend the Army War College. Upon completion, he was assigned to the Military Intelligence Division of the War Department. Almond attended the Army Air Corps Tactical School in 1939 and the Naval War College in 1940, then returned to the War Department General Staff.

In 1941 Almond was assigned as G-3 (Operations) of VI Corps and promoted to colonel. Shortly thereafter he became the chief of staff of the corps. In March 1942 Almond was promoted to brigadier general and assigned as assistant commander of the 93rd Infantry Division, a segregated unit of African American soldiers with white officers. Four months later, U.S. Army chief of staff Gen. George C. Marshall selected Almond to command the 92nd Infantry Division, another segregated unit. The 92nd Infantry Division saw action in Italy in 1944 and 1945. During an assault on Massa, Italy, in February 1945, the 92nd Infantry Division was forced to retreat. After the action the U.S. Army determined that its performance was substandard and the division was broken up and reorganized.

Almond's strongly held belief that "Negroes won't fight" explained his division's failure in his mind. Many in the U.S. Army at the time shared that belief. Most military historians, however, now agree that the main reason for the failure of the 92nd Infantry Division was the poor leadership of its white officers, many of whom were poor performers and were assigned to that division as a result.[1]

In 1944 personal tragedy struck Almond twice. On 25 June 1944 Maj. Thomas T. Galloway, a pilot with the Army Air Forces and Almond's son-in-law, was shot down and killed over St. Lô, France. In addition to Almond's daughter, Margaret, Galloway left behind a small son. Nine months later, on 19 March 1945, Almond's son, Capt. Edward M. Almond Jr., was killed while his unit, Company L, 167th Infantry Regiment, 45th Infantry Division, was engaged with the 17th Panzergrenadier Division. His only son's death left Almond shaken and embittered.[2]

In June 1946 Almond was assigned as assistant chief of staff for personnel to General of the Army Douglas MacArthur's Armed Forces Pacific Command, later redesignated the Far Eastern Command. Almond previously had turned down an assignment as military attaché to the Soviet Union because of his deep resentment of the Communist government.[3] MacArthur took an almost immediate liking to Almond. By that November Almond became deputy chief of staff, and in February 1949 he became the chief of staff of General Headquarters, Far Eastern Command (GHQ-FEC).

Following the outbreak of hostilities on the Korean peninsula, one of Almond's initiatives was the establishment on 14 July 1950 of the GHQ Target Group. The group

> consisted of a senior member from G-2 [intelligence] serving as chairman, an Air Force member, a Navy member from the Joint Strategic Plans and Operations Group, and a member of G-3 operations group. They advised on the employment of Navy and Air Force offensive airpower in accordance with the day-to-day situation; recommended air targets or target areas; recommended measures to ensure coordinated use of available air power; and maintained a continuing analysis of target systems and priorities assigned.[4]

The GHQ Target Group, in coordination with the Far East Air Force (FEAF) Target Committee, did the groundwork and made the recommendations to the FEC Target Selection Committee. That committee developed the interdiction programs designed to cut the flow of reinforcements and supplies to the (North) Korean People's Army (KPA) operating in South Korea.

Fifth Air Force and FEAF commander Lt. Gen. George E. Stratemeyer had problems dealing with FEC staff, and Almond in particular. Early in the war army officers dominated the FEC staff most having little experience with air force doctrine or operations. In running the war from Tokyo, Almond ordered all requests for air support to go through GHQ before passing them on to FEAF. As one would imagine, this produced unacceptable delays between air requests and actual air operations. MacArthur saw the fallacy of allowing army officers to run air force operations. Because of his confidence in Stratemeyer, MacArthur allowed him to run air force operations as he saw fit. By early August 1950, the FEAF Target Committee was providing most of the target identification in the theater. Almond's GHQ Target Group, meanwhile, had problems prioritizing target selection. To them every target was identified as "critical." The FEAF Target Committee, in coordination with the field commanders on the ground in Korea, made better use of air resources (air force, navy, and allied) by identifying those targets that were truly "critical." As a result, GHQ Target Group became redundant and subsequently was absorbed by FEAF Target Committee.

Thereafter, GHQ provided representatives from G-3 and G-4 (logistics) to the FEAF Target Committee.[5]

On 24 July 1950 Almond became "dual-hatted" as the chief of staff, U.S. FEC, and as chief of staff of the multinational United Nations Command (UNC). This was not an unusual arrangement, since in combined commands the overall commander also usually serves as head of his own nation's contingent. In Europe, for example, NATO's Supreme Allied Commander, Europe, is also the commander in chief (CinC) of the U.S. European Command. In 1950 MacArthur was both the CinC FEC and the CinC UNC. It was a logical extension of this command arrangement for MacArthur's chief of staff to be similarly dual-hatted. On 26 August, however, Almond assumed a third "hat" when he was given command of U.S. X Corps.[6] This was an unprecedented arrangement for any military organization. As chief of staff, Almond was responsible for planning Operation Chromite, the amphibious landing at Inch'on on the west coast of Korea, 30 kilometers from Seoul.[7] But as commander of X Corps, he also would directly command the landing force.[8] Thus, the roles of chief of staff and subordinate unit commander were combined under a single officer.

Prior to the landings the Eighth U.S. Army in Korea (EUSAK), commanded by Lt. Gen. Walton H. Walker, sat pinned into the Pusan Perimeter in the southeast corner of the country. Operationally, all U.S. Army forces should have come under EUSAK. MacArthur, however, retained the X Corps commander as his chief of staff so that Almond would report directly to FEC in Japan and not through EUSAK. This was a breech of the principle of unity of command, and it naturally produced a great deal of friction between Almond and Walker. One could make the argument that given MacArthur's ego, unity of command was maintained under MacArthur himself as overall commander in chief of U.S. and Allied forces in Korea. History recalls the accomplishments of MacArthur, not Almond, Walker, or even Ridgway until after MacArthur was relieved. As an interim measure, in the meantime, MacArthur appointed Maj. Gen. Doyle Hickey as acting chief of staff of FEC.

On 26 July, while acting in his capacity as FEC chief of staff, Almond had received a report from Walker stating that the situation of EUSAK was grim. Walker wanted to move Eighth Army headquarters from Taegu to Pusan immediately. He felt the enemy was so close that vital equipment and communications were endangered. His plan was to withdraw and redeploy along the Naktong River. Almond told Walker he would pass the request on to MacArthur, but he personally thought a move to Pusan would have a bad effect on both EUSAK and the Republic of Korea Army (ROKA). Withdrawal of U.S. forces would send a negative signal to ROKA that the Americans would not stay and fight, a factor North Korea certainly hoped for.[9]

Almond told MacArthur the situation in Korea was critical and urged MacArthur to go to Korea at once to meet with Walker. The next day MacArthur and Almond met with Walker in Taegu. MacArthur impressed upon Walker that the withdrawals must cease and that there would "no Korean Dunkirk." "MacArthur gave Walker a message: The Eighth Army was expendable. Regardless of how many men perished, and under what circumstances, it must stand or die—or stand and die."[10] "Stand or die" was Walker's order to all elements of EUSAK. The Pusan Perimeter was established on 4 August, and with the arrival later that month of the 1st Marine Brigade to secure the western portion of the perimeter against the North Korean 6th Infantry Division, the perimeter held until the second front was established at Inch'on.

The planning and execution of Operation Chromite were nearly flawless. The landings commenced at 0633 hours on 15 September, when the 5th Marine Brigade landed at Wolmi-do on the Inch'on peninsula. By nightfall the peninsula was secured. Almond's objective was to liberate Seoul by 25 September. He was so obsessed with this goal that he issued a communiqué at midnight on the twenty-fifth stating that Seoul had been liberated. In fact, street fighting raged on and it wasn't until the twenty-seventh that the capitol building was finally secured. On 29 September MacArthur presided in a ceremony at the capitol building marking the liberation of Seoul.

By 27 September elements of X Corps and Eighth Army's I Corps linked up near Osan. What had appeared as a near-hopeless situation for the UNC on the Korean peninsula in July turned favorable by that October, as UN forces crossed the 38th parallel and pursued the retreating KPA. In less than two months from the conception of Operation Chromite, X Corps had succeeded in regaining Seoul, had linked up with EUSAK, and had cut off the KPA in South Korea. The daring landings at Inch'on and the race to Seoul caught the KPA completely by surprise and forced North Korea to abandon any hope conquering South Korea. The success came despite the friction between army and Marine commanders, particularly between Almond and Maj. Gen. Oliver P. Smith, commander of the 1st Marine Division.

One reason that MacArthur kept his chief of staff as X Corps commander was the notion that should the Inch'on landing succeed and EUSAK and X Corps were successful in defeating the KPA, the war would be over by

Christmas. MacArthur then would regain his chief of staff back in Tokyo after the end of hostilities—hence Hickey's interim appointment as FEC chief of staff. Nonetheless, Hickey; Brig. Gen. Edward Wright, FEC G-3; and Maj. Gen. George L. Eberle, FEC G-4 all believed strongly that Almond's X Corps should have been integrated into the Eighth Army following the Inch'on landing and the liberation of Seoul.

Following Inch'on MacArthur laid the foundations for his next major operation, the movement of X Corps to Wonsan, a port city 175 kilometers north of the 38th parallel on the east coast of the Korean peninsula. From the very start of the planning, however, debate raged between Almond and Rear Adm. James H. Doyle, the commander of Amphibious Force Far East (Task Force 90). Ironically, Almond wanted to make an amphibious landing, while Doyle believed X Corps would make better time traveling overland. He argued that the waters around Wonsan would have to be cleared of mines. Maps and information on North Korea's east coast were sketchy at best. X Corps would have to re-embark at Inch'on, sail around the peninsula, and land at Wonsan. Doyle believed it would take a month.

Almond would not be deterred. He argued that resupplying X Corps from Wonsan would take pressure off Inch'on's port. An east coast landing also would hasten the advance to P'yongyang, with the Eighth Army advancing from the south and the X Corps driving from the east. Additionally, a land march over mountainous terrain would take a heavy toll on equipment as well as troops, and would invite opposing forces to launch ambush attacks on UN forces from the mountain passes. Almond saw the 1st Marine Division engaged in hard fighting in the hills near Uijongbu, north of Seoul, and realized his X Corps would be in for more of the same if it attempted an overland movement to Wonsan.

Almond prevailed and Operation Tailboard began on 7 October with the loading of the 1st Marine Division. The ships set sail on 15 October and arrived at Wonsan harbor on the twentieth. As Doyle predicted, the harbor was laden with mines. Five days later X Corps landed at Wonsan and was met by ROKA's Capital and 3rd Divisions, which had secured the port two weeks earlier.[11]

Upon completion of the landing, Almond commenced the drive north to the Yalu River, the boundary between North Korea and the People's Republic of China. The ROKA 26th Infantry Regiment was tasked to drive up the coast. The 7th Infantry Division advanced along the Iwon–Pukch'ong–Hyesanjin corridor, and the 1st Marine Division advanced northward toward the Changjin (Chosin) Reservoir. The 3rd Infantry Division was the last unit to arrive and had the mission of securing the Wonsan-Hungnam area, keeping the lines of communications open and the port facilities available.

By 21 November, three weeks after landing at Wonsan, the 7th Infantry Division was in sight of the Yalu River near the town of Hyesanjin, having made a 200-mile advance over mountainous terrain in subzero winter conditions. Excited, Almond flew there for a photographed meeting with the 7th Infantry Division commander Maj. Gen. David G. Barr and others in view of Chinese forces across the river. (Whether this was intended or not, it certainly taunted the Chinese.) MacArthur congratulated Almond and had him pass kudos to Barr and the 7th Infantry Division. But the drive to the Yalu had stretched Barr's supply lines and left his flanks exposed, which would prove disastrous in the coming days.

In late November the Chinese People's Volunteer Army (CPVA) crossed the Yalu River in two army groups numbering more than one-quarter-million troops. The 13th Army Group, with eight divisions, attacked Walker's Eighth Army in the west. The 9th Army Group, with twelve divisions, went after Almond's X Corps in the east. (By this time, X Corps was virtually the size of a numbered army, with the attachment of the ROKA I Corps from the Eighth Army to X Corps.) On 27 November elements of the Chinese East Liaodong Forty-Second Army engaged X Corps' 1st Marine Division. The Marines repelled the attack, defeating the 124th People's Liberation Army Division near Sudong and the 126th PLA Division near Hagaru-ri. The Chinese responded by deploying the PLA Twentieth and Twenty-Seventh Armies in the Changjin Reservoir area with the Twenty-Sixth Army held in reserve. This proved to be an overwhelming force for the 1st Marine Division and X Corps. The heavy Chinese attack took its toll on both UNC fronts. In the west the ROKA II Corps and the U.S. 2nd and 25th Infantry Divisions were mauled badly. The Eighth Army was pushed back below the 38th parallel.

In the east, X Corps, still a separate command from the Eighth Army, was driving north to the Yalu River when the Chinese attacked. As noted previously, the first units to meet the CPVA were elements from 1st Marine and 7th Infantry Divisions near the Changjin Reservoir. The fighting was intense. X Corps was pushed back from Yudam-ni and Hagaru-ri, down along the Koto-ri to Hamhung road.

On 28 November MacArthur summoned both Almond and Walker to Tokyo to discuss alternatives. Following the meeting, and knowing Almond could not sustain a prolonged campaign, MacArthur ordered the evacuation of X Corps from the Hamhung-Hungnam region to the Pusan area in southeastern Korea.

A naval evacuation, led by Doyle's TF 90, began at Hungnam on 10 December. The 3rd Infantry Division had the mission of holding the perimeter around the port of Hungnam, thereby securing an orderly evacuation of men and materiel. The 1st Marine Division was the first to go out. They had been in virtually continuous combat since the CPVA attacks. The next were the 7th Infantry Division and the ROKA divisions. To cover the evacuation of the last battalions of the 3rd Infantry Division, cruisers and destroyers of Vice Adm. Arthur D. Struble's Seventh Fleet provided supporting fires. This also provided cover for demolition units to destroy docks and port facilities, thereby denying their use to the enemy. The evacuation was completed on 24 December. As a result, Almond was able to withdraw more than 100,000 military personnel and 90,000 civilian refugees. Additionally, more than 17,000 tanks and vehicles and some 350,000 tons of cargo were sea-lifted out.

During the battle X Corps had tied down more than 120,000 CPVA troops, easing the pressure on Eighth Army's right flank. The CPVA 9th Army Group suffered more than 72,000 casualties, while X Corps sustained 11,500, half of which were killed or missing. On 7 December, under pressure from the U.S. Joint Chiefs of Staff in Washington, MacArthur finally placed X Corps under the Eighth Army, thereby giving EUSAK three complete corps. But the actual integration of X Corps into the Eighth Army did not take place until the completion of the evacuation to Pusan on 26 December.

By this time the 1st Marine Division had been moved to army reserve. The 2nd Infantry Division, which had been fighting north of P'yongyang, redeployed to Wonju, east of Seoul, and came under Almond's command. (Almond had established his advanced command post at Wonju.) Attached to the 2nd Infantry Division were one French and one Netherlands battalion. Additionally, the 7th Infantry Division and two ROKA divisions remained under X Corps. In April the 1st Marine Division (now commanded by Maj. Gen. Charles Thomas), rejoined X Corps, followed in May by the 3rd Infantry Division. The orderly and complete withdrawal of X Corps from Hungnam led to Almond receiving his third star the following February.

MacArthur's (and for that matter the Defense Department's) lack of trust in the effectiveness of Walker's leadership was another reason for Almond's unique combination of assignments. While in the Pusan Perimeter EUSAK's moral was poor. Walker was well known as a heavy drinker (coincidentally, his drink of choice was Johnny Walker scotch) who had frequent scrapes with colleagues and superiors. For Operation Chromite to work, MacArthur felt he needed direct reports from the field. He did not want Almond's reports filtered through Walker and the Eighth Army. Also, Almond as FEC chief of staff had clashed frequently with Walker.

With the command of U.S. ground forces in Korea divided, Walker suspected that his tenure as EUSAK commander was nearing an end. Walker, in fact, was on the verge of being relieved when he was killed in a traffic accident near Uijongbu, Korea on 23 December. That same day, U.S. Army chief of staff Gen. J. Lawton Collins, selected Lt. Gen. Matthew B. Ridgway as the new EUSAK commander. By 26 December Ridgway was at MacArthur's headquarters in Tokyo receiving his orders. On 27 December Almond flew to Ridgway's headquarters in Seoul. He reported that X Corps was reorganizing under Eighth Army command. Ridgway's orders to Almond were simple: "Fight cohesively and kill as many CCF as possible."

Ridgway told Collins he intended to be "ruthless with our general officers if they fail to measure up." One of the first to go was Maj. Gen. Robert B. McClure, commander of the 2nd Infantry Division. Ridgway sent Almond to the 2nd Infantry Division to assess its situation. Almond's report on 9 January 1951 indicated unmistakable evidence of a lack of command control by McClure. "[Almond] found artillery pieces strewn around the rear area with no protection against infiltrators. The division artillery officer was not at the front, and half of his 36 cannon were not in use. Conditions indicate not only a failure to operate in the full spirit of delay and destruction of enemy forces, but also careless control of divisional operations." Four days later, on 13 January, Almond was back at the 2nd Infantry Division, this time finding "men without gloves, sleeping bags, parkas or overcoats. Foxholes and fields of fire were poorly sited. One 57mm [gun] crew could not hit within 300 yards of a target 700 yards away."[12] Almond, with Ridgway's concurrence, relieved McClure the next day and placed his X Corps chief of staff, Maj. Gen. Clark L. Ruffner, in command of the 2nd Infantry Division. Colonel John S. Guthrie replaced Ruffner as Almond's chief of staff.

Some within the 2nd Infantry Division, including McClure's predecessor, Maj. Gen. Lawrence Keiser; the commander of the 23rd Infantry Regiment, Col. Paul Freeman; and the divisional G-3, Maurice Holden, suggested that Almond relieved McClure because of his close relationship with General Collins. Almond had blamed the army chief of staff when he first was passed over for lieutenant general. Nonetheless, McClure's replacement, Ruffner, was also a "Collins man" who had served with Collins in the 25th Infantry Division during World War II.

During the first half of 1951, X Corps operated against KPA and CPVA forces in central Korea, participating in the battles of Wonju, Chip'yong-ni, the Soyang River, and the Chinese Spring Offensive. During Operation Roundup, an assault in central Korea in preparation for the assault on Seoul, Almond ignored intelligence reports that X Corps would be the center of a major Chinese counterattack. When the attack came, it destroyed two ROKA divisions under his command and pushed the remainder of X Corps back below Hoengsong. Almond requested the 3rd Infantry Division to stabilize his front, which it did. Without the 3rd Infantry Division, Communist forces would have poured into the south, encircling the entire X Corps. By 1 June X Corps had managed disperse the equivalent of five armies numbering more than 150,000 Chinese and North Korean troops, the largest Communist force south of the Yalu River.[13] This counterattack became known as the "Battle of Soyang River" and was Almond's last major engagement as commanding general of X Corps. He relinquished command in July 1951 for rotation stateside. Communist forces casualties exceeded 65,000 Chinese and North Korean soldiers dead, while UNC casualties were 11,800, including 1,900 Americans.[14]

When MacArthur was relieved of command by President Harry Truman in April 1951, Ridgway became the commander of UNC and U.S. FEC. (Lt. Gen. James A. Van Fleet replaced Ridgway as commander of the Eighth Army.) One of Ridgway's first acts was to change the dual-position arrangement MacArthur set up with Almond. By that point, Almond was really little more than the FEC chief of staff on paper. Ridgway was sure that this arrangement was not satisfactory to either Hickey or Almond. As Ridgway later wrote,

> [MacArthur's] admiration for Almond's abilities, which I know to be well deserved and in which I fully concurred, actually made it appear that Hickey, upon whom devolved all the heavy responsibilities of the chief of staff of a major headquarters, was no more than an temporary fill-in. I am sure the arrangement was as little to Almond's taste at is was to Hickey's, but bold indeed was the subordinate who questioned such matters.[15]

Almond was a difficult character. He tended to be abusive to his subordinates both as chief of staff and X Corps commander. He was egotistical, overbearing, and tactless. His own X Corps chief of staff, Ruffner, once commented that Almond "could precipitate a crisis on a desert island with nobody else around." As previously noted, he often quarreled with Marine Maj. Gen. Oliver P. Smith, one of the key subordinates. Almond often belittled Smith and at times left him out of the decision loop during the planning of Operation

Chromite. The Almond-Smith feud raged throughout Almond's tenure as X Corps commander. On the other hand, when Major General Thomas brought the 1st Marine Division back to X Corps in April 1951, he and Almond got along superbly, to the point that at Almond's departure from Korea in July 1951, he praised Thomas as one of his best division commanders. Almond also had difficulties with Lt. Gen. Lemuel Shepherd Jr., commander of Fleet Marine Forces, Pacific. Almond had never witnessed an amphibious landing, let alone commanded one. Since such operations were the U.S. Marine Corps' specialty, it was extremely odd that Almond would alienate the division commander whose expertise should have been so valuable. As FEC chief of staff, Almond's popularity with his subordinate staff sections was virtually nonexistent. Throughout the FEC, "he was both feared and obeyed."[16]

Among his other personality quirks, Almond had strong racist inclinations, typical of many southerners of his time, but also a major handicap at the critical time when the U.S. military was just beginning the integration of the armed forces. Presumably, his beliefs about racial differences developed as he grew up in the South. They hardened during his period as commander of the 92nd Infantry Division and its failure during the Italian campaign in World War II. One particularly stark example of Almond's racism occurred in January 1951 when 2nd Infantry Division was tasked with securing the town of Wonju and the airfield south of town. The company commander leading the assault, Capt. Forest Walker, was black. Walker cleared the airfield in time for General Ridgway's plane to land. When his battalion commander, Cesidio V. Barberis, told Ridgway of Captain Walker's feat, Ridgway recommended award of the Silver Star. When Almond found out about it, he not only stopped the award process, but he also relieved Walker and reassigned him to the 3rd Battalion, 9th Infantry, an all-black unit in the rear.[17]

Despite his personality quirks, Almond was an effective commander in the field. Time and again when facing superior odds, he proved capable of holding fast, or when necessary organizing an orderly and complete withdrawal of men and materiel while inflicting greater casualties upon the enemy. During his tenure as chief of staff, Almond's organization and planning of the Inch'on landing were superb. Were it not for his bigotry and other personality quirks, Ned Almond just might have attained his fourth star.

Major General Clovis E. Byers replaced Almond as commanding general of X Corps on 13 July 1951. Almond returned to the United States as the commandant of the U.S. Army War College at Carlisle Barracks, Pennsylvania. He retired on 1 January 1953 and went to work for the Executive Life Insurance

Company of Alabama. From 1961 to 1968 he served as a member of the Board of Trustees for Virginia Military Institute and then became its president in 1968–69. Almond died on 11 June 1979 in San Antonio, Texas.

Despite Almond's not insignificant personality quirks and prejudices, he was a highly capable combat officer in three wars. In World War I he received the Silver Star and the Purple Heart. In World War II he received the Distinguished Service Medal, an Oak Leaf Cluster to the Silver Star, and the Legion of Merit. During the Korean War he received the Distinguished Service Cross with Oak Leaf Cluster, an Oak Leaf Cluster to the Distinguished Service Medal, the Distinguished Flying Cross with two Oak Leaf Clusters, and the Bronze Star Medal with V Device.

Notes

1. Before deploying to Italy, 92nd Infantry Division received nine months of training, as opposed to twelve months, the standard time frame needed to train a division prior to combat. U.S Army Military History Institute, Senior Officers Debriefing Program, Carlisle Barracks, Pa., 25 March 1975, 178.
2. Shelby L. Stanton, *America's Tenth Legion, X Corps in Korea, 1950* (Novato, Calif.: Presidio Press, 1989), 15.
3. Ibid., 16.
4. Robert Frank Futrell, *The United States Air Force in Korea, 1950–1953* (Washington, D.C.: Office of Air Force History, 1983), 50–51.
5. William T. Y'Blood, *The Three Wars of Lt. Gen. George E. Stratemeyer: His Korean War Diary* (Washington, D.C.: Air Force History and Museums Program, 1999), 54–55, 62n.
6. When Almond asked MacArthur for the name of the person to lead X Corps for the Inch'on landing, MacArthur looked up at Almond and said, "It's you." Stanton, *America's Tenth Legion,* 41.
7. An alternative landing at Wonsan would have put X Corps 135 miles from Seoul, across wooded mountains controlled by KPA forces. Also, a landing across Taegu, as General Collins proposed, would have done little more than extend EUSAK's defensive line. Retaking Seoul was paramount. Additionally, a September landing ensured that UN forces would obtain a firm hold before the Korean winter set it. MHI, Senior Officers Debriefing Program, 274–76.
8. The following are units, their commanding officers, and communications call signs assigned to X Corps ("Jade"):

   > 1st Marine Division, Maj. Gen. Oliver P. Smith, "Western"
   > 3rd Infantry Division, Maj. Gen. Robert H. Soule, "Kaiser"
   > 7th Infantry Division, Maj. Gen. David G. Barr, "Bayonet"
   > 2nd Engineer Special Brigade, Col. Joseph J. Twitty, "Wallace"
   > ROKA I Corps, Maj. Gen. Kim Paik Il, "Rogers."

Also one of his aides-de-camp was 1st Lt. (Capt.) Alexander M. Haig; Stanton, *America's Tenth Legion*, 325–26.

9. Joseph C. Goulden, *Korea, The Untold Story of the War* (New York: Times Books, 1982), 173–74.

10. Ibid.

11. Almond was given a prelude of Communist China's intervention on 29 October when the 26th Infantry Regiment (ROKA) captured sixteen Chinese soldiers near Hamhung, the first Chinese POWs of the war. MHI, Senior Officers Debriefing Program, 311.

12. Ibid., 437.

13. In his interview in 1975 Almond stated, "[T]he enemy was dispersed, disorganized, disheartened, and were being killed by every effort that our forces made. 'They are dying like flies' were my exact words." MHI, Senior Officers Debriefing Program, 368.

14. Spencer Tucker, *Encyclopedia of the Korean War* (Santa Barbara, Calif.: ABC-Clio, 2000), 37, 575.

15. Matthew B. Ridgway, *The Korean War* (Garden City, N.Y.: Doubleday, 1967), 169–70.

16. Roy E. Appleman, *South to the Naktong, North to the Yalu (June–November 1950)* in *U.S. Army in the Korean War* (Washington, D.C.: Government Printing Office, 1975), 490.

17. Walker, incidentally, happened to have been a member of the 92nd Infantry Division in Italy when Almond was commander. Clay Blair, *The Forgotten War: America in Korea 1950–1953* (New York: Times Books, 1987), 648. MHI, Senior Officers Debriefing Program, 416.

CHRONOLOGY OF WALTER T. KERWIN JR.

14 Jun 1917	Born in West Chester, Pennsylvania.
1939	Graduated U.S. Military Academy at West Point.
1939	Temporary service with 16th Infantry Regiment, Governor's Island, New York.
1939–44	Served with the 3rd Infantry Division.
1945	Assigned to War Department Staff.
1947	Assigned as student and instructor, Command and General Staff College.
1951	Served in Joint U.S. Military Mission for Aid to Turkey.
1953	Attended Armed Forces Staff College, Norfolk, Virginia.
1953	Assigned to Joint Task Force 7 (Nuclear Testing), Los Alamos Scientific Laboratory, Los Alamos, New Mexico.
1956	Attended U.S. Army War College, Carlisle Barracks, Pennsylvania.
1957	Assigned as commander, 56th Field Artillery Group, Fort Bragg, North Carolina.
1959–60	Attended National War College, Washington, D.C.
1960	Assigned as deputy director, Special Weapons, Research and Development, Department of the Army.
Aug 1961	Assigned as commander, Division Artillery, 3rd Armored Division.
1963	Assigned as chief of Nuclear Activities Branch, Operations Division, SHAPE, Paris.
Mar 1965	Assigned as commander, 3rd Armored Division.
1966	Assigned as assistant deputy chief of staff, Operations, Department of the Army.
May 1967	Assigned as chief of staff, MACV, South Vietnam.
1 Aug 1968	Assigned as commander, II Field Force, South Vietnam.
1969	Assigned as director for Civil Service Disturbance and Operations, Department of the Army.

1969	Assigned as deputy chief of staff for personnel, Department of the Army.
1973	Assigned as commander, Continental Army Command.
1973	Assigned as commander, Forces Command, Fort McPherson, Georgia.
21 Oct 1974	Assigned as vice chief of staff, U.S. Army.
1978	Retired from U.S. Army.

Walter T. Kerwin Jr.

James Jay Carafano

O n 9 June 1968, on the hot, sticky tarmac at Tan Son Nhut Air Base, South Vietnam, Gen. William "Westy" Childs Westmoreland bade farewell to his troops. He ended his tour as commander of the U.S. Military Assistance Command Vietnam (MACV) in the wake of America's greatest battle since the end of the Korean War. More than 500,000 Americans, along with South Vietnamese and other allied forces, had been embroiled in heavy combat during the harrowing Tet Offensive, when the North Vietnamese and Viet Cong launched simultaneous attacks across the country. The battles of Tet included the siege of the American base at Khe Sanh, recalling the famed but ill-fated disaster of the French garrison at Dien Bien Phu a decade earlier. As Westmoreland's plane departed in the twilight of a season of trial and turmoil, not far away at MACV headquarters the new commander, Gen. Creighton "Abe" Abrams, called for Maj. Gen. Walter "Dutch" Kerwin. Kerwin had served as MACV chief of staff throughout its most tumultuous and difficult year and he would remain as the head of Abrams' staff. Kerwin's tour under Westmoreland had been grueling and exhausting, but Abrams intended to make it even tougher. He planned big changes. Abrams said they were going to alter the course of the war, get the South Vietnamese back into the fight—and they were going to pull out of Khe Sanh. He knew he would be asking a lot from his chief of staff in the days ahead, but Abrams had never known an officer who thrived more on tough challenges and hard work. Kerwin's past had been a long tale of war and the disciplined life.

Born under the shadow of World War I in West Chester, Pennsylvania, on 14 June 1917, Walter T. Kerwin Jr. was heavily influenced in both outlook and leadership style by his life in the small rural town. Walter Jr. not only inherited his father's Pennsylvania "Dutch" nickname, but also Walter Sr.'s unshakable belief in the value of loyalty, discipline, competition, and hard work. Life was never easy for the Catholic family of modest means living in a fairly well-off Protestant community. Dutch's parents told him again and again, "if you want to get ahead you are going to have to work, and if you want to be a leader you are going to have to learn how to lead . . . you've got to make sacrifices and don't expect anything from anybody."[1]

The deprivations of the Depression years only reinforced his father's emphasis on self-reliance. They were hard times. When he was a teenager Kerwin's family could not afford to send him to Boy Scout summer camp and his father adamantly refused to borrow the money. One night while his dad was away looking for work, Kerwin and his mother walked across town to ask for a fifteen-dollar loan from a prominent local citizen who had been her high school classmate. Waiting until all his appointments had left the office, the man agreed to give her the money, but as an anonymous gift, not a loan. He didn't want anyone to find out that a Protestant was giving away money, certainly not to a Catholic. When Kerwin recalled the incident later in life he remembered it not for the unexpected act of charity, but as a reminder that such moments were few and far between. A man was expected to carry his own weight.

The Depression also shaped Kerwin's choice of a military career. Though Dutch's father had served in the Army, Walter Jr. wanted to be a doctor, but, lacking the money to pay for a college education, he sought a nomination to the U.S. Military Academy at West Point, New York. Cadets who attended the Academy got full tuition, room and board, and a small stipend from the government. After graduation the cadets received a lieutenant's commission. Established by Congress in 1802 to provide trained Army officers, the Academy had produced many of the nation's most famous military leaders including Ulysses S. Grant, John "Blackjack" Pershing, and Douglas MacArthur. Following in their footsteps, Kerwin arrived at the historic, fortress-like academy in the summer of 1935 for "beast barracks," the intense summer training subjected to the incoming class. His upbringing had prepared him well for the difficult life of a first-year "plebe," including hazing and harsh treatment liberally dispensed by upper-class cadets.

Kerwin discovered he liked West Point's challenge and stern discipline, though he found the Academy offered an ambivalent education. He thought the leadership training was quite good, but recalled that military and academic instruction proved to be of only marginal value for the Army's future leaders. West Point, like the army at large, had barely recognized the concepts of modern mechanized warfare. Cadets still conducted cavalry drills on horseback in the Academy's cavernous riding hall. Nor did cadets learn much about the larger aspects of war and international relations. "I suppose if I had come out of there [West Point]," General Kerwin recalled, "and had been asked to discuss the geopolitical strategic parts of the world, I would have been flabbergasted. We just didn't get to that sort of thing." West Point reinforced the fundamental importance of values and the attributes of selfless leadership, but provided only a smattering of the skills and knowledge needed for a lifelong career as a military officer. Kerwin had little expectation that he would need training as a future general or expertise in the higher levels of war; such possibilities seemed utterly remote from the thoughts of a young officer in the dawn of his career.

Kerwin graduated from West Point in 1939 and received a commission in the field artillery. His father had served in the artillery during World War I, but Kerwin selected the branch for his own reasons. The young lieutenant thought it would put him at the center of things. "I think you get a better idea of the entire capability of the army as an artilleryman," he reasoned. "First, you are a forward observer and you are working with the infantry, or you are working with the cavalry. Your whole fire planning is [an] integration of all the battle planning...you also work with the integration of the air battle plan. You really have a better opportunity to see what the whole thing is about."

Commissioned before the army buildup for World War II, Kerwin initially had little chance to practice the artillery trade. In his first tactical assignment as part of the 3rd Infantry Division, ammunition for the unit's 155mm howitzers was so scarce that when a single artillery battery fired its annual service practice most of the regiment's officers turned out to watch. Kerwin's life as an officer during the interwar period seemed unexceptional as he prepared to work his way slowly up through positions as a battery and battalion officer. Advancement in the division came at a metered, languid pace. His battery commander was over fifty. The division's senior leadership averaged almost sixty years old. The division's chief of staff was thirty-five years Kerwin's senior, graduating from West Point thirteen years before he was born.

Within a year the pace began to quicken. Returning from a lakeside picnic on the afternoon of 7 December 1941, Kerwin learned of the Japanese bombing at Pearl Harbor. Changes quickly followed as senior officers were moved out and young officers moved up with unprecedented quickness. Over the next two years, Kerwin received promotions that took him from lieutenant to lieutenant colonel. He became the division artillery operations officer, a post normally reserved for a very experienced senior officer.

In November 1942 the 3rd Infantry Division landed in North Africa, beginning a campaign that carried it to Sicily, Italy, southern France, and Germany, covering more miles, serving more days in combat, and suffering more casualties than any other American combat division in Europe. Kerwin's wartime experiences proved to be an extraordinary education in the military arts, in part due to the great responsibilities given to young officers, but more because of the tremendous variety and complexity of missions undertaken by the division, including four amphibious landings, multiple river crossings, mountain warfare, and fast-moving exploitation maneuvers. No operation was more trying than the landings at Anzio, Italy, in 1944.[2] After an almost effortless landing the Allies found the Germans holding the Alban Hills, blocking the route to Rome, and offering an unrestricted view of the beachhead. The advantage in observation made artillery fire a significant threat to Allied troops.

Anzio proved to be one of the defining moments in Kerwin's professional life. A month after the initial landings, the invasion commander was fired and Kerwin's division's commander, Maj. Gen. Lucian K. Truscott, was ordered to take over. One of the first tasks Truscott set for himself was doing something about the German artillery that continually peppered the beachhead from the Alban Hills. Truscott ordered Kerwin to report to the corps headquarters. In the damp and gloomy wine cellars and catacombs that housed the command post, Truscott gave him a simple order: organize all the artillery in the corps and silence the German guns. He then turned to the brigadier general who commanded the corps artillery and said, "You go along with Kerwin and make sure they do what he says."[3] Kerwin's plan massed twenty-three battalions and fired up to 20,000 rounds a day, banishing the scourge of artillery fire from the heights above.[4] In a few weeks, the German High Command in Italy gave up any hope of reducing the beachhead and pushing the Allies back into the sea. Truscott moved the corps headquarters above ground and began to make plans for going on the offensive.

Kerwin recalled his success not just as a great personal achievement, but an important lesson in leadership. He found Truscott's willingness to place such tremendous responsibility on a junior officer remarkable, though it was typical of the way the general got things done. Pick competent people. Teach them what they need to know. Tell them what you want. Trust them to get the job done. Don't worry about the details. Truscott's approach dovetailed well with Kerwin's own notions of what made good leader—men who were competent, selfless, and resolute. Truscott became a role model whom Kerwin emulated throughout his career.

World War II ended for Kerwin in Mutzig, France. He was seriously wounded while reconnoitering a German stronghold.[5] The crippling leg injury was so severe that Kerwin couldn't walk, and doctors wanted him to consider having the leg amputated. He refused. Surgery at Walter Reed Army Hospital in Washington, D.C., proved sufficiently successful to return Kerwin to active duty, though poor circulation in the leg would trouble him for the rest of his life.

Back on regular duty, like many of his contemporaries Kerwin received his formal senior military education only after the war ended. In 1947 he attended the Army's Command and General Staff College at Fort Leavenworth, Kansas, first as a student and then as an instructor. The Staff College was supposed to school mid-grade officers in the fundamentals of planning large-scale operations and staff planning. Like many of his fellow students, Kerwin found that experience had outstripped education. The instruction consisted of "dull and boring" auditorium lectures, Kerwin recalled. Meanwhile, every veteran thought he was an expert, offering solutions to every tactical problem reflecting his own personal experience, whether it was island hopping in the Pacific or large-scale European maneuvers. The course material only reinforced these preconceptions, replaying World War II with an emphasis on field army operations and little thought that the army might be required to conduct other missions in the postwar world. Kerwin also attended the Armed Forces Staff College in Norfolk, Virginia. He found the course there largely redundant, with classes on joint operations differing little from Leavenworth's stale teachings on army tactics.

Kerwin was also a student at the Army War College at Carlisle Barracks, Pennsylvania, followed later by attendance at the National War College in Washington, D.C. The war colleges are the American military's most senior formal schools, designed to teach officers to think at the operational and strategic levels of war. But after his education in real war with the 3rd Infantry Division, Kerwin found the schools uninspiring, valuing the experiences more for the friendships and spirited informal debates between students that inspired critical thinking and cemented professional relationships that lasted throughout his career.

Interspersed between bouts of military education, Kerwin had a wide variety of operational assignments, including a tour on the War Department Staff, an overseas assignment, work on developing tactical nuclear munitions at Los Alamos Laboratory, New Mexico, and overseeing nuclear testing in the Pacific. None of these duties was considered a "premier" assignment, and since he had missed combat duty during the Korean War, the field artillery branch personnel management officers in Washington assured Kerwin that his career was a "dead dog." In fact, as he prepared to graduate from the Army War College, he had no projected assignment. Kerwin, on the other hand, had no doubts about his abilities or his value to the army. The week before graduation he asked for permission to go the Pentagon in Washington, to talk personally with the army's chief personnel officer. Now a full colonel, Kerwin rehearsed his speech all the way down to Washington. "I had the highest efficiency average of any artillery officer in my peer group," he recalled, "with over two years in combat in a infantry division and I had been to more schools than anybody else. . . . I just considered it inconceivable that I didn't have a job." After hearing Kerwin's speech, the general offered him the only vacant assignment available, commander of an artillery group at Fort Bragg, North Carolina, part of the Army's elite XVIII Airborne Corps.

A successful command at Fort Bragg led to a series of more prestigious assignments, including promotion to general officer rank and division command. After a decade of successful assignments, Kerwin reported to MACV in May 1967 to serve as the chief of staff. The assignment was no accident. Kerwin had served under MACV's deputy commander General Abrams before.

In 1961, newly appointed to the rank of brigadier general, Kerwin was assigned to command the 3rd Armored Division Artillery in Germany. The division commander was Creighton Abrams. An authentic World War II hero, the cigar-chomping, plain-spoken Abrams' rise through the postwar ranks was certain and steady. He carried with him a reputation as a fierce and difficult boss. "Many [officers] were afraid of Abe," one officer recalled. "They were actually afraid of him."[6] Kerwin recalled meeting Abrams for the first time shortly after he took command of the 3rd Division Artillery. From Abrams' outer office, Kerwin could hear the general loudly complaining, obviously upset about the results of recent readiness exercise. Kerwin thought he should come back another time, but was told that would be unwise. The interview that followed was brief. Abrams said almost nothing. After a few awkward minutes Kerwin asked, "Is there anything you want me to do?" Abrams shot back, "Aren't you a general?" Dismissed, Kerwin left shaking his head and thinking, "I'm not long for this job."[7]

Despite Kerwin's initial impression, the two officers quickly earned each other's respect and confidence. Kerwin found that Abrams' command style was much like Truscott's. "They were both blunt, but they were people-oriented, and they listened," Kerwin recalled. "If you knew what you were doing, they'd leave you alone. If you didn't, they would teach you. . . . Abe was a great teacher. He would tell stories. Each story had a lesson."[8] Over the course of Abrams' tenure as division commander he became Kerwin's friend and mentor.

In 1967 Abrams was selected to replace Westmoreland as commander of MACV and he selected Kerwin to serve as his chief of staff. The two departed for South Vietnam on three days' notice. Major General Kerwin arrived in Vietnam as the U.S. military's participation in the war was increasing substantially. While military operations expanded, the theater's complicated organizational arrangements strained to keep up. Though General Westmoreland was the military leader most visibly connected with the war, he did not directly control all the forces involved. The air and naval forces, for example, in part answered to the theater commander in chief (CinC) in Hawaii. Kerwin was appalled by the complexity and inefficiency of the organization. "The Marines," Kerwin observed when he arrived, "were sitting up there in I Corps almost entirely by themselves. The bombing and other fire support was being run out of many other organizations. It was split . . . initially MACV was in a small headquarters downtown [Saigon], and in my opinion," he recalled, "not organized to get the best out of everything." The staff was simply not getting the most out of the preponderance of power available from the various forces crammed into the theater. Theater rotation policies that moved officers through the MACV staff in less than a year didn't help. "In retrospect," Kerwin recalled, "the one-year tours was a mistake." The staffs were never as cohesive and competent as the ones he had seen during World War II.

When he took over Kerwin saw two major obstacles in trying to manage the large and unwieldy staff ensconced in an office building in Saigon. MACV's rotation policy was his biggest headache. In practice, officers spent far less than a year on the staff. The time given to in-and-out processing and rest-and-recuperation leave shaved more than a month off the tour. Halfway through their assignments many officers rotated to combat duties with field units. At best, most served only four or five months at their desks in Saigon. Kerwin wanted to change the staff policy and prohibit officers from leaving the staff during their year-long tour, but he faced overwhelming opposition. Many saw their assignment in Vietnam as an opportunity to gain choice combat jobs in the field, which had become almost a prerequisite for promotion and advancement in the wartime military. Kerwin was never able to get the policy changed.

The short time officers spent in Saigon exacerbated the second great limitation Kerwin found in the way MACV managed the war. The staff included officers from every branch of the service and a large corps of civilians who had to coordinate with the commands in Honolulu and Washington; direct the ground war; manage a horde of civil affairs and support programs; and liaison with the South Vietnamese and the contingents from each of the foreign countries that had sent troops to Vietnam. Kerwin found few of the attributes necessary to conduct this kind of staff work resident in the personnel assigned to MACV. They simply lacked the experience and training for the job.

Kerwin could do little to address the personnel shortfalls. He directed his energies to managing the flow of information between MACV's senior leadership and the staff. Kerwin saw his principal role as ensuring the staff understood what the leadership wanted and then informing the command group on what the staff was doing. While the staff might not have operated as effectively as he would have like, as chief he could at least be confident that the right priorities were being addressed.

Determining what the leadership wanted to do, however, was another major challenge for the chief of staff. Kerwin found that the command relationships at MACV were not nearly as cohesive as they should have been. Abrams had left for Vietnam believing that he would shortly replace Westmoreland as MACV commander, with Kerwin his own hand-picked chief of staff at his side. The change in command, however, was delayed by the president for more than one year.[9] Abrams found himself in a difficult position, particularly since he was skeptical about Westmoreland's approach to the war. Before heading to Vietnam, Abrams had read a study prepared the Army Staff, called PROVN. The PROVN report made 140 recommendations, most of which called into question how the conflict was being fought.[10]

Despite their differences, however, Abrams was determined not to be a disruptive influence at MACV. Still tensions remained. "Although General Abrams was completely loyal to Westmoreland," Kerwin recalled, "there was not the closeness that there probably should have been between the two of them. There were many times, which I knew of being the chief of staff, that General Westmoreland did not take General Abrams into his confidence. General Abrams knew that he wasn't being utilized in the true sense of being a deputy commander."

In addition to supporting both generals, Kerwin performed duties for Ellsworth Bunker, the ambassador to South Vietnam, and Ambassador Robert

William Komer, MACV's civilian deputy commander in charge of Civil Operations and Revolutionary Development Support (CORDS) programs. Kerwin greatly respected Bunker, but he found working with Komer difficult. Komer, Kerwin, and Abrams had all flown to Vietnam together. On the plane, Kerwin could tell that the ambassador and Abrams were going to be like "oil and water." Abrams didn't like small talk. Komer never stopped talking, mostly boasting about himself and his ideas. Kerwin saw from watching Abrams' body language that the two would never get along, and that he was destined to be caught in the middle.

Day-to-day life at MACV headquarters bore out Kerwin's concerns. Though Kerwin, tireless and demanding as ever, ran the staff well, it was no easy task considering these men all seemed to have different agendas, personalities, philosophies, priorities, and, Kerwin lamented, "didn't necessarily speak the same language." From the quiet and introspective Westmoreland, to the blunt and down-to-earth Abrams, to the abrasive and volatile Komer, it was usually Kerwin who was caught in the crossfire. "It took an inordinate amount of time," the MACV chief of staff discovered, "that I, as the chief of the whole headquarters, working for Westy, was able to exercise some sort of coordination and staff functioning, and all those things that should be done in that headquarters." Moving MACV from its cramped facilities in Saigon to larger and better organized quarters near Tan Son Nhut helped, but staff coordination remained a chronic challenge.

Supporting Westmoreland, Abrams, and Komer proved particularly frustrating because each was running a different aspect of operations with, at times, little inclination to integrate or coordinate their efforts. Westmoreland focused on the "big war," primarily large-scale conventional combat operations. Abrams spent much of his time on developing the capabilities of the South Vietnamese forces to better provide for their own security and defense. Komer took on responsibility for the South Vietnamese pacification programs, with particular focus on improving operations against the Viet Cong insurgency movement.

In this array of activity, Kerwin found the command least prepared for the latter two missions.[11] Ironically, the U.S. Army did have a foundation of experience in tasks ranging from counterterrorism to military assistance to nation-building. The Army had conducted counter-guerrilla, pacification, and civil-military operations from its inception.[12] Kerwin's generation in particular had considerable experience in many such operations during the postwar occupations of Germany, Austria, Trieste, Japan, and South Korea. In addition, with the onset of the Cold War American military assistance programs had expanded exponentially. Kerwin, for example, had served two years on a joint U.S. military mission to Turkey, an experience that left him with a deep appreciation for the difficulties and sensitivities of working with foreign governments. The U.S. Army, however, never incorporated this experience into its doctrine, military education, or professional development programs. In addition, these assignments were not viewed as career enhancing, and the best of the "up and coming" leaders usually were not assigned to these duties. As a result, the Army found itself unprepared for Vietnam's complex civil-military challenges. Competition for priorities and resources among the MACV leadership exacerbated the problem.

As far as Kerwin was concerned, Komer's presence on the staff only made things worse. "Komer was smart and energetic with lots of ideas," the chief of staff recalled, "but he was also volatile and often had difficulty separating good ideas from bad ones. Komer was trying to run his own war, without coordinating CORDS activities with the rest of MACV." Keeping tabs on him and his disruptive influence on the staff was one of Kerwin's greatest trials.

Even in the conventional "big war," which held top priority for Westmoreland, Kerwin found serious problems. "We were all taught," Kerwin recalled, "that once you start it [a war] you go after him [the enemy] with everything; surprise, swiftness, speed, mass and so forth. We weren't able to do that in Vietnam."

The problem, as Kerwin saw it, was clearly at the operational level of war. Though he and his contemporaries had been exposed to operational planning during World War II and their postwar military education, the U.S. Army during the course of the Cold War gradually lost interest in the operational art. The army's attention was on the defense of Europe and the North Atlantic Treaty Organization (NATO), focused on the initial tactical engagements with the Warsaw Pact and the employment of nuclear weapons. Indeed, in the army's thinking nuclear weapons gradually supplanted operational maneuver as the solution to the problems of campaign planning. In the years before Vietnam, Kerwin, with his background as an artilleryman, found much of his time consumed by the requirements for planning, training, and securing the Army's ever-growing inventory of nuclear rockets and artillery. Nuclear weapons were never far from the military mind. In fact, in the wake of the Tet Offensive Kerwin assembled a small planning team to consider the potential for employing tactical nuclear weapons against North Vietnam.[13]

While the U.S. Army had dissipated its doctrinal and educational grounding in operational warfare, veterans of major combat operations like Kerwin were quick to point out flaws in MACV's approach to conventional military operations. MACV's campaigns consistently failed to retain the initiative, to bring the enemy to battle at a time and place where the U.S. forces could be used to best advantage. Part of the problem, Kerwin believed was that "we never understood the [South] Vietnamese. We think we know best. We tried to force on them what they should to do. . . . We never really got them into the war."

The second major problem was the geographical limits of the operational theater. The prohibition against conducting ground operations in North Vietnam, Cambodia, and Laos, while the North Vietnamese Army exploited the South's 900 miles of border to move in and out of the combat zone, made MACV's approach fatally flawed. Unless you have a plan, Kerwin reasoned, "that allows you to go after the enemy, then you are just sitting there and that really is just a defensive situation." Kerwin recognized that the limits of Vietnamese participation in major military operations and the theater's geographical boundaries were the product of political constraints over which MACV had no control. Nevertheless, he reasoned, if these obstacles meant that MACV's plans couldn't work, they should have changed their plans.

The chief of staff also recognized that MACV's inability to deal effectively with the media exaggerated the command's shortfalls and fueled the growing unpopularity of the American effort. He was appalled by the sheer number of correspondents in the theater and that many lacked substantive journalistic experience. "We lost the media war." Kerwin concluded. "One of the problems was there were over 450 correspondents in the country. I can even remember being interviewed by one ex-soldier who took his discharge in Hawaii, and came back to work for one of the free-lance magazines."

Kerwin recalled that the chairman of the Joint Chiefs of Staff, Gen. Earle Wheeler, told Westmoreland, "What you have to do is try to turn the adverse media thing around. At least get them so that they understand what is going on." In response, Westmoreland, with Kerwin (who worked with the press on a daily basis) by his side, started holding private weekly meetings with small groups of correspondents. After a few sessions, Westmoreland found that what he thought had been discussed in the meetings and the resulting articles were often "miles and miles apart." Discouraged, he told the chief of staff to discontinue the effort. Even when the leadership was frank with the press, Kerwin concluded, the army simply had great difficulty getting balanced and objective reporting. The problems with the press, however, were more complex and deep-rooted than Kerwin suspected. The real problem, as one historian concluded, was that the leadership at MACV allowed itself to be "drawn progressively into politics to the point that by late 1967 they had become involved in 'selling' the war to the American public."[14] As the military lost legitimacy in the eyes of the press, in turn the U.S. Army became more mistrustful and frustrated in its dealings with the media, feeding a death-spiral in relations between the two. This breakdown had serious implications for the conduct of the war. The proliferation of television and other mass media had created a global information environment, reducing the span of time and distance among far-off military operations, domestic public opinion, and public-policy decisions. The lack of a constructive relationship with the press exacerbated rapidly declining public support.

Despite a losing battle with the media and the many other challenges facing MACV, Westmoreland was content with the performance of his chief of staff. The two were rarely intimate and the MACV commander seldom delved into Kerwin's management of the staff. Kerwin once asked if there was anything in particular he should be doing. Westmoreland replied, "You know, I go out in the field a lot. When I'm out there, I want you here." "When I'm back here at the headquarters," the MACV commander added, "I want you here."[15] Kerwin accepted the remark as Westmoreland's version of a compliment.

After he had been on the job for months, Kerwin's confidence in his ability to manage the staff grew. He felt particularly well supported by MACV's J-2, Brig. Gen. Phillip B. Davidson, a West Point classmate, and J-3, Marine Brig. Gen. John R. Chaisson. Davidson served as the command's chief intelligence officer. As the MACV operations officer, Chaisson managed the Combat Operations Center, a huge, sprawling, single-story concrete building at the new headquarters complex near the airport. Kerwin considered both men outstanding staff officers, brilliant, energetic perfectionists.

Kerwin's appreciation for the staff and his own abilities was put to the test on 31 January 1968 during the Tet ceasefire, which marked the traditional Vietnamese celebration of the Lunar New Year. Kerwin remembered that Tet was like no holiday he had seen anywhere else in the world. "People," he recalled, "simply took off and went home." Awakened at 0200 hours at his quarters in downtown Saigon by what he thought were firecrackers set off during the celebration, an urgent phone call from the MACV command center reported that fighting had broken out in the city and across the country.[16]

Kerwin and his driver quickly collected their gear for the short trip to headquarters. Armed with a pistol, an M-16 rifle, and M-60 machine gun mounted on the back of their jeep, they left well prepared, or so they thought.

Firefights were blazing up and down the main avenues. Every few moments the dark night would explode with flashes of light and a haze of acrid smoke, enough evidence for Kerwin that they had driven headlong into a battle zone.

Before Tet, as a show of confidence, the Americans largely relied on the South Vietnamese to assume responsibility for the protection of the Saigon area, but security was notoriously lax during the celebrations and despite protests by MACV, South Vietnamese commanders had furloughed many soldiers so they could go home for the holidays. As a result, the initial responses to the attacks were chaotic and uncoordinated. No one knew the full extent of the incursions as episodic battles erupted across the city with security forces blundering into enemy agents fanning out to strike their designated targets. Rather than risk running a gauntlet of firefights, Kerwin decided to turn around and go back to his quarters, where he anxiously waited for the route to the MACV command post to be cleared.

By first light, reports of attacks from across the country were streaming into the MACV Combat Operations Center. By the time Kerwin arrived at the command post the staff had only barely begun to piece together what was going on. Before dawn on 31 January, Viet Cong insurgent forces and the regular North Vietnamese Army had launched a series of surprise coordinated attacks across South Vietnam, targeting more than 100 cities, towns, and hamlets, as well as military bases and the American embassy in Saigon. Although MACV had suspected a major Vietnamese offensive for some time, the exact timing of the attack and scope of the operation had caught them off guard.[17] By mid-morning Westmoreland had directed Kerwin to send a message to all U.S. units announcing cancellation of the ceasefire and placing all troops on maximum alert. Meanwhile, Kerwin scrambled to get MACV headquarters fully operational as enemy activity throughout the city prevented many staff members from reporting in during the first hours and days of the battle.[18]

During the first hectic hours of battle and many days to follow, Kerwin's most important role was providing the MAVC commander an accurate tactical picture of what was happening in the theater. This was no simple task, particularly during the opening hours of the battle, as scattered, incomplete reports streamed in from throughout the country. The challenge at MACV was always distilling the massive volumes of information coming in into a usable form for the commander to make decisions. While the staff had responsibility for assembling and analyzing the data, it was Kerwin's job to coordinate their efforts and make sure they provided a coherent, comprehensible picture.

Meanwhile, Westmoreland himself had gone to the scene of the attack on the American embassy in Saigon. The embassy, he felt, was a critical psychological objective. It would be an incredible blow to American prestige if the enemy destroyed the symbol of the American presence in Vietnam. Westmoreland called Kerwin from the scene and ordered the chief of staff to dispatch more combat troops to the battle for the embassy.

Back at MACV headquarters, one of the first calls Kerwin received was from the Joint Chiefs of Staff in Washington, demanding a situation report. Kerwin replied honestly he had no idea what was going on and that he would get back to them. By mid-morning, Kerwin had pieced together the scope of the enemy operation and had updated the MACV commander and the JCS in Washington. While there were some serious battles in the south, including roaring firefights in downtown Saigon, the primary concern was keeping the major north-south main supply routes (MSRs) open. As long as MACV could keep control of the highways and continue to move troops and supplies, the command believed the situation in the south could be stabilized. Operationally, Westmoreland was most worried about the attack on the city of Hue and the ongoing siege of the U.S. base at Khe Sanh, both in the northern part of the country. Worried that the northern provinces might fall to North Vietnamese invasion, Westmoreland at Kerwin's suggestion extended his operational control over the region by establishing a MACV Forward headquarters at Phu Bai, just south of Hue. Troops in the area were under command of Marine Lt. Gen. Robert E. Cushman of the III Marine Amphibious Force (III MAF). Westmoreland, however, ordered the MACV deputy commander General Abrams to assume control over all the forces in the area and conduct the fight for the northern provinces.[19]

In addition to the Marine forces, MACV redeployed the U.S. Army's 1st Cavalry Division from South Vietnam's central coast to the fighting in the north.[20] Kerwin recalled it was a difficult decision, mixing Army and Marine forces on the fly, throwing up an ad hoc headquarters and tossing in a new commander. "It could have gone down the tube up there," Kerwin recalled. The Marines, the Vietnamese forces, and the more than 45,000 army troops MACV funneled into the area strained both the theater's tactical control and logistical support. MACV also found itself battling incessantly to ensure that commanders gave the South Vietnamese forces adequate air and artillery support, so that they could make real contributions to the operation. Despite these obstacles, within the week American and Vietnamese forces were on the offensive.

While Abrams pushed to recapture Hue, Westmoreland anxiously monitored the events at Khe Sanh, where attacks had been ongoing since 21 January. The year before, Westmoreland had directed a buildup at Khe Sanh as a potential jumping-off point to interdict North Vietnamese forces and supplies moving through neighboring Laos. The base was not vital to defending the northern provinces, but he decided holding Khe Sanh had become an opportunity to fix and engage a large number of North Vietnamese regular forces. The Tet campaign appeared to give the battle for Khe Sanh even greater political significance as a test of American resolve.[21]

Since mid-January the air forces had conducted a series of punishing air attacks as part of Operation Niagara to reduce enemy pressure on Khe Sanh. On 31 January, Westmoreland moved into MACV's Combat Operations Center to track operations minute by minute. Coordinating control of close air support between the air force and the Marines became a particularly vexing issue that drove him to distraction.[22] At one point, recalling the story of how Kerwin had been called on to work out the complicated artillery support plan for the Anzio beachhead during World War II, Abrams suggested that Westmoreland send his chief of staff to resolve the dispute. Kerwin was dispatched to resolve the controversy, a rare moment away from the command post. He arrived to find a large tent filled with a throng of officers from all the services. The chief of staff quickly realized that productive results could never be achieved with such a gaggle. After a day of arduous debate, Kerwin returned to MACV headquarters and reported that it was tough going. Anzio had been easier. Kerwin returned to Saigon and ordered each service to send a single representative to the second meeting, and he didn't let them out until they hammered out a workable agreement.

Throughout these tense weeks, Kerwin carefully watched his commander, demonstrating another aspect of serving as a commander's advisor and counselor. Concentrating on the operations center left Westmoreland physically and mentally exhausted. Westmoreland's wife, Kitsy, was at Clark Air Base in the Philippines. Kerwin tried to arrange for her to come to MACV, reasoning it would be the only way to get the general to go back to his quarters and relax.[23] Meanwhile, Kerwin continued to manage the blitzkrieg of coordination and logistical tasks required to keep the counteroffensive going.

In the month following the outbreak of the Tet Offensive, Kerwin rarely left the command center. He had bunks installed in one of the side rooms. On a good day he would manage four hours sleep, but such luxuries were rare. Workdays with only two hours of sleep were not uncommon, and a complete night of rest was impossible. There was always someone, somewhere, in some time zone that needed to speak to the chief of staff, day and night.

During the long weeks after Tet, Kerwin's respect for his fellow principal staff officers only grew. Davidson shrugged off the surprise of the timing and scope of the North Vietnamese attack and focused assessing the situation in the North, as well as what appeared to be crushing defeat to the Viet Cong infrastructure throughout the country. Chaisson, composed and tireless, directed the myriad of ongoing activities in the Combat Information Center with his usual sureness and efficiency.

On 2 March, while the North Vietnamese continued to concentrate forces on Khe Sanh, joint operations by South Vietnamese, U.S. Marine, and U.S. Army forces completed recapturing Hue. As the enemy retreated to Laos, the army's 1st Cavalry Division prepared to conduct Operation Pegasus, the relief of the Marines at Khe Sanh. The operation began on 1 April and was completed within a week.

In the wake of Tet, Westmoreland requested 200,000 additional troops. Kerwin discounts claims that the proposal was foisted on MACV by the chairman of the JCS, General Wheeler.[24] Westmoreland saw higher troops' strengths as the key to seizing the opportunity to exploit the advantages gained by crippling the Viet Cong infrastructure during the Tet campaign. But, after briefing the new requirements to representatives from Washington, Kerwin had little optimism that the request would be well received. In the United States the proposal was met with a wave of negative reaction, as many Americans interpreted the call for more troops as a sign of defeat, believing the war had become an intractable quagmire.

Tet offered ambivalent lessons for Kerwin and the MACV staff. Despite all its shortcomings and obstacles, MACV had launched an effective counteroffensive under difficult conditions, demonstrating great operational agility and flexibility. On the other hand, though the invasion had been successfully repulsed the campaign again highlighted the flaws Kerwin saw in MACV's operational design—the challenges of getting the South Vietnamese army fully into the fight, the cost of not thoroughly coordinating all warfighting; Vietnamization and pacification efforts; and, finally, the difficulty of holding the initiative when the enemy had the freedom to withdraw behind safe borders. Most damaging, however, was MACV's rapidly deteriorating relations with the press, their portrayal of Tet as a horrendous military setback, and the resulting increasing disillusionment of Americans with the war effort.[25]

After Tet, Kerwin remained as chief of staff during the transition between Westmoreland and Abrams, helping the new commander begin to address the flaws they saw in MACV's operational approach to the war.[26] Abrams' first order was to withdraw from Khe Sanh. Later, Kerwin served in combat as the commanding general of II Field Forces.[27] After returning to the United States, he held a succession of important posts, retiring as the vice chief of staff of the U.S. Army in 1978. In retirement Kerwin remained an influential figure, supporting the post-Vietnam revitalization of the army, encouraging the renaissance in thinking on the operational art, and, most important, supporting a return to an emphasis on the basics of soldiering, professionalism, integrity, and character. He had always believed the fundamentals of a strong disciplined life—selfless service, hard work, values—were the secrets of his success as a military leader. For Kerwin war and the disciplined life would always go together.

Notes

1. Unless noted otherwise information and quotations on Kerwin's early life and career are from General Walter T. Kerwin Jr., oral history, vols. 1 and 2, U.S. Army Military History Institute, Carlisle Barracks, Pa., 1980.

2. For a summary of combat operations at Anzio see Martin Blumenson, *Salerno to Cassino*, reprint (Washington, D.C.: Center of Military History, 1993), 385–94, 419–29.

3. General Walter T. Kerwin, interview with author, 17 July 2002, Alexandria, Va. (hereafter Kerwin interview).

4. Patrecia Slayden Hollis, "Yesterday and Today: 50 years of the Army," *Field Artillery* (August 1993): 6; Lucian King Truscott, *Command Missions: A Personal History* (New York: Dutton, 1954), 325.

5. For an account of Kerwin's wounding see John A. Heintges, oral history, MHI, 1974, 169.

6. Lewis Sorley, *Thunderbolt, General Creighton Abrams and the Army of His Times* (New York: Simon and Schuster, 1992), 146.

7. Kerwin interview.

8. Ibid.

9. For more on the controversy surrounding Abram's assignment see Samuel Zaffiri, *Westmoreland: Biography of General William C. Westmoreland* (New York: William Morrow, 1994), 210; Sorley, *Thunderbolt*, 195. Kerwin had known Westmoreland only briefly before his assignment to MACV, during an assignment at Fort Leavenworth.

10. For more on the PROVN Study see Lewis Sorley, "To Change a War: General Harold K. Johnson and the PROVN Study," *Parameters* (Spring 1998): 93–109.

11. Kerwin's papers are at the U.S. Army Military History Institute at Carlisle Barracks, Pennsylvania. The records deal primarily with his term as U.S. Army vice chief of staff. For a summary of Abrams' role at MACV see Sorley, *Thunderbolt*, 145–51, 161–66. See also Zeb B. Bradford Jr., "With Creighton Abrams in Vietnam," *Assembly* (May/June 1998): 28–32. Komer discusses his role in Robert W. Komer, *Bureaucracy Does Its Thing: Institutional Constraints on U.S.-GVN Performance in Vietnam* (Santa Monica, Calif.: Rand, 1972). For Westmoreland's view on pacification see William Childs Westmoreland, oral history, vol. 1, MHI, 1982, 145–51 and 161–66. See also James Lawton Collins Jr., *The Development and Training of the South Vietnamese Army, 1950–1972* (Washington, D.C.: Department of the Army, 1975), 85–122; Jeffrey J. Clarke, *Advice and Support: The Final Years, 1965–1973* (Washington, D.C.: Center of Military History, 1988), 127–340.

12. Andrew J. Birtle, *U.S. Army Counterinsurgency and Contingency Operations Doctrine 1860–1941* (Washington, D.C.: Center of Military History, 1998).

13. See Kerwin oral history, 2:392. See also William C. Westmoreland, *A Soldier Reports* (Garden City, N.Y.: Doubleday, 1976), 338.

14. William M. Hammond, *The Military and the Media, 1962–1968* (Washington, D.C.: Center of Military History, 1988), 388. See also Peter Braestrup, *The Big Story* (New Haven: Yale University Press, 1983).

15. Kerwin interview.

16. Ibid.

17. For an overview of the Tet battles and the controversy surrounding the intelligence failure to anticipate the campaign see Don Oberdorfer, *Tet! The Turning Point of the Vietnam War* (New York: Da Capo, 1983); Phillip B. Davidson, *Vietnam at War* (Novato, Calif.: Presidio Press, 1988), 473–528; John Prados, *The Hidden History of the Vietnam War* (Chicago: Ivan R. Dee, 1995), 129–51; Ronnie E. Ford, *Tet 1968: Understanding the Surprise* (London: Frank Cass, 1995); Marc Jason Gilbert and William Head, eds., *The Tet Offensive* (Westport, Conn: Praeger, 1996).

18. Westmoreland, *A Soldier Reports*, 323; Bruce Palmer Jr., *The 25-Year War: America's Military Role in Vietnam* (Lexington: University of Kentucky Press, 1984), 76–77. During this period, U.S. Army Headquarters, Vietnam (HQ USARV), at Long Binh served as the alternate MACV headquarters. Palmer suggests HQ USARV played a decisive role. Kerwin recalled only that the assistance was helpful.

19. Zaffiri, *Westmoreland*, 291, claims all the MACV leadership was dissatisfied with the pace of Cushman's efforts to secure Hue and break the siege at Khe Sanh. Westmoreland, *A Soldier Reports*, 345, denies it. See also Sorley, *Thunderbolt*, 213–17. Kerwin recalled that the command was dissatisfied with the progress of operations, but saw the problem primarily as the result of the lack of centralized command and control over all the joint forces in the area. See Kerwin interview.

20. For a discussion of the division's operations in Tet see Shelby L. Stanton, *Anatomy of a Division: The 1st Cav in Vietnam* (Novato, Calif.: Presidio Press, 1987), 111–32. For the battles of Hue and Khe Sanh see Eric Hammel, *Fire in the Streets: The Battle for Hue, Tet 1968* (New York: Contemporary Books, 1991); John Prados and Ray W. Stubbe, *Valley of Decision: The Siege of Khe Sanh* (New York: Houghton Mifflin, 1991); Robert Pisor,

The End of the Line: The Siege of Khe Sanh (New York: Norton, 1982); Eric Hammel, *Khe Sanh, Siege in the Clouds: An Oral History* (New York: Crown, 1989).

21. See, for example, MFR, subject: President's Position on Khe Sanh, 16 February 1968, William C. Westmoreland Papers, History Files, MHI. Westmoreland provided a summary of calls from the chairman of the Joint Chiefs of Staff General Wheeler relaying a conversation between President Lyndon B. Johnson and Secretary of Defense Robert S. McNamara, relating the political concerns over Khe Sanh and that the president wanted early warning if Westmoreland decided to withdraw from the base so that he could "prepare the political defenses." Westmoreland sent detailed daily reports on Khe Sanh to the joint chiefs. See COMUSMACV, "Eyes Only" message File, 1968, Westmoreland Papers. Kerwin called Khe Sanh Westmoreland's "pet project." He did not see the battle of Khe Sanh as a major component of the Tet offensive. "The situation in Khe Sanh had stabilized before Tet started," he recalled.

22. Shelby L. Stanton, *The Rise and Fall of an American Army: U.S. Ground Forces in Vietnam, 1965–73* (Novato, Calif.: Presidio Press, 1985), 243. See also History File, 28 December–31 January 1968, Westmoreland Papers; Air Power Chronology, Messages and Correspondence, 1965–1968, Westmoreland Papers.

23. Westmoreland, *A Soldier Reports*, 339. History File, 28 December–31 January 1968, 30. Westmoreland stayed at MACV headquarters from 31 January to 22 March and then went Clark Air Base in the Philippines to see his family.

24. Kerwin interview.

25. For a cogent analysis of the military's response to Tet see Robert Buzzanco, *Master of War: Military Dissent and Politics in the Vietnam Era* (Cambridge: Cambridge University Press, 1996), 311–40.

26. For an overview of Abram's tenure as MACV commander see Lewis Sorley, *A Better War: The Unexamined Victories and Final Tragedy of America's Last Years in Vietnam* (New York: Harcourt Brace, 1999).

27. Before his departure Westmoreland recommended Kerwin for command of II Field Force. See Message, Westmoreland to Johnson, 19 March 1968, MACV, Top Secret, Eyes Only, 1967–68, Westmoreland Papers.

Contributors

Colonel (Ret.) Donald W. Boose Jr. has taught at the U.S. Army War College since 1990. He spent a substantial part of his thirty years of military service in Northeast Asia in infantry and Foreign Area Officer assignments. He is the co-author of *Great Battles of Antiquity*, a major contributor to the *Encyclopedia of the Korean War*, and the author of articles on Northeast Asia security issues, Asia-Pacific history, and the Korean War.

James Jay Carafano is a senior fellow at the Center for Strategic and Budgetary Assessments in Washington, D.C. A retired Army officer with over twenty-four years of active service, he is the former executive editor of *Joint Force Quarterly*. He also served as the head speechwriter for the chief of staff, U.S. Army, and as the head of military studies at the Center for Military History. Before coming to Washington, he was the chief of Task Force 2000 at the U.S. Field Artillery School, where he was responsible for developing future operational concepts for land warfare. Before assuming this position he had a range of assignments in the United States and overseas. He has also taught history at Georgetown University, the U.S. Military Academy at West Point, Mount St. Mary's College, and the U.S. Army Field Artillery School. Dr. Carafano is a graduate of the U.S. Army War College and received his MA and PhD at Georgetown University. He has contributed many articles to academic and professional military journals. His books include *After D-Day: Operation Cobra and the Normandy Breakout; "Soldiers Are Our Credentials": The Collected Works and Selected Papers of General Dennis J. Reimer, Army Chief of Staff* (edited volume); and *Waltzing into the Cold War: The Struggle for Occupied Austria*. He is currently writing a book on U.S. civil-military relations.

Philip Green was commissioned in the Royal Artillery. He also joined the Commandos and commanded 79 (Kirkee) Commando Battery. He served with the Trucal Oman Scouts and in Singapore and Borneo. He also served as an exchange gunnery instructor at the U.S. Field Artillery School at Fort

Sill, Oklahoma. Retiring from the army as a lieutenant colonel, he completed an Honours Degree in History and International Politics. From 1989 to 1997 he was the branch director of the Hereford and Worcester Red Cross. He contributed to a wide range of military history publications, including *World War II in Europe: An Encyclopedia*. Lieutenant Colonel Green died in 1999.

Russell Hart is an associate professor of history at Hawaii Pacific University where he teaches in the university's Diplomacy and Military Studies program. He holds a PhD from Ohio State University and is the author of the award-winning book *Clash of Arms: How the Allies Won in Normandy, June–August, 1944*. Dr. Hart has also co-authored five additional books on the Second World War. He is currently working on a monograph entitled *Hitler's Last Hope: The German Military's Efforts to Rescue Hitler in Berlin, April–May 1945*.

Dr. Stephen Hart is a senior lecturer in the War Studies Department at the Royal Military Academy Sandhurst. He is the co-author of several works on the German army in World War II and the author of *Montgomery and "Colossal Cracks": The 21st Army Group in Northwest Europe, 1944–45* (Praeger, 2000).

Robert H. Larson received his BA from The Citadel and his MA and PhD from The University of Virginia. He has been a member of the faculty of Lycoming College in Williamsport, Pennsylvania, since 1969, where he is currently Robert and Charlene Shangraw Professor of History. Among his other publications is *The British Army and the Theory of Armored Warfare, 1918–1940*, which was awarded the Templer Medal by the Society for Army Historical Research in the United Kingdom.

Geoffrey P. Megargee received his undergraduate degree in history from St. Lawrence University in 1981. Following stints as an army officer and in the business world, he entered San Jose State University, where he received a master's in European history in 1991, and then Ohio State University, from which he graduated with a doctorate in military history in 1998. He is the recipient of, among other honors, a Fulbright grant for research in Germany, and he is the author of *Inside Hitler's High Command* (University Press of Kansas, 2000; a Main Selection of the History Book Club and winner of the Society for Military History's 2001 Distinguished Book Award) and *War of Annihilation: Combat and Genocide on the Eastern Front, 1941* (Rowman and Littlefield, 2007). Dr. Megargee currently holds the position of applied research scholar at the

Center for Advanced Holocaust Studies, United States Holocaust Memorial Museum, where he is editing a multivolume encyclopedic history of the camps and ghettos in Nazi Germany and Nazi-dominated Europe.

Julius A. Menzoff serves as an adjunct instructor at Embry-Riddle Aeronautical University, Saint Leo University, and Columbia College, at these institutions' Hunter Army Airfield campuses located in Savannah, Georgia, teaching history and criminal justice administration courses. He also served as an adjunct instructor of history and criminal justice administration at the Fort Worth Campus of Columbia College, Tarrant County College, Southeast Campus, Arlington, Texas, and Texas Christian University, Fort Worth. He has published entries in encyclopedias and has given papers at various conferences. He graduated from Texas Christian University with a BA in history. He received his master's in criminal justice administration from Oklahoma City University and his master's in history from Texas Christian University. After retiring from the U.S. Army, he earned his PhD in history from Texas Christian University. He and his wife, Lee, and daughter Melissa reside in Richmond Hill, Georgia.

Michael Orr taught war studies at the Royal Military Academy at Sandhurst and is currently a senior lecturer at the British Army's Conflict Studies Research Centre. His publications for CSRC include *Russian Armed Forces as a Factor in Regional Stability* (1998) and *The Russian Heliborne Desant Force in Theory and Practice* (1997). He is currently working on a history of Russia's wars in Chechnya and a biography of Marshal Zhukov.

Captain Carl O. Schuster is a native of Hanahan, South Carolina. He was commissioned at the Navy ROTC battalion at the University of South Carolina in 1974. From there he served in a diverse range of naval positions aboard a variety of American and Allied warships and staffs before finishing his career as director of operations at the Joint Intelligence Center Pacific in Pearl Harbor, Hawaii. He retired from the Navy in 1999 and currently works as the director of a Commercial Information Analysis Center in Hawaii. He is also a widely published author of military history and assistant editor of *World War II in Europe: An Encyclopedia*.

William Van Husen is a twenty-four-year veteran of the U.S. Air Force. He received a BS, magna cum laude, from the University of Maryland and an MS in international relations from Troy State University. From 1989 to 1994 he taught history and American government for Central Texas College and the University of Maryland in the European region. He was assistant editor and contributor to *World War II in Europe: An Encyclopedia* and a contributor to the *Encyclopedia of the Korean War*. Currently, he is communications contract manager with Headquarters, U.S. Air Forces in Europe at Ramstein Air Base, Germany.

Stephen Walsh is a research associate with the Centre for Defence and International Security Studies. He graduated from Lancaster University with a master's in defense and strategic studies, and then attended the Royal Military Academy at Sandhurst, where he won the Trust Medal for best overall academic performance. In 1994 he was commissioned into the Adjutant General's Corps of the British Army.

David T. Zabecki is the author of *Steel Wind: Colonel Georg Bruchmüller and the Birth of Modern Artillery*; the author of *The German 1918 Offensives: A Case Study in the Operational Level of War*; the editor of *World War Two in Europe: An Encyclopedia*; the editor of *Vietnam: A Reader*; and the editor and co-translator of *On the German Art of War: Truppenführung*. He is also the editor of *Vietnam* magazine, the only regularly published periodical devoted to the military history of the Vietnam War. He enlisted in the U.S. Army in 1966 and served as an infantry rifleman in Vietnam in 1967 and 1968. He continued serving in the regular Army, the Army National Guard, and the Army Reserve, until his retirement in 2007. He is a 1988 graduate of the U.S. Army Command and General Staff College, and a 1995 graduate of the U.S. Army War College. He has commanded as a captain, lieutenant colonel, colonel, brigadier general, and major general. From 1998 to 2000 he was the chief of staff of the 7th Army Reserve Command in Germany. From 2000 to 2002 he was one of the deputy chiefs of the U.S. Army Reserve. In 2002 and 2003 he was the commanding general of the 7th Army Reserve Command, and during the buildup and first months of the war with Iraq he served simultaneously as the director of the U.S. Army Europe Deployment Operations Center, which moved 33,000 soldiers and their equipment from Europe to the Middle East. During the last half of 2003 he served in Israel as the senior security advisor to the multiagency U.S. Coordinating and Monitoring Mission, also known as the Roadmap to Peace in the Middle East. In 2004 he commanded all U.S. forces in Normandy, France, committed to supporting the observances of the sixtieth anniversary of the D-Day landings. In 2005 and 2006 he commanded the U.S. Southern European Task Force Rear (Airborne) and served as the senior U.S. Army commander south of the Alps. He holds a PhD in military science, technology, and management from Britain's Royal Military College of Science.

Bibliography

Ambrose, Stephen E. *Eisenhower: Soldier and President*. New York: Simon and Schuster, 1991.

Appleman, Roy E. *Disaster in Korea: The Chinese Confront MacArthur*. College Station: Texas A&M University Press, 1989.

———. *South to the Naktong, North to the Yalu (June–November 1950): U.S. Army in the Korean War*. Washington, D.C.: Government Printing Office, 1961.

Balck, Hermann. *Ordnung im Chaos: Erinnerungen 1893–1948*. Osnabrück: Biblio Verlag, 1981.

Barnett, Correlli. *The Desert Generals*. London: William Kimber, 1960.

Belchem, David. *All in the Day's March*. London: Collins, 1978.

Bidwell, Shelford. *Gunners at War: A Tactical Study of the Royal Artillery in the Twentieth Century*. London: Arms and Armour, 1970.

Blair, Clay. *The Forgotten War: America in Korea, 1950–1953*. New York: Crown, 1987.

Blumenson, Martin. *Breakout and Pursuit*. In *U.S. Army in World War II: The European Theater of Operations*. Washington, D.C.: Department of the Army, 1961.

———. *Mediterranean Theater of Operations: Salerno to Cassino*. Reprint. Washington, D.C.: Department of the Army, 1993.

———, ed. *The Patton Papers*. 2 vols. Boston: Houghton Mifflin, 1972, 1984.

Bor, Peter. *Gespräche mit Halder*. Wiesbaden: Limes Verlag, 1950.

Carell, Paul. *The Foxes of the Desert: The Story of the Afrikakorps*. New York: Bantam Books, 1967.

Carlson, Verner R. "Portrait of a German General Staff Officer." *Military Review* (April 1990): 69–70.

Chalfont, Alun. *Montgomery of Alamein*. London: Athenaeum, 1976.

Chandler, Alfred D. *The Papers of Dwight David Eisenhower: The War Years*. 5 vols. Baltimore: Johns Hopkins University Press, 1970.

Churchill, Winston S. *The Second World War*. 6 vols. London: Cassell, 1959.

Colby, John. *War from the Ground Up: The 90th Division in World War II*. Austin, Tex.: Nortex Press, 1991.

Cole, Hugh M. *The Ardennes: The Battle of the Bulge*. In *The U.S. Army in World War II: The European Theater of Operations*. Washington, D.C.: Department of the Army, 1965.

———. *The Lorraine Campaign*. In *The U.S. Army in World War II: The European Theater of Operations*. Washington, D.C.: Department of the Army, 1950.

Collins, J. Lawton. *War in Peacetime: The History and Lessons of Korea*. Boston: Houghton Mifflin, 1969.

Cray, Ed. *General of the Army: George C. Marshall, Soldier and Statesman*. New York: Caper Square Press, 2000.

Crosswell, D. K. R. *The Chief of Staff: The Military Career of General Walter Bedell Smith*. Contributions in Military Studies. New York: Greenwood, 1991.

de Guingand, Francis. *From Brass Hat to Bowler Hat*. London: H. Hamilton, 1979.

———. *Generals at War*. London: Hodder and Stoughton, 1964.

———. *Operation Victory*. Rev. ed. London: Hodder, 1960.

Ent, Uzal W. *Fighting on the Brink: Defense of the Pusan Perimeter*. Paducah, Ky.: Turner Publishing, 1996.

Erickson, John. *The Road to Berlin*, vol. 2 of *Stalin's War with Germany*. London: Weidenfeld and Nicolson, 1983.

———. *The Road to Stalingrad*, vol. 1 of *Stalin's War with Germany*. New York: Harper and Row, 1975.

Fraser, David. *Knight's Cross: A Life of Field Marshal Erwin Rommel*. New York: HarperCollins, 1993.

Futrell, Robert Frank. *The United States Air Force in Korea, 1950–1953*. Rev. ed. Washington, D.C.: Office of Air Force History, 1983.

Gaglov, I. I. *Army General A. I. Antonov*. Moscow: Sovestskii Pisatel, 1987.

Garfield, Brian. *The Thousand-Mile War: World War II in Alaska and the Aleutians*. Garden City, N.Y.: Doubleday, 1969.

Garland, Albert N., and Howard M. Smyth, with Martin Blumenson. *Sicily and the Surrender of Italy*. In *The U.S. Army in World War II: The Mediterranean Theater of Operations*. Washington, D.C.: Office of the Chief of Military History, 1965.

Gay, Hobart R. Papers. U.S. Army Military History Institute, Carlisle Barracks, Pa.

Gelb, Norman. *Ike and Monty: Generals at War*. New York: William Morrow, 1994.

Glantz, David. *From the Don to the Dnepr: Soviet Offensive Operations, December 1942–August 1943*. London: Routledge, 1991.

———. *Soviet Military Deception in the Second World War*. London: Routledge, 1989.

———. *Zhukov's Greatest Defeat: The Red Army's Epic Disaster in Operation Mars, 1942*. Lawrence: University Press of Kansas, 1999.

Glantz, David, and Jonathan House. *When Titans Clashed: How The Red Army Stopped Hitler*. Lawrence: University Press of Kansas, 1995.

Goulden, Joseph C. *Korea: The Untold Story of the War*. New York: Times Books, 1982.

Greacen, Lavinia. *Chink, a Biography*. London: Macmillan, 1989.

Greenwood, Alexander. *Field-Marshal Auchinleck: A Biography of Field-Marshal Sir Claude Auchinleck*. Durham, UK: Pentland Press Ltd, 1991.

Guderian, Heinz. *Panzer Leader*. New York: Ballantine Books, 1957.

Hamilton, Nigel. *Monty*. 3 vols. London: Hanish Hamilton, 1982–86.

Hammond, William M. *The Military and the Media, 1962–1968*. Washington, D.C.: Center for Military History, 1988.

Handleman, Howard. *Bridge to Victory: The Story of the Reconquest of the Aleutians*. New York: Random House, 1943.

Hansen, Chester B. Papers. U.S. Army Military History Institute, Carlisle Barracks, Pa.

Harkins, Paul D. Papers. U.S. Army Military History Institute, Carlisle Barracks, Pa.

Hart, Russell A. *Clash of Arms: How the Allies Won in Normandy, June–August 1944*. Boulder, Colo.: Lynne Rienner, 2001.

Hart, Stephen. *Montgomery and "Colossal Cracks": The 21st Army Group in Northwest Europe 1944–45*. Westport, Conn.: Praeger, 2000.

Hastings, Max. *The Korean War*. New York: Simon and Schuster, 1987.

Higgins, Trumbull. *Korea and the Fall of MacArthur*. New York: Oxford University Press, 1960.

Hoffmann, Peter. *Widerstand-Staatsstreich-Attentat: Der Kampf der Oppositionen gegen Hitler*. 3rd ed. Munich: R. Piper and Co. Verlag, 1979.

Howe, George F. *Northwest Africa: Seizing the Initiative in the West*. In *The U.S. Army in World War II: The Mediterranean Theater of Operations*. Washington, D.C.: Department of the Army, 1957.

Irving, David. *The Trail of the Fox: The Search for the True Field Marshall Rommel*. New York: E. P. Dutton, 1977.

Kesselring, Albert. *Kesselring: A Soldier's Record*. New York: William Morrow, 1954.

Kurowski, Franz. *Das Vermächtnis. Siegfried Westphal: Als Generalstabschef dreier Feldmarschälle im Krieg 1939–1945*. Bochum: Heinrich Pöppinghaus Verlag, 1982.

Love, Edmund G. *The Hourglass: A History of the 7th Division in World War II*. Nashville, Tenn.: Battery Press, 1988.

MacDonald, Charles B. *The Last Offensive*. In *The U.S. Army in World War II: The European Theater of Operations*. Washington, D.C.: Department of the Army, 1973.

Mackintosh, Malcolm. *The Soviet Union and the Warsaw Pact*. London: Routledge, 2006.

Macksey, Kenneth. *Rommel: Battles and Campaigns*. New York: Da Capo Press, 1997.

Maddox, Halley G. Papers. U.S. Army Military History Institute, Carlisle Barracks, Pa.

Mellenthin, F.-W. von. *German Generals of World War II as I Saw Them*. Norman: University of Oklahoma Press, 1977.

———. *Panzer Battles: A Study of Employment of Armor in the Second World War*. Norman: University of Oklahoma Press, 1956.

Mitcham, Samuel W. *Rommel's Greatest Victory. The Desert Fox and the Fall of Tobruk, Spring 1942*. Novato, Calif.: Presidio Press, 1998.

Montague, Ludwell L. *General Walter Bedell Smith as Director of Central Intelligence, October 1950–February 1953*. University Park: Pennsylvania State University Press, 1992.

Montgomery, Bernard L. *Memoirs*. London: Collins, 1958.

Morgan, Frederick. *COSSAC's Memoirs: Overture to OVERLORD*. London: Hodder and Stoughton, 1951.

———. *Peace and War, a Soldier's Life*. London: Hodder and Stoughton, 1961.

Müller, Klaus-Jürgen. "Witzleben, Stuelpnagel and Speidel." In *Hitler's Generals*, ed. Corelli Barnett, 43–74. New York: Grove Weidenfeld, 1989.

Murray, G. E. Patrick. *Eisenhower and Montgomery: The Continuing Debate*. Westport, Conn.: Praeger, 1996.

Oberdorfer, Don. *Tet! The Turning Point of the Vietnam War*. New York: Da Capo, 1983.

Palmer, Bruce, Jr. *The 25-Year War: America's Military Role in Vietnam*. Lexington: University Press of Kentucky, 1984.

Patton, George S., Jr. *War as I Knew It*. Boston: Houghton Mifflin, 1947.

Reinhardt, K. *Moscow: The Turning Point? The Failure of Hitler's strategy in the winter of 1941–42*, Studies in Military History. Oxford: Oxford University Press, 1992.

Richardson, Charles. *Flashback: A Soldier's Story*. London: William Kimber, 1985.

———. *Send for Freddie: Story of Montgomery's Chief of Staff Major-General Sir Francis de Guingand*. London: William Kimber, 1987.

Ridgway, Matthew B. *The Korean War*. Garden City, N.Y.: Doubleday, 1967.

Ritgen, Helmut. *Die Geschichte der Panzer-Lehr-Division im Westen*. Stuttgart: Motorbuch Verlag, 1979.

Rommel, Erwin. *Krieg ohne Hass*. Edited by Lucie Rommel and Fritz Bayerlein. Heidenheim, Germany: Verlag Heidenheimer Zeitung, 1950.

———. *The Rommel Papers*. Edited by Basil H. Liddell Hart. New York: Harcourt Brace, 1953.

Schofield, B. B. *Operation Neptune*. London: Ian Allen, 1974.

Schwarz, Eberhard. *Die Stabilisierung der Ostfront nach Stalingrad: Mansteins gegenschlag zwischen Dontez und Dnirpr im Frühjahr 1943*. Göttingen: Hansen-Schmidt, 1985.

Shtemenko, S. M. *The Soviet General Staff at War 1941–1945*. Moscow: Progress Publishers, 1985.

Smith, Walter Bedell. *Eisenhower's Six Great Decisions*. New York: Longmans, Green, 1956.

———. *My Three Years in Moscow*. New York: Lippincott, 1950.

Sorley, Lewis. *A Better War: The Unexamined Victories and Final Tragedy of America's Last Years in Vietnam*. New York: Harcourt Brace, 1999.

———. *Thunderbolt, General Creighton Abrams and the Army of His Times*. New York: Simon and Schuster, 1992.

Spayd, P. A. *Bayerlein: From Afrikakorps to Panzer Lehr*. Atgen, Pa.: Schiffer Military Books, 2003.

Speidel, Hans. *Aus unserer Zeit: Erinnerungen*. Frankfurt/Main: Propyläen, 1977.

———. *Invasion 1944: Ein Betrag zu Rommels und des reiches Schicksal*. Tübingen: Wunderlich, 1949.

Stanton, Shelby L. *America's Tenth Legion, X Corps in Korea, 1950.* Novato, Calif.: Presidio Press, 1989.

Summers, Harry G. *Korean War Almanac.* New York: Facts on File, 1990.

Taggart, Donald G., ed. *History of the Third Infantry Division in World War II.* Nashville, Tenn.: Battery Press, 1987.

Truscott, Lucian K. *Command Missions: A Personal History.* New York: E. P. Dutton, 1954.

Tucker, Spencer. *Encyclopedia of the Korean War.* Santa Barbara, Calif.: ABC-Clio, 2000.

U.S. War Department. *FM 101-5 Staff Officers Field Manual: The Staff and Combat Orders.* Washington, D.C.: Government Printing Office, 1940.

Vasilevskiy, A. M. *A Life-Long Occupation.* Moscow: Politizdat, 1974.

Volkogonov, Dmitri. *Stalin, Triumph and Tragedy.* London: Weidenfeld and Nicolson, 1991.

Weigley, Russell, F. *Eisenhower's Lieutenants.* Bloomington: Indiana University Press, 1981.

Westphal, Siegfried. *Erinnerungen.* Mainz: Hase und Koehler Verlag, 1975.

Williamson, Gordon. *The Afrikakorps 1941–43.* London: Osprey Publishing, 1991.

Y'Blood, William T. *The Three Wars of Lt. Gen. George E. Stratemeyer: His Korean War Diary.* Washington, D.C.: Air Force History and Museums Program, 1999.

Zabecki, David T. and Bruce Condell. *On the German Art of War: Truppenführung.* Boulder, Colorado: Lynne Rienner Publishers, 2001.

Zhukov, G. K. *Reminiscences and Reflections.* Moscow: Novosty, 1974.

Index

Abrams, Creighton, 205, 219, 221; command style of, 210–11; reputation of as a difficult boss, 210; tension with Westmoreland, 212

Across the River and Into the Trees (Hemingway), 78

Alexander, Harold, 32, 97, 103, 146

Allen, Leven C., 179

Almond, Edward M., 1, 178, 190, 200–201; as assistant and deputy chief of staff of the Armed Forces Pacific Command, 191–92; and the Battle of Soyang River, 199; as chief of staff of General Command, Far Eastern Command (GHQ-FEC), 192–93; as chief of staff of United Nations Command (UNC), 193; as chief of staff of VI Corps, 191; and the Chinese attack across the Yalu River, 196, 197; as commander of the 2nd Infantry Division, 197; as commander of the 92nd Infantry Division, 191; as commander of X Corps, 193, 198–99; and establishment of the GHQ Target Group, 192; and the evacuation of X Corps, 196–97; feud of with Smith, 199–200; friction of with W. Walker, 193–94, 198; military career of, 190–91; and Operation Tailboard, 195–96; personal tragedies of, 191; and the planning and execution of Operation Chromite, 193–94, 197–98; racism of, 191, 200

Almond, Edward M., Jr., 191

American Expeditionary Force (AEF), 4, 16–17

Antonov, Alexsey Innokentevich: as chief of General Staff, 150; as chief of staff of the Black Sea Group, 144–45;

as chief of staff of the Southern Front army group, 144; and the concept of *maskirovka* camouflage, 150, 162; difficult personality of, 199; education and military career of, 143–44; and the organization of the Soviet General Staff, 146; as an organizer of the Kiev Maneuvers, 144; planning of the Byelorussian offensive (Operation Bagration), 149–50; preparation of for the defense of the Kursk salient, 148–49, rehabilitation of after Stalin's death, 151; reputation of for competence, 144; role of in briefing Stalin, 148; Stalin's jealousy of, 150–51

"Appreciation of the Situation in the Western Desert" (Dorman-Smith), 86

Arnim, Hans-Jürgen von, 33

Auchinleck, Claude, 77, 78, 79, 84, 103; on the death of Dorman-Smith, 86; dismissal of from Eighth Army, 85

Badanov, Vasily M., 161–62

Bagramyan, Ivan K., 161–62

Balck, Hermann, 9; brilliant counterattacks of against the Soviets, 68; as commander of the Fourth Panzer Army, 70; relationship with Mellenthin, 68–69

Barker, Raymond, 105, 107

Barnett, Correlli, 77, 80

Barr, David G., 196

Battle Studies (du Picq), 130

Bayerlein, Fritz: as chief of staff of the DAK, 30; as chief of staff of the Italian First Army, 33–34; as chief of staff of Panzerarmee, 31–32, 34; as a combat commander, 34; command function